Accents of English 3

Accents of English is about the way English is pronounced by different people in different places. Volume 1 provides a synthesizing introduction, which shows how accents vary not only geographically, but also with social class, formality, sex and age; and in volumes 2 and 3 the author examines in greater depth the various accents used by people who speak English as their mother tongue: the accents of the regions of England, Wales, Scotland and Ireland (volume 2), and of the USA, Canada, the West Indies, Australia, New Zealand, South Africa, India, Black Africa and the Far East (volume 3). Each volume can be read independently, and together they form a major scholarly survey of considerable originality, which not only includes descriptions of hitherto neglected accents, but also examines the implications for phonological theory.

Readers will find the answers to many questions: Who makes 'good' rhyme with 'mood'? Which accents have no voiced sibilants? How is a Canadian accent different from an American one, a New Zealand one from an Australian one, a Jamaican one from a Barbadian one? What are the historical reasons for British–American pronunciation differences? What sound changes are currently in progress in New York, in London, in Edinburgh? Dr Wells has written principally for students of linguistics, phonetics and English language, but the motivated general reader will also find the study both fascinating and rewarding.

An illustrative cassette accompanies volume 1.

The author is Reader in Phonetics, University College London

Cover design by Jan van de Watering

The depth of shading on the world map indicates those areas where English is to a greater or lesser degree the mother tongue of the population.

Accents of English 3

Beyond the British Isles

J. C. WELLS

CAMBRIDGE
UNIVERSITY PRESS

Published by the Press Syndicate of the University of Cambridge
The Pitt Building, Trumpington Street, Cambridge CB2 1RP
40 West 20th Street, New York, NY 10011–4211, USA
10 Stamford Road, Oakleigh, Melbourne 3166, Australia

First published 1982
Reprinted 1985, 1990, 1993, 1996

Library of Congress catalogue card number: 81-10127

British Library cataloguing in publication data

Wells, J. C.
Accents of English.
3: Beyond the British Isles
1. English language – Pronunciation
I. Title
421.5'2   PE1137

ISBN 0 521 22919 7 hard covers Volume 1
ISBN 0 521 29719 2 paperback Volume 1
ISBN 0 521 24224 X hard covers Volume 2
ISBN 0 521 28540 2 paperback Volume 2
ISBN 0 521 24225 8 hard covers Volume 3
ISBN 0 521 28541 0 paperback Volume 3

Transferred to digital printing 1999

Contents

Volume 1: An Introduction

Contents

Contents

Volume 2: The British Isles

Contents

Volume 3: Beyond the British Isles

Contents

To the memory of my father,
Philip Wells (1909–1974),
who encouraged me

Preface

I believe that the three volumes of *Accents of English* represent the first attempt ever to offer a reasonably comprehensive account of the pronunciation of English in all its native-speaker varieties.

I have of course exploited my own familiarity with the various accents – such as it is, varying in depth in accordance with the varying exposure to them which life has happened to give me. These biases will no doubt be apparent. But I have also endeavoured to make appropriate use of all kinds of scholarly treatments of particular regional forms of speech, wherever they have been available to me and to whatever tradition they belong (philological, dialectological, structuralist, 'speech', generativist, sociolinguistic, variationist). My aim has been to bring together their principal findings within a unified and integrated framework.

My own descriptive standpoint, as will be seen, lies within the University College London 'phonetic' tradition of Daniel Jones, A. C. Gimson, and J. D. O'Connor. I am fortunate to have been their pupil. This standpoint could be said to involve an eclectic amalgam of what seems valuable from both older and newer theoretical approaches.

Where surveys based on substantial fieldwork exist, I have made use of their findings. Where they do not, I have had to rely partly on my own impressions. The reader must bear in mind that some of the statements I make are for this reason necessarily tentative.

Inevitably I may be laying myself open to the charge of rushing in where angels fear to tread. Many readers will know more about the socially sensitive pronunciation variables of their home areas than I can hope to. The Rotherham native will look here in vain for a discussion of the features which distinguish his speech from that of Sheffield a few miles away – features obvious to the native, but opaque to the outsider (vol. 1, 1.1.4). There is a great deal of descriptive work remaining to be done.

I see the original contribution of these volumes as lying principally in the following areas: (i) the description of certain neglected accents, including certain accents of the British Isles and the West Indies; (ii) the identification and naming of a number of phonological processes, both historical and synchronic; (iii) the bringing together into a single descriptive framework of accounts by scholars working in many different places and in many different traditions.

Many people have helped me through discussion or correspondence, and in some instances by reading parts of the manuscript. In this regard I would mention particularly D. Abercrombie, K. Albrow, C.-J. N. Bailey, A. Bliss, N. Copeland, R. Easton, A. C. Gimson, T. Hackman, J. Harris, S. Hutcheson, L. Lanham, R. Lass, F. MacEinrí, J. D. McClure, J. Milroy, J. D. O'Connor, H. Paddock, S. M. Ramsaran, H.-H. Speitel, P. Trudgill and J. Windsor Lewis. Our views do not always coincide, nor have I accepted all their suggestions; responsibility for the facts and opinions here presented remains mine. I am aware that these are far from the last word on the subject. For any shortcomings I beg indulgence on the grounds that something, however inadequate, is better than nothing.

I am also grateful to J. L. M. Trim for first suggesting that I write this work, and to G. F. Arnold and O. M. Tooley – not to mention Cambridge University Press – for enquiring so assiduously after its tardy progress.

London, January 1981   JOHN WELLS

Typographical conventions and phonetic symbols

Examples of pronunciation are set in *italics* if in ordinary spelling, otherwise in / / or [ ]. Sometimes methods are combined, thus *disapp*[ɪə]*rance* (which draws attention to the quality of the diphthong corresponding to orthographic *ea* in this word).

/ / is used for **phonemic** transcriptions: for representations believed to be analogous to the way pronunciations are stored in the mental lexicon (= underlying phonological representations); for transcriptions in which only significant sound units (phonemes) are notated.

[ ] is used for **allophonic** transcriptions: for representations believed to include more phonetic detail than is stored mentally (= surface phonetic representations); for transcriptions involving the notation of certain non-significant phoneme variants (allophones); also for **general-phonetic** or **impressionistic** notation of unanalysed data.

Note that symbols enclosed in [ ] are only selectively 'narrowed'. Thus on occasion [r] is used to stand for the ordinary English voiced post-alveolar approximant, more precisely written as [ɹ]; similarly [i] or [iː] may sometimes stand for [ɪi], etc. But where the quality of /r/ or /i(ː)/ is the topic under discussion, then the precise symbols are employed.

Phonetic symbols are taken from the International Phonetic Alphabet (see chart, p. xx). The following additional symbols are employed:

ɝ   r-coloured ɜ
ɷ   unrounded ʊ
ɪ   lowered close central unrounded vowel (= ï)
ʟ   voiced velar lateral
Cˀ   unreleased C
C⁼   unaspirated C
C   any consonant

V   any vowel
→   goes to, becomes, is realized as
~   or
x   varying socially with
$ \
. }   syllable boundary (indicated only when relevant)
\#   stem boundary, word boundary
‖   sentence boundary, end of utterance
Ø   zero
/   in the environment:
   X → Y / A ⎯ B   X becomes Y in the environment of a preceding A and a following B, i.e. AXB → AYB.

Words written in capitals

Throughout the work, use is made of the concept of **standard lexical sets**. These enable one to refer concisely to large groups of words which tend to share the same vowel, and to the vowel which they share. They are based on the vowel correspondences which apply between British Received Pronunciation and (a variety of) General American, and make use of **keywords** intended to be unmistakable no matter what accent one says them in. Thus 'the KIT words' refers to 'ship, bridge, milk . . .'; 'the KIT vowel' refers to the vowel these words have (in most accents, /ɪ/); both may just be referred to as KIT.

RP	GenAm		
ɪ	ɪ	1. KIT	ship, sick, bridge, milk, myth, busy . . .
e	ɛ	2. DRESS	step, neck, edge, shelf, friend, ready . . .
æ	æ	3. TRAP	tap, back, badge, scalp, hand, cancel . . .
ɒ	ɑ	4. LOT	stop, sock, dodge, romp, possible, quality . . .
ʌ	ʌ	5. STRUT	cup, suck, budge, pulse, trunk, blood . . .
ʊ	ʊ	6. FOOT	put, bush, full, good, look, wolf . . .
ɑː	æ	7. BATH	staff, brass, ask, dance, sample, calf . . .

ɒ	ɔ	8. CLOTH	cough, broth, cross, long, Boston ...
3:	3r	9. NURSE	hurt, lurk, urge, burst, jerk, term ...
i:	i	10. FLEECE	creep, speak, leave, feel, key, people ...
eɪ	eɪ	11. FACE	tape, cake, raid, veil, steak, day ...
ɑ:	ɑ	12. PALM	psalm, father, bra, spa, lager ...
ɔ:	ɔ	13. THOUGHT	taught, sauce, hawk, jaw, broad ...
əʊ	o	14. GOAT	soap, joke, home, know, so, roll ...
u:	u	15. GOOSE	loop, shoot, tomb, mute, huge, view ...
aɪ	aɪ	16. PRICE	ripe, write, arrive, high, try, buy ...
ɔɪ	ɔɪ	17. CHOICE	adroit, noise, join, toy, royal ...
aʊ	aʊ	18. MOUTH	out, house, loud, count, crowd, cow ...
ɪə	ɪ(r	19. NEAR	beer, sincere, fear, beard, serum ...
ɛə	ɛ(r	20. SQUARE	care, fair, pear, where, scarce, vary ...
ɑ:	ɑ(r	21. START	far, sharp, bark, carve, farm, heart ...
ɔ:	ɔ(r	22. NORTH	for, war, short, scorch, born, warm ...
ɔ:	o(r	23. FORCE	four, wore, sport, porch, borne, story ...
ʊə	ʊ(r	24. CURE	poor, tourist, pure, plural, jury ...

THE INTERNATIONAL PHONETIC ALPHABET

(Revised to 1979)

	Bilabial	Labiodental	Dental, Alveolar, or Post-alveolar	Retroflex	Palato-alveolar	Palatal	Velar	Uvular	Labial-Palatal	Labial-Velar	Pharyngeal	Glottal
Nasal	m	ɱ	n	ɳ		ɲ	ŋ	ɴ				
Plosive	p b		t d	ʈ ɖ		c ɟ	k g	q ɢ		k͡p g͡b		ʔ
(Median) Fricative	ɸ β	f v	θ ð s z	ʂ ʐ	ʃ ʒ	ç ʝ	x ɣ	χ ʁ	ɥ	ʍ	ħ ʕ	h ɦ
(Median) Approximant		ʋ	ɹ	ɻ		j	ɰ		ɥ	w		
Lateral Fricative			ɬ ɮ									
Lateral (Approximant)			l	ɭ		ʎ	ʟ					
Trill	ʙ		r					ʀ				
Tap or Flap			ɾ	ɽ				ʀ				
Ejective	p'		t'				k'					
Implosive	ɓ		ɗ				ɠ					
(Median) Click	ʘ		ʇ									
Lateral Click			ʖ									

(pulmonic air-stream mechanism)
(non-pulmonic air-stream)

VOWELS

	Front		Back	
	Unrounded	Rounded	Unrounded	Rounded
Close	i	y	ɯ	u
Half-close	e	ø	ɤ	o
Half-open	ɛ	œ	ʌ	ɔ
Open	a	ɶ	ɑ	ɒ

(Also central vowels: ɨ ʉ, ə, ɐ)

OTHER SYMBOLS

c, ʑ Alveolo-palatal fricatives
ʎ, ʓ Palatalized ʃ, ʒ
ɾ Alveolar fricative trill
ɺ Alveolar lateral flap
ɧ Simultaneous ʃ and x
ʄ Variety of ʃ resembling s, etc.

ɪ = ι
ʊ = ω
ɜ = Variety of ə
ɚ = r-coloured ə

DIACRITICS

° Voiceless n̥ d̥
ˬ Voiced s̬ t̬
ʰ Aspirated tʰ
ᵬ Breathy-voiced b̤
̪ Dental t̪
̫ Labialized t̫
ʲ Palatalized t̫
˞ Velarized or Pharyngealized ɫ, ɫ̵
ˌ Syllabic n̩ l̩
ˌ or ˎ Simultaneous ʃ (but see also under the heading Affricates)

˙ or ˓ Raised e˙, e̝, e̜ w
˳ or ˒ Lowered e˳, e̞, e̞ ɐ
+ Advanced u+, u̟
- or ̠ Retracted i̠, i-, t̠
¨ Centralized ë
~ Nasalized ã
˞ r-coloured a˞
ː Long aː
˙ Half-long a˙
˘ Non-syllabic ŭ
˒ More rounded ɔ̹
˓ Less rounded y̜

STRESS, TONE (PITCH)

ˈ stress, placed at beginning of stressed syllable:
ˌ secondary stress:
˥ high level pitch, high tone:
˩ low level:
ˊ high rising:
ˏ low rising:
ˋ high falling:
ˎ low falling:
ˆ rise-fall:
ˇ fall-rise.

AFFRICATES can be written as digraphs, as ligatures, or with slur marks: thus t͡s, t͡ʃ, d͡ʒ:
ʦ ʧ ʤ: t͡ʃ d͡ʒ.
c, ɟ may occasionally be used for t͡ʃ, d͡ʒ.

6

North America

6.1 GenAm revisited

6.1.1 Introduction

In North America it is along the Atlantic coast that we find the sharpest regional and social differences in speech. This is where the earliest European settlements were established. This is where the thirteen colonies were which came together in 1776 to constitute the United States. The inland areas, including the vast tracts of the mid west and then the far west, were settled from the east. Hence we find that the important isoglosses in North America tend to run horizontally, east to west. The principal speech areas can be seen as essentially horizontal bands stretching across the country. In the long-settled east they are sharply distinguished from one another; as we move towards the recently settled west they become progressively more confused and intermingled.

Following Kurath (1949) dialectologists usually recognize three principal speech areas in the east. This tripartite division rests mainly on differences of vocabulary, although it is claimed as valid for morphology and syntax and also for pronunciation as well. The **north** comprises New England and New York State; it extends from Maine through the Yankee heartland down to northern New Jersey. It includes New York City and Boston, Massachusetts. The **midland** area extends inland from the Middle Atlantic states of New Jersey and Pennsylvania, and includes Philadelphia. The **south** extends southwards from about Washington, DC, and includes Virginia and the Carolinas, with the cities of Richmond, Norfolk, and Charleston. These speech areas and their subdivisions, as seen by Kurath, are shown in the map, fig. 15. (The concept of the midland group of dialects has been called 'perhaps the most fruitful contribution Kurath has made to the study of

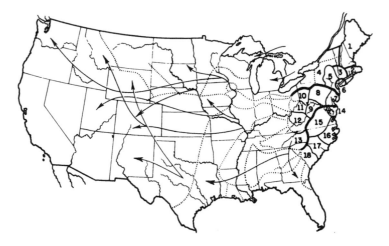

Fig. 15 Dialect areas of the United States (after Francis 1958)

THE NORTH	THE MIDLAND	THE SOUTH
1. Northeastern New England	*North Midland*	14. Delmarva (Eastern Shore)
2. Southeastern New England	7. Delaware Valley (Philadelphia)	15. The Virginia Piedmont
3. Southwestern New England	8. Susquehanna Valley	16. Northeastern North Carolina (Albemarle Sound and Neuse Valley)
4. Inland North (western Vermont, Upstate New York and derivatives)	10. Upper Ohio Valley (Pittsburgh)	
	11. Northern West Virginia	
	South Midland	17. Cape Fear and Peedee Valleys
5. The Hudson Valley	9. Upper Potomac and Shenandoah	18. The South Carolina Low Country (Charleston)
6. Metropolitan New York	12. Southern West Virginia and Eastern Kentucky	
	13. Western Carolina and Eastern Tennessee	

American dialects' (McDavid 1979: 141); it has also been strongly attacked (Bailey 1968a).)

By 1700, only part of the territory included in the original thirteen colonies had been settled: eastern Massachusetts, Connecticut, the Hudson Valley and New York, New Jersey, the areas around Philadelphia and Baltimore, Maryland; and, further south, Virginia and the area around Charleston, South Carolina. Most of the population lived in the larger cities – Boston, New York, Philadelphia, and Charleston.

Over the next hundred years settlement spread: westwards as far as the Appalachian Mountains, and southwards to cover the piedmont (non-mountainous) part of the Carolinas. The original settlers had come from England; they were now joined by Scotch-Irish from Ulster and (particularly in Pennsylvania) by Welsh and German settlers. The Germans brought their language with them; it remains, as 'Pennsylvania Dutch', to the present day. The midland area is supposed to owe some of its speech characteristics to the influence not only of the Germans but also of the Scotch-Irish and the Welsh. There is backing for this view in vocabulary, but it is difficult to find real support for it in the phonetics of midland speech; perhaps the absence of an /ɑ/ vs. /ɔ/ distinction (LOT–THOUGHT Merger), which is characteristic of western Pennsylvania, might be traced to the Scotch-Irish.

In the south social conditions were very different from those obtaining in the north and the midland. There was still a landed gentry, who retained a strong association with England and continued to send their sons to be educated there. Black slave labour was brought in to supplement or replace indentured white labour, and the plantation economy flourished. Poor whites made what living they could on the poorer land away from the great plantations. A merchant class grew up, but social stratification remained more rigid than in the north.

Then came the expansion westward. The first area beyond the Appalachians to be settled was the Ohio valley. Midlanders pushed not only westwards to southern Ohio, Indiana, and Illinois but also southwards to the inland parts of Virginia (now West Virginia), the Carolinas, and Georgia. Meanwhile New Englanders (particularly those from the western part of New England and its offshoot, upstate New York) moved into the Great Lakes area: northern Ohio, Michigan, Wisconsin, northern Illinois.

The coastal cities continued to exert their prestige. This is hardly surprising when we consider that at the time of American Independence Boston and Philadelphia were the second and third

469

largest English-speaking cities in the world. The influence particularly of Boston in the north, and of Richmond and Charleston in the south, was very great at this period. Later, however, it waned; and by the nineteenth century we start to find a new pattern: English innovations in pronunciation, brought in through the great seaports of the east coast, were being imitated there and in their immediately surrounding areas, but not spreading through the country, not being carried westward by the pioneers, and finally falling back again in the face of the usage of the majority of Americans. This is what we find with R Dropping (vol. 1, 3.2.2), which came from England to Boston, to New York, and to the coastal south, but has remained in American eyes an anglicism, an easternism, or a southernism. The same applies to BATH Broadening (vol. 1, 3.2.6), which is even more of a minority pronunciation in America today. On the Atlantic coast, Pennsylvania remained immune to these new pronunciation habits, as did western New England. And R Dropping and BATH Broadening never penetrated inland very far.

It is this fact that gives some residual legitimacy to the older classification of American accents as eastern, southern, and General American. '**Eastern**' refers to the non-rhotic accents of (i) Boston and eastern New England, and (ii) New York City. We discuss these in 6.4 and 6.3 below respectively. '**Southern**' refers in the first instance to the non-rhotic accents of the lowland south; they are treated in 6.5. '**General American**' comprises that majority of American accents which do not show marked eastern or southern characteristics, including both those deriving basically from the northern speech of the Hudson Valley and upstate New York and those deriving from the midland speech of Pennsylvania: it is to this 'General American' (GenAm for short) that the rest of this section is devoted.

Obviously, GenAm is not a single unified accent. But as a concept referring to non-eastern non-southern accents, the label has its uses. It corresponds to the layman's perception of an American accent without marked regional characteristics. It is sometimes referred to as '**Network** English', being the variety most acceptable on the television networks covering the whole United States.

In the opening up of the west in the nineteenth century it was this GenAm type of pronunciation which was carried into the new

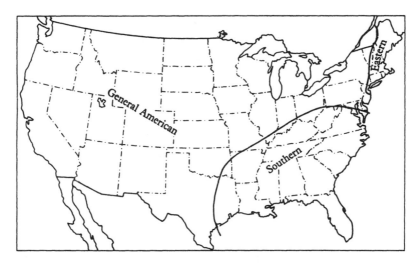

Fig. 16   The three major speech areas, as noted before the 1940s (from
Bronstein 1960). Reprinted by permission of Prentice-Hall

settlements stretching across the continent to the Pacific. As the
various waves of colonization met and merged, northern, midland,
and southern-deriving accents also merged and blended. The map,
fig. 15, from Francis (1958), is an attempt to show the directions of
migrations and the resulting 'dialect areas'. On the west coast, it
appears that Idaho and Washington states are relatively northern in
speech, Oregon relatively midland, and California mixed (Reed &
Reed 1972: 135).

There is a problem about how best to classify the 'southern
mountain' accents of West Virginia, Kentucky, Tennessee, and the
westernmost parts of Virginia and the Carolinas. Historically
speaking, these can be considered midland settlements strongly
influenced by the speech of the coastal south. In the layman's view
today, they are considered a kind of southern accent, although
Kurath classifies them as 'South Midland'.

Thomas (1958) proposes an analysis of the United States into ten
major regional speech areas (fig. 17). He sets off the Middle Atlantic
area around Philadelphia (C) and western Pennsylvania (E) from
the central midland (G) (all regarded by Kurath as 'North midland'), and on the Pacific coast distinguishes the north-west (H)
from the south-west (I). On the other hand he does not distinguish

471

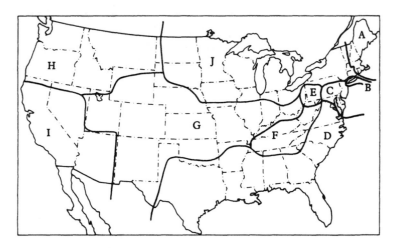

Fig. 17   The major regional speech areas (from Thomas 1958) A:
Eastern New England; B: New York City; C: Middle Atlantic; D:
Southern; E: Western Pennsylvania: F: Southern Mountain; G: Central
Midland; H: Northwest; I: Southwest; J: North-Central

between western New England and the inland north (both combined as 'North Central' (J)), nor between various subareas of the
south (D) such as tidewater Virginia, the South Carolina low
country, or eastern Texas.

The twentieth century has seen two further important move-
ments of population: the migration of blacks from the south to the
cities of the north, and the arrival of large numbers of Hispanics,
speakers of Spanish, both from Puerto Rico and from Mexico and
further south. The blacks have brought with them such typical
southern features as non-rhoticity, which has tended to come to be
seen in the north as a substandard characteristic, even as a speech
defect – notwithstanding its older high prestige in Boston and the
east (and, of course, in England).

The vowel and consonant systems were set out in volume 1,
2.1.3–5; the vowel system is repeated here for convenience (223),
with the addition of reference to certain systemic variables.

(223)

ɪ ʊ	i		u			
ɛ ʌ	eɪ	ɔɪ	o	(eə)	ɜ	(ɔ)
æ	aɪ		aʊ	ɑ		

One relates to the opposition between /ɑ/ and /ɔ/ (LOT vs. THOUGHT), which is lacking in some varieties of GenAm. The other concerns the possible splitting of TRAP–BATH into /æ/ and a new /eə/. Apart from these points, variability in the vowels of GenAm is a matter either of realization or of lexical incidence. Special considerations apply, though, in the environment /—r/.

Some older speakers have a falling diphthong /ɪu/ (discussed in volume 1, 3.1.10), with minimal pairs such as /tʃɪuz/ *chews* vs. /tʃuz/ *choose*; compare also *abuse* /ə'bɪuz/ with *misuse* /mɪs'juz/. Although Kenyon (1958: §341–48) includes /ɪu/ as one of the diphthongs of GenAm, and had it in his own speech, it is now rather rare. According to *PEAS* (168), it is entirely absent from the Atlantic seaboard, though traces remain inland in the New England settlement area.

6.1.2 The THOUGHT–LOT Merger

A well-known diagnostic for distinguishing the northern speech area of the United States from the midland and southern areas is the pronunciation of the word *on*. In the northern area it is /ɑn/, with the vowel of LOT; elsewhere it is /ɔn/, with the vowel of THOUGHT. For an increasing number of Americans, however, this is a distinction without a difference. Asked whether *on* rhymes with *John* (i.e. /ɑn/) or with *lawn* (i.e. /ɔn/), they may reasonably reply, 'With both'. These speakers entirely lack the opposition between /ɑ/ and /ɔ/.

In the east most speakers preserve the opposition. An unrounded vowel, /ɑ/, is used in LOT (also in PALM and, with following /r/, in START). It contrasts with a rounded vowel, /ɔ/, used in THOUGHT (also in CLOTH and, with following /r/, in NORTH – but see discussion below, 6.1.5). There are minimal pairs such as *collar* vs. *caller*, *cot* vs. *caught*, *stock* vs. *stalk*, *don* vs. *dawn*, *knotty* vs. *naughty*: in each pair the first item has /ɑ/, the second /ɔ/. In the eastern states covered by *PEAS*, Kurath & McDavid report the existence of the opposition in all except two areas: eastern New England (which we discuss in 6.4 below), and western Pennsylvania. By the expression 'western Pennsylvania' they refer principally to the Pittsburgh area; northernmost and southernmost Pennsylvania, as well as the eastern part of the state, retain the opposition (see maps in

Wetmore 1959), while the merger certainly extends into neighbouring parts of Ohio such as Youngstown (Hankey 1972). In 'western Pennsylvania', then, *cot* and *caught* are homophones, [kɒt], and similarly with the other pairs mentioned above.

Where LOT and THOUGHT are merged, Kurath & McDavid symbolize the merged vowel as /ɒ/. They comment (*PEAS*: 17) that in western Pennsylvania 'this /ɒ/ has a considerable range of allophones; it is usually a raised low-back vowel [ɒ˙], more or less rounded and prolonged, but may be positionally short and even unrounded ...'. Wetmore (1959) shows that in both lexical sets qualities occur ranging from fully back unrounded [ɑ] (in *PEAS* notation [ɑ]) to an open variety of [ɔ]. Before /r/, /ɒ/ also has realizations ranging to retracted front unrounded [a-].

What may once have been a western Pennsylvania regionalism is now clearly very much more widespread. It is well-known as a feature of Canadian pronunciation. I have frequently encountered it in the speech of Americans from the far west, particularly Utah and Nevada, but often also California. With these westerners the merged vowel is often phonetically unrounded, so that *law* is pronounced [lɑ] (compare the traditional GenAm [lɔ]). (This suggests the preferability of the symbol /ɑ/ for the merged phoneme rather than Kurath & McDavid's /ɒ/). In Utah, Cook (1969) reports low central unrounded [ɑ] as the usual quality for the merged vowel, but with an optional [ɒ] allophone before velars (*dog*) and after /w/ (*water*); in careful speech [ɑ] is used in all environments. In California and Nevada, according to Reed & Reed (1972) *on* and *wash* (and presumably other such words) have [ɑ] in urban speech but [ɒ] in rural areas.

Attempting to specify the geographical spread of the merger, Hockett (1958: 345–6) attributes it to 'the northernmost Middle West (northern Michigan, Wisconsin, Minnesota)', Canada, and 'an indeterminately large region of the American northwest stretching into Utah'. In the *Linguistic atlas of the Upper Midwest*, Allen finds (1976: 24) that the informants almost all preserve the opposition. But he continues,

actually, the limitation of *Atlas* data to the midcentury and to older speakers ignores an apparently rather rapid and highly noticeable development in the Upper Midwest since the time of the field investigation.

During the past 30 years I have observed in my classes at the University of Minnesota a steadily increasing proportion of students who have no low-back rounded vowel except before /r/. Annually, more and more students have only [ɑ] or even [a] [sc. an open back or central unrounded vowel, my [ɑ] or [ɑ+]__JCW] in *law*, *jaw*, *fall*, and the like, and hence lack any distinction between, for example, *caller* and *collar*, *tot* and *taught*, and *don* and *dawn*. The rapid extension of this development among younger speakers for whom it is not an inherited pattern clearly calls for rather intensive research.

Describing the merger as a sound change in progress, Bailey (1973: 19) claims that the shift from [ɔ] to [ɑ] first affects the environment '__tV, e.g. *naughty*, which thereby comes to sound identical to *knotty*; then other environments involving a following alveolar, e.g. *caught* and *dawn* (making them like *cot* and *don*); and lastly those involving a following velar, e.g. *hawk* (making it like *hock*). In any community undergoing the change, there will be a time (he claims) when the oldest speakers have [ɑ] in *naughty*, formal [ɔ] but allegro-speech [ɑ] in *caught* and consistent [ɔ] in *hawk*; while the youngest speakers have only [ɑ] in *naughty* and *caught*, but fluctuate between formal [ɔ] and allegro [ɑ] in *hawk*. Whether this claim is true I do not know.

6.1.3 Further issues relating to THOUGHT and LOT

For that majority of Americans who retain the opposition between the /ɔ/ of THOUGHT and the /ɑ/ of LOT, there are certain words whose pronunciation varies between the two depending on regional factors. Among them are not only *on* (6.1.2 above) but also *fog*, *frog*, *hog*, *log*; *gong*; *water*, *wash*; and *pa*, *ma*. There is also regional variability in the phonetic realization of the two vowel phonemes in question.

As with *on*, the prevailing pattern is for the words listed above to have unrounded /ɑ/ in northern speech, rounded /ɔ/ in midland. *Fog*, *log*, *hog* and *frog* generally conform to this pattern; compare *dog* (very generally /ɔ/) and *cog* (generally /ɑ/). *Gong* and *tongs* tend to have /ɑ/ in the north and east, /ɔ/ in the south and west (whereas *long* and *strong* generally have /ɔ/ in the north and midland, with /ɑ/ quite common in the south). *Water* generally has /ɔ/, but /ɑ/ in the south midland; in New Jersey *PEAS* also reports /ʌ/ in several localities. Conversely, *wash* generally has /ɔ/ in the south midland, /ɑ/ elsewhere in the Atlantic states (though with a good deal of mixed usage and sometimes, particularly in the midland area, it has /-rʃ/). Further west, the vowel in both *water* and *wash* is predominantly rounded. For *ma* and *pa*, the north has /ɑ/, the midland area often /ɔ/.

There are many speakers (in western New England, for example) who retain the LOT vs. THOUGHT opposition in most environments, but have it neutralized in the environment __rV, as in *tomorrow*, pronounced with a quality [ɒ] which is intermediate between the usual [ɑ] of LOT and the usual [ɔ] of THOUGHT. Further west, where LOT and THOUGHT rhyme, with the opposition neutralized, such words tend to have a rounded [ɔ]-type vowel which may be qualitatively very different from the [ɑ ~ ɒ] used in other environments; thus [lɑ] *law*, [kɑt] *cot–caught*, but [tə'mɔrou] *tomorrow*, ['kɔrə'spɑnd] *correspond*. With this kind of pronunciation, it may well be correct to regard [ɔ], occurring only before /r/, as an allophone of /o/. For other speakers again, who preserve the opposition between LOT and THOUGHT before prevocalic /r/ as well as elsewhere, it makes sense to discuss the incidence of /ɑ/ and /ɔ/ in this environment; in *tomorrow*, *borrow*, *sorrow*, and *sorry* /ɑ/ prevails, whilst /ɔ/ is commoner in *forest*, *orange*, *warrant*, *horrible*, /ɑ/ in these words being found mainly along the Atlantic coast. Dwellers in *Oregon* are supposed to be able to recognize outsiders by their tendency to pronounce the name of the state with [ɑ] instead of [ɔ]. *Chicago*ans, similarly, pronounce the name of their city /ʃə'kɔgo/, while outsiders usually prefer /ʃə'kɑgo/ (Mencken 1963: 662).

Turning to the question of the realization of /ɑ/ and /ɔ/, we can say that where they contrast in the GenAm area /ɑ/ is usually an open central, or somewhat backer than central, unrounded [ɑ+] (much as RP /ɑː/), while /ɔ/ is a lightly rounded half-open back [ɔ] (and therefore opener and less rounded than the usual RP /ɔː/). In the north central area, however, /ɑ/ tends to be noticeably less back, being fronted to [a–] or even [a], thus ['baɫ əv 'skatʃ] *bottle of scotch* (elsewhere ['bɑɫ əv 'skatʃ]). The THOUGHT vowel, in turn, is often as open as [ɒ], particularly away from the Atlantic coast. (In eastern New England, though, it is [ɒ], with loss of the LOT–THOUGHT opposition – see 6.4 below.) But in Philadelphia and Baltimore, as also in New York City, it is no opener than [ɔ], and is well rounded.

6.1.4 BATH Raising

A change is under way in American English affecting the quality of the vowel in certain words which have traditionally been regarded as having GenAm /æ/. An example is the word *half*. Alongside the usual GenAm [hæf ∼ hæəf] (and the [a ∼ ɑ] and [æɪ] variants associated with eastern New England and the south respectively) pronunciations such as [hɛəf], [heəf], [hẽəf], and even [hiəf] can now be heard.

To British ears this is a very striking characteristic of American pronunciation, and can already be said to form part of the British stereotype of an American accent. Yet there is no real trace of it in the published Linguistic Atlas materials (*PEAS*, *LAUM*) or in such well-known descriptions of American phonetics as Kenyon (1958) and Thomas (1958). It is obviously quite a recent development.

Although there is a reference to this in New York City speech as far back as 1896 (Babbitt 1896, cited by Labov 1972a: 145), the first phonetician to give detailed attention to the question was Trager (1930). He detected a special allophone of /æ/, phonetically longer, tenser, and slightly closer, used in a range of stressed environments. He identified the relevant environments as follows: word-finally, before voiced plosives /b, d, g, dʒ/; before fricatives /f, v, θ, s, z, ʃ/; and before two nasals, /m, n/; and also before final clusters involving one of these as the first member. Thus [æᶥ] is to be found in words such as *cab, bad, half, halve, pass, lash, lamb, man, past*. Among disyllables words containing a morpheme boundary may differ from those without; thus for example *tabby* has [æ] but *tabbing* [æᶥ], *badger* [æ] but *badges* [æᶥ]. He also pointed out that [æᶥ] is not used before /ŋ/ or /l/, where if anything a lowered allophone of /æ/ occurs, as in *sang* [sæ̞ːŋ], *pal* [pæɫ]; and that the words *have, has, had* are exceptional in containing ordinary [æ] in spite of constituting environments in which [æᶥ] would be expected.

In the light of these 'exceptions' and others which he discovered, Trager quickly became convinced that there was ample evidence to claim that a phonemic split had occurred. In a 1934 article he listed further pairs such as *bade* with [æ] vs. *bad* with [æᶥ], *can* 'be able' vs. *can* 'tin container', *having* vs. *halving*. By 1940 he confidently entitled an article 'One phonemic entity becomes two'. Coming as he did from Newark, NJ, Trager was among that minority of Americans who have a three-way distinction /ɛ–æ–ɛə/ (*merry* vs. *marry* vs. *Mary*). He was able to identify the [ɛə] of *Mary* (and in general of all words in our standard lexical set SQUARE) as identical with the vowel of *half*, etc., thus adding pairs like *marry* vs. *Mary* to the list of minimal pairs exemplifying [æ] vs. [æ˞]. It was at about this time that he devised his 'binary' analysis of English vowels; henceforth he symbolized the two vowels as /æ/ (*cat*) and /eh/ (*bad, bare*) (cf. Trager 1941).

Most Americans do not have any centring-diphthong phoneme in their vowel system. For them, *pace* Trager, it is much less clear that a phonemic split is involved; rather, we may be dealing with a realizational change in the phoneme /æ/. The precise set of environments in which the new realization occurs, the phonetic nature of the new realization, and the degree to which the use of the new realization is optional or stylistically sensitive – all these vary from place to place and from accent to accent.

Trager's [æ˞] quality is only the earliest stage in the phonetic development. Mid qualities come next, usually with a centring offglide, thus [ɛˑə], [eˑə]. At this stage *Graham* and *gram* typically become homophonous, while *man* is identical with the first part of *mayonnaise*. In some areas the raising process has continued, so that the quality may now be a glide from a close tense starting-point, thus [iˑə]. There is anecdotal evidence (Labov 1972a: 156) of New York City children complaining that a boy, *Ian*, had been given a girl's name (*Ann*)! These close realizations are not found nearly so widely as the [eə] type; they seem in fact to be restricted to the eastern United States.

In some other places, the range of environments in which the new realization is found is wider. Labov hypothesizes (1971: 427) that the change always first affects the environments /__m/ and /__n/, next /__f/, /__θ/, and /__s/, and then successively spreads to other environments, which can be arranged in an implicational hierarchy, (224).

(224)   __m, n; __f, θ, s; __d; __b; __ʃ; __g; __v, z; __p, t, k; __l.

Buffalo, in upstate New York, has Raising in all these environments, i.e. including in words like *cap*, *cat*, *back*, *canal* – in fact the sound change now applies to all cases of /æ/ in the environment /__

$C_0 \# /$, i.e. to all monosyllabic TRAP and BATH words. But New York City has the Raising only in the environments up to /__g/, and variably in /__v, z/ (not in /__p, t, k/, or /__l/). Philadelphia has Raising only in the environments /__m, n/, and /__f, θ, s/, and variably in /__d/. Other localities have been discovered with the various intermediate stages; and Birdsboro, Pa., is reported to be in an early stage of the development, with raising just before /m/ and /n/ and variably before /f, θ, s/.

In Detroit and Chicago, according to Bailey (1973: 60), the Raising rule has been extended to all environments mentioned; this leaves the phoneme /æ/ with two sharply distinct realizations, [eə] in monosyllables (and other final stressed syllables), [æ] elsewhere. But the alternation remains on the whole subject to the influence of social context, since the [eə] alternant is held in low repute and replaced by [æ] in careful, monitored speech.

In Buffalo, upstate New York, not only is the rule extended to all /__C_0 \# / environments, but also the extent of change of quality is greater, variably reaching [iə] (as in New York City). This leads Bailey to hypothesize (1973: 60) that Buffalo may be the place of origin of the sound change.

6.1.5 Vowels before /r/

In considering the problems raised by vowels in the environment of a following /r/, it is helpful first to consider the restricted environment /__rV/ and the subsystem of vowels occurring before 'intersyllabic /r/' (as *PEAS* calls it).

Words such as *spirit, mirror* have /ɪr/; words such as *cherry, merry, herald* usually have /ɛr/. There is no problem in identifying the first as the vowel phoneme KIT and the second as DRESS. Other vowels in this environment, though, are not always so readily identified with the vowel phonemes established on the basis of contrasts in other environments. We have seen above (6.1.3) that on the whole *tomorrow, sorry*, etc., have [ɑ], identified with the /ɑ/ of LOT, while *forest, orange* tend to have a rounded vowel, [ɒ ~ ɔ]. Where THOUGHT and LOT are unmerged, this vowel may be regarded as an allophone of the /ɔ/ of THOUGHT; where they are merged, provided that NORTH and FORCE are also merged, it may be preferable to regard it as an allophone of the /o/ of GOAT. (In RP, and generally in England and Wales, all these words unquestionably have the /ɒ/ of LOT; hence the existence of rounded vowels in some of them in America implies a failure to extend LOT Unrounding to all pre-/r/ environments.)

Words such as *married, narrow, barrel* would be expected, on the basis of the situation in all non-American accents, to have the /æ/ of TRAP. This is not uncommon in America; but it faces a widespread rival in /ɛ/, recorded by *PEAS* in western New England and upstate New York and obviously very frequent in the middle and far west. This leads to the well-known American possibility of homophony in pairs such as *merry–marry, herald–Harold*, distinct otherwise as DRESS vs. TRAP. (Certain words in this group also have rural variants with /ɑ/, thus /'bɑrə/ *barrow*.)

In words such as *furrow, worry, hurry, courage*, we would expect to find /ʌ/, i.e. the vowel of STRUT, thus /'hʌri/ *hurry*, etc. It can be argued that phonemically speaking this is what we always do find in American accents. Phonetically, though, [ʌ] plus /r/ is quite rare, being virtually restricted to New York City and scattered parts of the east and south. Elsewhere we get an r-coloured mid central vowel [ɝ], thus ['hɝi], or else a vowel of the [ɜ] type plus /r/, thus ['hɜɹi]; in each case this is phonetically the same as in words such as *nurse* [nɝs ~ nɜɹs], as can be seen from the fact that in such accents *hurry* rhymes with *furry*. Phonemically, one of two conclusions can be drawn: either *hurry*, etc., have the same /ɜ/ as NURSE, and we write /nɜrs/, /'hɜri/ (or, with Kenyon & Knott 1953, /nɝs/, /'hɝi/); or, alternatively, [ɜ] can be regarded as a positional allophone of /ʌ/ and [ɝ] as a realization of /ʌr/, from which it follows that there is no separate phoneme /ɜ/ (or /ɝ/) in this most usual type of GenAm. The latter seems the most economical analysis, and is logically unassailable; it means that *nurse* [nɝs] is to be phonemicized /nʌrs/. (Since GenAm also usually lacks a proper opposition between [ʌ] and [ə], it follows that the phoneme may equally well be written /ə/; which leads to the phonemicization of *hurry* ['hɝi] as /'həri/. Following my usual practice of taking the pronunciation of the simple keyword as the guide to appropriate notation, though, I shall write the GenAm STRUT phoneme as /ʌ/, and *hurry*, therefore, as /'hʌri/. In view of the above argument, it is admittedly inconsistent to write NURSE words in GenAm with /ɜr/, as I have done everywhere else in these volumes; but it makes for easier comparisons with other accents.)

American accents are unique in their treatment of historically long vowels before /r/. In GenAm, at least, these vowels have undergone a series of phonetic developments (vol. 1, 3.3.1) which culminated in the replacement of monophthongs from part-systems B and C by vowels from part-systems A and D in this environment.

In words such as *serious, mysterious, weary, Vera*, the vowel before /r/ is generally identical with that of words such as *nearer, fearing*, in which a suffix beginning with a vowel is attached to a stem ending in /r/ (*near#er, fear#ing*). The GenAm vowel in all these words ranges between an [ɪ] much as in *kit* to something slightly closer (though not as close as the [i] of FLEECE). Phonologically, though, the crucial question is obviously whether the [ɪr] sequence is identical with that of *spirit, miracle, Syria*, etc. In GenAm, it is; and in consequence *mirror* and *nearer* are perfect rhymes, as are *Syria* and *diphtheria*; the phrase *spear it* (in which *it*, being a clitic, is phonetically exactly like a suffix) sounds identical with *spirit*. It is this fact which defines the GenAm vowel system as belonging to type III (vol. 1, 2.3.6). Nowhere outside North America do *nearer* and *mirror* categorically rhyme. Within North America, they do not rhyme in southern and eastern accents, in which *nearer* has either [i(ə)] or [ɪə], as against the [ɪ] of *mirror*.

Given that *nearer* is /ˈnɪrər/, one would expect *near* to be /nɪr/. Compared, though, with the environment /__rV/, the vowel in the environments /__r‖/ and /__rC/ (*beard*) is usually diphthongal and often rather closer in quality: a typical version of *near* might be transcribed [nɪəɹ] or [nɪɹ˞]. The opposition between /i/ and /ɪ/ is neutralized in this environment in GenAm, as in most kinds of English; but given that *nearer* has /ɪr/ (as evidenced by its rhyming with *mirror*) it is clearly more satisfactory to phonemicize [ɪəɹ ~ ɪɹ˞] as /ɪr/ than as /ir/. This accords with the practice of Kenyon & Knott, Thomas, and many others.

The sequence /i/ plus /r/ can occur across morpheme boundaries, as in *key#ring* /ˈkiriŋ/ (which does not rhyme with *clear#ing* /ˈklɪrɪŋ/ in GenAm). Certain words, notably *hero* and *zero*, are sometimes pronounced by Americans as if they contained #, thus

/'hiro, 'ziro/ rather than the expected /'hɪro, 'zɪro/; compare RP (and some New York City) /'hɪərəʊ, 'zɪərəʊ/.

If NEAR has /ɪr/, the prevailing GenAm pronunciation of SQUARE is /ɛr/. This makes *Mary* a homophone of *merry* /'mɛri/ and *sharing* a perfect rhyme of *herring*: /'ʃɛrɪŋ, 'hɛrɪŋ/. Again, such rhymes and homophones are unique to North America: compare RP *M*[ɛə]*ry* vs. *m*[e]*rry*, *sh*[ɛə]*ring* vs. *h*[e]*rring*.

There are, however, two other possibilities for SQUARE in the GenAm area: /ær/ and /eɪr/. The first of these makes *Mary* a homophone of *marry*, /'mæri/, both being distinct from *merry* /'mɛri/. Describing his own Ohio speech, Kenyon (1958: §362) transcribes /ær/ in *fairy, barbarian, precarious, hilarious*, but /ɛr/ in *vary, various, Hungarian, librarian*. In our terms these are all members of the same lexical set, SQUARE; Kenyon himself comments, 'I do not attempt to explain the inconsistencies', and expresses the view that /ɛr/ is now commoner than /ær/ in GenAm as a whole. In discussing the pronunciation of *Mary* and *dairy*, *PEAS* (124–5) does not mention /æ/ as a possibility.

In the New York City area SQUARE words usually have /ɛə/, a distinct phoneme. But GenAm has no such phoneme. For the GenAm minority who distinguish *Mary* from both *merry* and *marry*, *Mary* must be regarded phonologically as /'meɪri/, with the FACE vowel, whatever its realization (usually [e] or [eə]). This remains in scattered parts of the northern area (New England, upstate New York); in the upper midwest Allen (*LAUM*: 34) reports that it is 'headed for obsolescence', as more and more speakers standardize on /'mɛri/ for *Mary*.

It seems that pronunciations other than /ɛr/ are slightly more widespread in SQUARE words where the vowel is in the environment /—r#/, as in *care, fair*, etc., and their derivatives *caring, fairer*, etc. But here, too, the GenAm area overwhelmingly has /ɛr/.

GenAm is thus often characterized by three-way homophony in sets such as *merry–marry–Mary*, all /'mɛri/: compare RP /'meri/ vs. /'mæri/ vs. /'mɛəri/, Scottish /'mɛre/ vs. /'mare/ vs. /'mere/, etc. The vowels of all three lexical sets, DRESS, TRAP, and SQUARE neutralize as /ɛ/ before a following /r/. (In Philadelphia, however, *merry* can reportedly be homophonous with *Murray* /'mʌri/.)

In START words, GenAm regularly has /ɑr/, thus *bar* /bɑr/, *barring* /'bɑrɪŋ/, *sharp* /ʃɑrp/. Qualitatively, this ranges from a fronted central [a-] to a back and slightly rounded [ɒ]. The backed realization is particularly associated with the Philadelphia area. Most Americans have a central [ɑ+] quality. For some mid westerners the vowel itself is noticeably r-coloured in certain environments, thus *barn* [bɑ˞ɹn] (or perhaps rather [bɑ˞n̩]).

In some rural speech the distinction between START and NORTH is neutralized (perhaps variably). This makes *barn* and *born* homophonous, or at least makes them sound each like the other to outsiders, leading to jokes about being *barn* in a *born*. *PEAS* (121) mentions this as a 'unique' feature of the Delmarva peninsula (to the south of Wilmington, Del.), where both have [ɒ]. It is also found in the west, where Cook (1969) demonstrated it to be characteristic of rural, but not urban, speakers in Utah; in the south it is widespread west of the Mississippi (6.5.8 below). It is also reported by *LAUM* (32) for parts of southern Iowa.

The NORTH words have [ɔ] in nearly all kinds of GenAm speech, thus [nɔ˞θ] *north*, [fɔ˞ɾi] *forty*. For those speakers who have preserved the LOT vs. THOUGHT contrast, this is clearly the |ɔ| of THOUGHT plus |r|. For those who have not, the phonemic analysis is not always clear-cut; it depends on whether NORTH and FORCE are merged.

In FORCE words, there is a reasonably clear geographical variation in the Atlantic states: FORCE is merged with NORTH in the north midland area (Pennsylvania, Ohio, New Jersey; also New York City), but the distinction is maintained, though sometimes variably, in the Atlantic states to the north and south. In the mid west and far west, survey fieldworkers almost everywhere report that some speakers do merge pairs such as *hoarse* and *horse*, *mourning* and *morning*, while others keep them distinct. It seems that it is not unusual for speakers to be able to perceive the distinction, and know which words belong in which lexical set, while not actually producing it themselves, or producing it only in case of threatening ambiguity. The quality of the merged vowel is typically slightly closer than the [ɔ] of traditional GenAm THOUGHT.

Some speakers distinguish FORCE–NORTH pairs not by vowel quality but by duration, thus [hɔ˙rs] *hoarse* vs. [hɔrs] *horse* (*LAUM*: 31).

Otherwise, those who have the distinction use a vowel somewhere between [o] and a raised [ɔ] in FORCE, so that *hoarse* is [ho˞s ~

hɔʊ̯s], as against *horse* [hɔʊ̯s]; compare also the first and last syllables of *forty-four* /'fɔrti'for/.

Since a following /r/ usually has a lowering rather than a raising effect on a preceding vowel, it seems reasonable to analyse the [ǫ] of merged FORCE–NORTH as /o/ rather than as /ɔ/, if obliged to choose one or the other. This is obviously correct in the case of accents with merged THOUGHT–LOT, since it is START which has the /ɑ ~ ɒ/ of THOUGHT–LOT plus /r/. There is an interesting situation for any speakers who keep START, NORTH, and FORCE distinct yet merge THOUGHT and LOT. If they have /ɑ/ (or /ɒ/) in START, THOUGHT and LOT, /o/ in FORCE and GOAT, NORTH must be regarded as /ɔ/, and their /ɔ/ is then restricted to the environment /__r/: *fork* /fɔrk/ rhymes with neither *park* /pɑrk/ nor *pork* /pork/.

The CURE words have a closish back rounded vowel in GenAm; it is generally regarded as /ʊ/, although the distinction between /u/ and /ʊ/ is neutralized in this environment. *You're* and *your* are both pronounced /jʊr/ (with weak form /jər/); *tourist* is /'tʊrɪst ~ 'tʊrəst/. This is the pronunciation throughout the northern and north midland parts of the GenAm area; but the south midland (like the south) usually has /o/, i.e. merges CURE and FORCE so that *poor* rhymes with *door* /dor/. Another possibility is for CURE words to have the NURSE vowel; this seems particularly common with the words *yours* and *sure*, so that *surely* then becomes a homophone of *Shirley* /'ʃɜrli/. Europeans notice the way some Americans seem to pronounce *Europe* as 'Yurrup', i.e. /'jɜrəp/ rather than the expected /'jʊrəp/ (compare RP /'jʊərəp ~ 'jɔːrəp/).

Words such as *fire*, *tired* generally have the expected PRICE vowel plus /r/. In the midland area, however, *fire* tends to be pronounced [fɑʊ̯], making it identical with *far*; *tired*, similarly, may be a homophone of *tarred* [tɑʊ̯d]. According to *PEAS*, words such as *power*, *towered* generally keep /aʊ/ even in the midland area (except for 'a few speakers in . . . Pennsylvania'); but Hankey (1972: 55) describes the possibilities in western Pennsylvania and Ohio of *tire*, *tower*, and *tar* (i) being all distinct, or (ii) being all identical, or (iii) having *tire* and *tar* distinct, [tar] and [tɑr] respectively, but *tower* being identical either with one or with the other. Structurally, this parallels the situation in RP and many accents of England (vol 1, 3.2.9, Smoothing); it is not known whether it reflects independent innovations in the American midland and England, or whether the former has imported an innovation initiated by the latter. (The authors of *PEAS* were evidently unaware of the existence of [faː] *fire*, etc., in England.) In western Pennsylvania–Ohio the neutralization can also apply to /aɪ/ and /aʊ/ before /l/, so that *tile* and *towel* can merge as [tɑ+ɫ]; but they remain distinct from *tall*.

As in England, *our* and *ours* quite often have /ɑ/ for speakers who would always retain /aʊ/ in *hour*, *power*, etc.

From the foregoing it can be seen that GenAm tends overall to reduce the subsystem of vowels operating in the environment /___r/ to six (eight if we include /aɪ/ and /aʊ/), as shown in (225):

(225) /ir ~ ɪr/ merge as /ɪr/   *near, spirit*
       /eɪr ~ ɛr ~ ær/ merge as /ɛr/   *fairy, ferry, marry*
       /ɑr/ (START, LOT)   *bar, sorry*
       /ɔr ~ or/ merge as [ɔr]   *war, bore, orange*
       /ur ~ ʊr/ merge as /ʊr/   *you're, poor*
       /ʌr ~ ɜr/ merge as [ɝ]   *current, furry*

6.1.6 Other vowels

Typical phonetic values for the GenAm vowels are plotted in figs. 18 and 19. In part-system A, /ɛ/ is somewhat opener than the corresponding RP /e/ (though the difference is not as great as the use of different phonemic symbols might imply); GenAm /ʌ/ is a centralized back vowel, the fronted qualities ([a–] etc.) which are found in some parts of the south of England being unknown in North America.

The vowels /ɪ, ɛ, ʊ, ʌ/, while normally monophthongal, tend to have centring-diphthong allophones when prosodically salient and when in the environment of a following final voiced consonant, thus *He's wearing a ˈbib* [bɪəb]! In the east, this variant is not very widespread except in the south midland area; in the United States as a whole, it seems to grow commoner as one moves further towards the west and south. Illustrations involving /ɛ, ʊ, ʌ/ are *ˈbed* [bɛəd], *ˈgood* [gʊəd], *ˈrub* [rʌəb]. Under the same environmental and prosodic constraints, /æ/ may be found with diphthongal realizations of the [æə] and [æɪ] types, as well as the [eə] type discussed above (6.1.4).

Before /ʃ/ and /ʒ/, certain vowels have variants involving an assimilatory off-glide to the [ɪ] area. This particularly affects /ɛ, æ, ʊ,

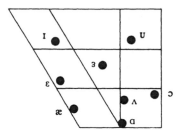

Fig. 18   GenAm vowel qualities (part-systems A and D)

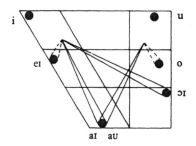

Fig. 19   GenAm vowel qualities (part-systems B and C)

ɔ/, and is associated with the south midland region (and the south); it is common in the mid and far west. Examples include *measure* ['mɛɪʒɚ], *splash* [splæɪʃ], *push* [pʊɪʃ], *wash* [wɔɪʃ]. For some speakers a similar diphthonging affects /ɛ/ and/or /æ/ before certain velars, giving pronunciations such as *egg* [ɛɪg ~ ɛj], *back* [bæɪk ~ bæc] (the latter variant in each case having palatal rather than velar contact for the final consonant). In the case of /ɛ/, there may be a loss of phonemic contrast between /ɛ/ and /eɪ/ (so that *egg* rhymes with *vague*); this pronunciation is found in the folk speech of part of New England (*PEAS*: 132) as well as being a well-known southernism. In the case of *wash* and *Washington*, pronunciations involving /r/ before the /ʃ/ are quite widespread in the mid west. *PEAS* (173) calls this 'rather general' in Pennsylvania west of the Susquehanna River and in West Virginia, and in the Pennsylvania settlements further south. Its origins presumably lie in hypercorrection of [ɔɪ] arising from the vocalization of /r/ before palato-alveolars in words such as *scorch*; an identical [ɔɪ] developed from [ɔ] before [ʃ] in *wash* is reinterpreted as /ɔr/ and realized accordingly.

The close /i/ and /u/, FLEECE and GOOSE respectively, are usually either monophthongs or very narrow diphthongs: [iˑ ~ ɪi], [uˑ ~ ʊu]. More clearly diphthongal variants are associated with the Middle Atlantic area (New Jersey, Philadelphia, Baltimore, Pittsburgh), where under appropriate prosodic/environment conditions there may even be diphthongs of the types [ɪi], [ʊu], thus *There were* `three* [θrɪi]! *It's* `true* [trʊu]! Fronting (with or without diphthongization) is also characteristic of the Middle Atlantic area, as well as of the south. In Chicago fronted variants, of the [ʉ] type, are reportedly (Pederson 1965) associated with educated speech, the back [u] type with uneducated. (British elocutionists strive in just the opposite direction, considering the backest variety of /uː/ the most beautiful!)

Before final /l/, the vowels in part-systems B and C develop a centring offglide in much mid western speech. This is particularly noticeable with /i/ and /u/, as in *feel* [fiəɫ], *rule* [ruəɫ]. There may be the auditory impression of an intrusive semivowel; and words of this kind may optionally be disyllabic: [fijəɫ, ruwəɫ]. Some speakers have the same kind of thing with /eɪ/ and /o/, as in *fail* [fe(j)əɫ], *coal* [ko(w)əɫ]. This Pre-L Breaking may apply in the environment of a word-internal #, as in *feel#ing, rul#ing*.

The mid /eɪ/ and /o/, FACE and GOAT respectively, exhibit a degree of regional variation. Monophthongs or very narrow diphthongs are associated particularly with the northernmost mid west (Wisconsin, Minnesota, the Dakotas); also with the Pennsylvania German settlement area (e.g. Reading, Pa.; compare the widish [ɛɪ]-type diphthong of Philadelphia and adjacent New Jersey). The most usual quality is a narrow diphthong, [eɪ], [oʊ].

The starting-point of /o/ is fairly back in GenAm as a whole. Certain areas, though, are characterized by a central starting-point to the diphthong, giving [ɜʊ] or (with rounded starting-point) [ɵʊ]. This variant is very reminiscent of typical British pronunciation (RP etc): *road* [rɜʊd], *slow* [slɜʊ]. It is associated particularly with part of the Middle Atlantic area, notably Philadelphia in eastern Pennsylvania and Pittsburgh in western Pennsylvania. It is not known whether this is an indigenous American development or derived from British models (GOAT Advancement, vol. 1, 3.2.8).

The /aɪ/ of PRICE is generally [aɪ], with an open front starting-point. Some speakers have a central starting-point, [a-ɪ ~ ɑ-ɪ]; this is common along the Atlantic coast from New Jersey southwards. Some speakers in New England and New York State have starting-points which are mid rather than fully open, such as [ʌɪ]; this may be restricted to the environment of a following voiceless consonant, and is becoming uncommon.

The /aʊ/ of MOUTH may have much the same starting-point as /aɪ/, thus [aʊ ~ ɑʊ]. In New Jersey and parts of Pennsylvania and the south midland area, the starting-point is usually [æ], giving [æʊ] (PRICE–MOUTH Crossover, vol. 2, 4.2.4). This variant is also reported in parts of Nebraska and Iowa, where it is regarded as resulting from midland, as against northern, influence (*LAUM*: 26). It is also found in much of the south and south-west; in Salt Lake City, Utah, it is reported that [aʊ] is currently giving way to [æʊ] (Cook 1969). The [æʊ] type is also known in rural parts of New England, (*PEAS*: 110), and in Philadelphia (where there may even be variable homophony of *council* and *cancel* with [æə]).

There remains one interesting question of lexical incidence in the GenAm speech area: the question of /ʊ/ or /u/ in words such as *coop*, *Cooper*, *hoop*, *broom*, *room*, *hoof*, *roof*, and *root*. In *coop* and *Cooper*, the vowel is predominantly /u/ in the north and north midland, /ʊ/ in the south and south midland; the southern limit of /u/ follows the state line between Pennsylvania and Maryland (*PEAS*: Map 108). In Philadelphia and adjacent parts of New Jersey and Delaware, *coop* has a variant /kʊb/. In *hoop*, the /ʊ/ form is much more widespread, though educated midwesterners are reported to consider /hup/ more correct (*LAUM*: 251). In *broom* and *room* the predominant vowel is /u/, although /ʊ/ forms are widespread in New England and also in Maryland and Virginia. Some speakers seem to use a compromise vowel phonetically intermediate between [ʊ] and [u] (*PEAS*: 152; *LAUM*: 249–50). In *roof* /u/ is very much more common than it is in *hoof*; anyone who has /ʊ/ in *roof* is virtually certain to have it in *hoof*, but the converse does not hold. The /rʊf/ variant is particularly common in New England, as is /rʊt/ for *root* (elsewhere /rut/).

6.1.7 Consonants

With the exception of a possible /ʍ/ (alternatively analysed as /hw/), discussed in volume 1, 3.2.4, there are no deviations in

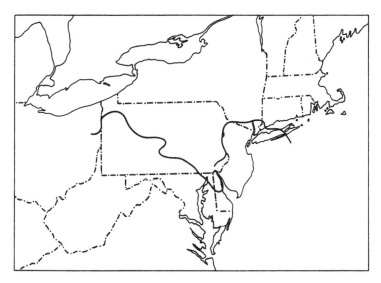

Fig. 20   Southern boundary of the predominance of /s/ in *greasy* (after *PEAS*)

GenAm from the consonant system set out in 2.1.5. The question of Yod Dropping has also been discussed in volume 1, 3.3.3; the GenAm preference for /tu, du, nu/ in *tune, duke, new* is, however, subject to pressure from schoolteachers who often prescribe /tju, dju, nju/ as correct. The tendency of midwestern radio announcers to hypercorrections such as /njun/ *noon* is notorious.

The question of T Voicing has also been discussed in volume 1, 3.3.4, where the possible variants [ṭ] and [ɾ] for /t/ in the environment V—V were mentioned, as was the possibility of [ɾ̃] as a realization of /nt/ in the same environment.

Among the other plosives, mention should perhaps be made of implosive [ɓ] as a possible occasional realization of initial /b/. I associate this with the cowboy, western stereotype: *I ('ve) come for my* [ɓ]*oy*. (Perhaps it ought to be counted a southernism rather than included in the section on GenAm.)

The adjective *greasy* and the verb *to grease* are well-known for regional variation in the United States, /-s-/ being the prevailing northern forms and /-z-/ the southern. The noun *grease* almost always has /s/. The map, fig. 20, shows that /s/ in *greasy* (in the phrase *my hands are greasy*) predominates in New England and in

489

the New England settlement area (including a New England enclave around Marietta, Ohio), as well as in eastern Pennsylvania (but not in Philadelphia itself); /z/ is universal in the south and south midland, and predominates in New York City, New Jersey, and Philadelphia, as well as in south-western Pennsylvania and southern Ohio.

GenAm /l/ tends to be rather dark. Before stressed vowels it is neutral or only slightly velarized; preconsonantally and finally definitely dark (velarized). The difference vis-à-vis southern accents (and RP etc.) is particularly noticeable in the environment V—V, as in *valley, jelly, rely*: compare GenAm ['dʒɛɫi], southern ['dʒɛlɪ]. The sequence /lj/, however, is frequently subjected to a kind of coalescent assimilation in GenAm, being realized as [ʎ] or just a long [jj], as in *failure, battalion, William* ['wɪjjəm].

GenAm /r/ has distinct positional variants for many speakers: apical post-alveolar [ɹ] prevocalically, elsewhere an r-coloured vocoid [ɚ] articulated without raising of the tongue tip but by bunching the tongue backwards and upwards in the mouth and pressing it rather tensely against the rear molars (Uldall 1958). According to *PEAS*, western Pennsylvania differs from other rhotic American accents in using [ɹ] in postvocalic position, where others have [ɚ].

GenAm is of course rhotic, retaining historical /r/ in all environments. There are certain cases, however, where historical /r/ is commonly lost through a process of **R Dissimilation**. This affects historical /r/ (orthographic *r*) in unstressed non-final syllables adjacent to /r/ in another syllable: examples include *surprise* /sə'praɪz/, *governor* /'gʌvənər/ (compare *govern* /'gʌvərn/), *caterpillar* /'kætəpɪlər/, *thermometer* /θə'mɑmətər/. In all cases there exist alternatives with /r/, generally preferred in careful speech.

6.2 Canada

6.2.1 Introduction

Canada has two official languages, English and French. Two in every three native-born Canadians – some eleven million – have

English as their mother tongue. The other third speak French; there are also small communities speaking Scottish Gaelic, Eskimo, and Amerindian languages. The languages brought in by recent immigrants (notably Ukrainian, German, Italian, and Polish) have not generally persisted beyond the foreign-born generation.

The British usually take English-speaking Canadians for Americans. This is upsetting to some Canadians, who tend to feel that the speech of Americans is, or should be, clearly distinguishable from their own. It was after all the Canadians who remained loyal to Britain when the United States broke away two centuries ago. Yet the British can be forgiven for this error: a typical Canadian accent agrees with GenAm rather than with RP at almost every point where these reference accents differ from one another: amongst other things, it is rhotic, with flat BATH and T Voicing.

When Canadians argue about British versus American pronunciations, the phonology is not discussed but taken for granted; the questions at issue are just those of lexical incidence. Does *schedule*, they ask, begin with /ʃ/ or with /sk/? Does (or should) *leisure* rhyme with *seizure* or with *pleasure*? Is *news* /nuz/ or /njuz/? Equally those who insist that Canadian English is something distinctively Canadian, not just a reflection of American or British models, concentrate on incidence, perhaps demonstrating that Canadians often pronounce *khaki* as /ˈkɑrki/, which differs both from RP /ˈkɑːki/ and from GenAm /ˈkæki/.

Yet there exists one particular combination of accent characteristics which constitutes a reasonably reliable diagnostic for distinguishing (most) Canadians from Americans. It depends on the use of a mid central starting-point for the PRICE and MOUTH diphthongs in the environment of a following voiceless consonant, together with the absence of the THOUGHT vs. LOT opposition (both discussed in more detail below, 6.2.3–4). Thus to pronounce the sentence *I saw the White House* as [aɪ ˈsɑ ðə ˈhwəit ˌhʌʊs] may be regarded as un-American, but typically Canadian.

Canadian pronunciation is extremely homogeneous, considering the vastness of the territory over which it extends and the varied history of settlement. From Ottawa to Vancouver is more than 3000 kilometres; their accents are virtually the same. Not only is there very little geographical variation, but what social variation there is in accent seems to be confined to trivial details of lexical incidence.

Only to the east of Ontario do we begin to find more variety. Newfoundland, in particular, stands quite apart from the rest of Canada (see below, 6.2.7–9).

Close contact between Canada and the United States is of long standing, and the border has never been a great barrier to the movement of populations. After the expulsion of the Acadians from Nova Scotia, their farmlands were taken over by New Englanders; Americans loyal to Britain during the War of Independence (the Revolution) settled in the Maritime provinces and Ontario. Today United States influence dominates the mass media in Canada as well as much of its commercial life. Yet membership of the Commonwealth, together with continuing immigration from Britain, has meant that Canada is and has been more receptive to British ways, and British habits of speech, than those living further south. And now Canadians can look with a sense of national pride on their own unique blend of British and American culture and speech.

Dialectologists divide Canada into three principal dialect areas: Newfoundland, eastern Canada (including the Maritimes and Ontario) and western Canada. The differences between the latter two areas hardly involve pronunciation. Consequently, it will be convenient here first to deal with all of Canada except Newfoundland, and then to discuss Newfoundland separately.

6.2.2 The vowel system

The stressed vowels of Canadian English can be represented as (226).

(226)

ɪ	ʊ	i		u	
ɛ	ʌ	eɪ		o	ɜ
æ		aɪ	ɔɪ	aʊ	ɑ

Allophonic variation in the phonetic realization of certain vowels is discussed below, either in 6.2.3 or (in the case of /aɪ, aʊ/ in 6.2.4. There follows, (227), a table of lexical incidence for the vowels:

(227)

KIT	ɪ	FLEECE	i	NEAR	ɪr
DRESS	ɛ	FACE	eɪ	SQUARE	ɛr
TRAP	æ	PALM	ɑ[1]	START	ɑr
LOT	ɑ	THOUGHT	ɑ	NORTH	or
STRUT	ʌ	GOAT	o	FORCE	or
FOOT	ʊ	GOOSE	u	CURE	ʊr
BATH	æ	PRICE	aɪ[1]	*happ*Y	i
CLOTH	ɑ	VOICE	ɔɪ	*lett*ER	ər [ɚ]
NURSE	ɜr [ɝ]	MOUTH	aʊ[1]	*comm*A	ə

[1] discussed below.

6.2.3 The open back vowel(s)

As mentioned above, most Canadian accents have one single merged vowel phoneme for all five reference sets THOUGHT, CLOTH, LOT, PALM, and START (in the last of these, it is followed by /r/). This phoneme is here transcribed /ɑ/. In phonetic quality it is most usually back, close to cardinal 5. It may be lightly rounded, [ɒ]. Before /r/, i.e. in the reference set START, it has a central, unrounded allophone, [ɑ₊ ~ a–]. Durationally all allophones are rather long. As far as notation goes, it could of course alternatively be transcribed /ɒ/ or /ɔ/.

The THOUGHT–LOT Merger (6.1.2 above) is reflected in homophones such as *caught–cot* /kɑt/, *stalk–stock* /stɑk/. However, one pre-war report (Scott 1939) claims a distinction of length in such pairs; there may be older speakers who make such a distinction, but for most Canadians the merger is certainly complete and the pairs homophonous.

A failure of the PALM–LOT Merger (vol. 1, 3.3.2) is reported for some Nova Scotia speech, with a front [a–] in START and PALM, but a back [ɒ] in LOT–CLOTH–THOUGHT. The word *father* in this area is ['faːðɚ], as against the ['fɑːðɚ] type found in New Brunswick and westwards.

The word *palm* itself, like *calm*, may sometimes be found with /æ/ or a compromise vowel of the [a] type. (As elsewhere in North America, the reference set PALM is actually better represented by the keyword *father* than by *palm* itself.) Among British-influenced circles, the same compromise vowel, or even /ɑ/, may sometimes be encountered in certain BATH words, though inconsistently and

493

perhaps only in careful speech. One oddity is the word *salmon*, in Canada often pronounced /'sɑmən/ (compare RP-GenAm /'sæmən/).

6.2.4 PRICE, MOUTH Raising

In Canadian English the PRICE and MOUTH vowel phonemes, /aɪ/ and /aʊ/, have special allophones used in the environment of a following voiceless (fortis) consonant. These allophones are diphthongs with a mid starting-point (half-open or somewhat closer): [əi] (or more precisely [ɐi]) and [ʌʊ] respectively. They are used in words such as *pipe, white, like, life, nice; out, couch, south, house*. The distinction can be heard clearly when one compares pairs such as *write* [rəit] vs. *ride* [raɪd], *out* [ʌʊt] vs. *loud* [laʊd]; so also *knife–knives, house–houses* ['haʊzɪz].

Historically, it is not clear whether this is an innovation (as the name Raising implies), or an archaism retaining the earlier qualities of these diphthongs (vol. 1, 3.1.11) in a restricted environment only. If the latter, a rule inversion would seem to have taken place, since it is now simpler to write a rule raising the first element of the diphthongs before a voiceless consonant than one lowering it before voiced consonants, vowels, and major morpheme boundaries.

The [ʌʊ] allophone is sometimes perceived by Americans as a variety of /u/, leading to popular claims that Canadians say 'oot and aboot' for *out and about*.

Certain delicate questions arise in connection with the precise specification of the environment in which this Raising occurs. In general, it does not apply where the diphthong is shielded from a following fortis consonant by a major morpheme boundary: so *tie-clip*, for example, has unraised [aɪ]. But for some speakers there are occasional exceptions to this principle where the two morphemes in question are lexically close-bound, e.g. *high school* ['həiskul].

Probably the crucial factor is the syllable affiliation of the fortis consonant. As long as it is part of the same syllable as the diphthong, then Raising applies. Intersyllabic (ambisyllabic) consonants will be 'captured' by a more strongly stressed syllable from a less stressed following syllable. The examples adduced and discussed by Chambers (1973) can, I believe, be accounted for in this way: raised [əi] in *bicycle, cite, hypodermic, titan, psycho* with stressed diphthong; but unraised [aɪ] in *bisexual, citation, hypothesis, titanic, psychology*, where the stressing of the following syllable protects the fortis consonant after the diphthong from capture.

A few examples, though, seem likely to remain as exceptions to any proposed rule formulation, e.g. (for some speakers) *Cyclops* ['saɪklɑps] vs. *micron* ['mǝikrɑn].

6.2.5 Consonants

The Canadian consonant system offers no surprises. It agrees with that of GenAm throughout.

T Voicing and D Tapping (vol. 1, 3.3.4) are clearly usual, leading to the neutralization of the /t–d/ opposition in the relevant environments, so that pairs such as *matter–madder, petal–pedal, I hit it–I hid it* are homophonous. Often, though, informants deny that this is the case: in a recent survey, only 40 per cent of parents and 60 per cent of teenagers questioned reported themselves as using a voiced /t/ in *butter*. And Canadian English furnishes an interesting paradox, well-known to phonological theorists, in pairs such as *writer* vs. *rider*, which are ['rǝirɚ] and ['raɪrɚ] respectively. Thus *writer* has the /aɪ/ allophone appropriate for the environment of a following voiceless consonant, but *rider* the allophone appropriate for a following voiced consonant, even though their following consonants are phonetically identical: hence the consonantal opposition /t/ vs. /d/ is realized as a distinction between surface vowels. This paradox was first pointed out by Joos (1942), and its implications for phonological theory later developed by Chomsky (1964: 74) (cf. vol. 1, 1.2.13).

Canadian /l/ is dark in all positions. The other liquid, /r/, is a constricted coronal approximant, as is its syllabic congener /ɜr/ [ɚ]. Generally, of course, Canadian English is firmly rhotic; but there is a small (recessively) non-rhotic enclave in the 'post-German' speech of Lunenburg, NS.

In *wh-* words the /hw-/ pronunciation appears to be sharply recessive, remaining principally in Ontario. Further west and further east /w-/ is usual, and no distinction between pairs such as *whale–wail* is made. Less than half of the Canadians questioned in a recent survey claimed to use [hw] in *whine*, even though this is a matter where over-reporting would be expected. While 49 per cent of those with college or university education claimed to use [hw], only 35 per cent of those with no more than high school did so.

In words such as *tune, duke, new,* Yod Dropping (vol. 1, 3.3.3) is widespread, although the pronunciation with /j/ enjoys higher prestige. In the same survey the respondents divided roughly equally on *student* /st(j)u-/; but over two-thirds claimed *new* as /nju/ rather than /nu/. In Ontario, hypercorrection to /-ju/ in *moon, noon, too,* etc., has been reported. Along the 'middle border', on the other hand – from Thunder Bay to Saskatchewan – Yod Coalescence, thus *tune* /tʃun/, is rather common.

6.2.6 Questions of incidence

There are a fair number of words where Canadian English shows divided usage. These words have two rival pronunciations, one of which corresponds to mainstream American usage and the other of which to mainstream British usage. An important step towards quantifying this variability was taken with the carrying out of the survey mentioned in the previous section.

This was the Survey of Canadian English, conducted in 1972. It was based on a postal questionnaire distributed to 1000 native-born school students aged between fourteen and fifteen in each Canadian province. As well as an answer sheet for his or her own use, each teenager selected was also given two answer sheets to be filled in by his or her parents. Over 14,000 answer sheets were returned for analysis. The questionnaire consisted, amongst other matters, of forty-two questions concerning pronunciation. The results must be interpreted with certain reservations, bearing in mind that they depend entirely on self-reporting. For example, there can be little doubt that a very much larger percentage of the parents customarily use a voiced /t/ in *butter* than the 40 per cent who reported themselves as doing so; and certainly more than the 60 per cent of teenagers who reported it. In general, the teenagers give the impression of more accurate self-reporting than the parents, no doubt because the parents have had greater exposure to normative pressures from prestige accents. For example, over two-thirds of the parents claimed to use /tʃ/, not /dʒ/, in the word *congratulate* /kən'græ‿əleɪt/, while only just over half of the students claimed this. Ten times as many students as parents reported /dif/ for *deaf* (though even they were a very small minority: /dɛf/ was overwhelmingly preferred).

The general trend is for an increase in the use of the 'American' variants at the expense of the 'British' ones. Thus *lever* with /ɛ/, *lieutenant* with /lu/, *either* with /i/ are all reported more frequently by the younger age group (students) than by the older one (parents).

The other general trend revealed by the Survey was for an association between American variants and a lower level of education, and between British variants and a higher educational level. For example, 77 per cent of those with only a high school education reported /sk/ in *schedule*, while the smaller figure of 68 per cent of those with college or university education did so (the remainder, in each case, reporting the 'British' /ʃ-/). For *leisure* with /i/ as against /ɛ/ the corresponding figures were 71 per cent and 60 per cent, for *anti-* with /aɪ/ as against /i ~ ɪ/ 18 per cent and 12 per cent. For *progress*, on the other hand, the figures were the other way round: 49 per cent of the more highly educated reported the American /prɑ-/ (as against British /pro-/), but only 39 per cent of the less highly educated. The two groups were nearly the same in the proportion (about one-sixth) who reported American /-əl/ rather than British /-aɪl/ in *missile*.

Overall it is clear that in many of these words the British-style lexical incidence has an established place in Canadian speech in a way it does not in the speech of the United States. Other examples of this, not covered by the Survey of Canadian English but believed to be characteristic of Canadian pronunciation and different from typical American pronunciation, include *been* /bin/, *shone* /ʃɑn/, and *suggest* /sə'dʒɛst/. Another well-known supposedly British-Canadian characteristic, /zɛd/ for the name of the letter *Z* (American /zi/) was revealed by the Survey to be true only of mainland Canada; Newfoundland prefers /zi/.

It is supposed to be possible to identify speakers from western Canada by their pronunciation of *slough* ('large body of residual water') as /slu/, as against the form /slɑʊ/ used by those from central and eastern Canada. The Survey revealed an east–west difference in *apricot*, which is pronounced with initial /eɪ/ in British Columbia, but /æ/ elsewhere. And over half the respondents from Saskatchewan reported *bury* as ['bɝi], a form reported by less than one third of the respondents overall.

6.2.7 Newfoundland: general

Lying off the east coast of the Canadian mainland, Newfoundland was Britain's oldest colony (founded 1583) and is now Canada's newest province (since 1949). There are about half a million inhabitants, and their speech covers a spectrum ranging from Standard English to varieties which are perhaps the only ones in North America to count as traditional-dialect in the sense in which this term is employed in volume 1, 1.1.3.

Newfoundland speech has affinities with the English of Ireland and of the south of England, especially the south–west. It is generally fully rhotic, as is other Canadian speech; but in several other respects it differs quite strikingly from the Canadian and North American mainstream. The vowel of STRUT is back and often rounded, near to [ɔ]: to avoid confusion with the vowel written with this symbol in other accents, I transcribe this Newfoundland STRUT vowel /ɔ̆/. The vowels of LOT and THOUGHT are not merged; they are both unrounded. Some Newfoundland speech, uniquely in North America, has /l/ clear in all positions and shows a failure to undergo the FACE Merger (vol. 1, 3.1.5: *pate* /pɛːt/ does not rhyme with *bait* /bɛɪt/). In broad accents, PRICE and VOICE are merged as /əi/. Among the consonants, broad local accents lack the [θ] and [ð] of standard accents, either dental plosives [t̪, d̪] or else [f, v] being used in their place. Many final clusters have undergone simplification, e.g. *post* and *nest* end in /s/ rather than in /st/. These last characteristics, as well as certain morphological and syntactic features of popular Newfoundland speech, are shared with many black people in the United States (6.6 below); the fact that they occur in the folk speech of white Newfoundlanders shows clearly that there is nothing exclusively Black about them.

6.2.8 Newfoundland: vowels

There is a great deal of regional and social variation in the quality and rounding of open and back vowels. What is presented below, (228), is to be interpreted just as an example of a Newfoundland vowel system, rather than as part of a comprehensive analysis of the speech of the whole island. It is the vowel system of the broad accent of Carbonear, an old-established town on the Avalon peninsula.

(228)

ɪ ʊ	iː		uː		
ɛ ɔ̈		əi	əu	ɛː	3
æ ɑ	ɛɪ		ʌʊ	æː	ɑː

The incidence of these vowels is shown in (229).

(229)

KIT	ɪ	FLEECE	iː	NEAR	ɛr
DRESS	ɛ	FACE	ɛː, ɛɪ	SQUARE	ɛ̈r
TRAP	æ[1]	PALM	æ, ɑː	START	ær
LOT	ɑ	THOUGHT	ɑː	NORTH	ɔ̈r
STRUT	ɔ̈	GOAT	ʌʊ	FORCE	ɔ̈r
FOOT	ʊ	GOOSE	uː	CURE	ɔ̈r
BATH	æː	PRICE	əi	happY	[i]
CLOTH	ɑː	CHOICE	əi	lettER	ər [ɚ]
NURSE	ɜr [ɜː]	MOUTH	əu	commA	ə

[1] discussed below.

The regional standard accent shows various modifications of this vowel system in the direction of RP and, especially among the young, towards GenAm–Canadian. The long monophthongs /ɛː, æː/ disappear as separate phonemes, being merged with /ɛɪ/ and /æ/ respectively. A diphthong /ɔɪ/ is used for CHOICE, so that in standard speech the homophony between PRICE and CHOICE words disappears: *boy* and *buy* are then [bɔɪ] and [bəi], as against the broad accent [bəi] for both. Nevertheless the PRICE vowel often remains phonetically [əi] in all environments; this is one of the characteristics distinguishing the pronunciation of some educated Newfoundlanders from that of other Canadians. Typically we have (230).

(230)

	GenAm	Other Canadian	Newfoundland
write, like, nice ...	aɪ	əi	əi
ride, time, buy ...	aɪ	aɪ	əi

Broad Newfoundland speech exhibits several mergers before /r/, not all of which are found in the regional standard. In the latter, NEAR words have a variety of [ɪr] which is just sufficiently distinct from [ɛr] to keep NEAR distinct from SQUARE: *beer* [bɪr] vs. *bare–bear* [bɛr] (but in the broad accent all three words [bɛr]). On the opposite side of the vowel area CURE is represented by [ʊr ∼ ɔr]: *boor* [bʊr ∼ bɔr] vs. *bore–boar* [bɔ̈r] (but in the broad accent all three [bɔ̈r]).

Word-finally, the *happy* vowel is [i], a short allophone of /iː/, thus *body* ['bɑdi] etc. In broad speech, pairs such as *studied–studded* are, interestingly, nevertheless homophones, since both have [-id] /-iːd/. In the regional standard, they are kept apart.

In the larger but less populous 'mainland', i.e. away from the Avalon Peninsula, KIT and DRESS are reportedly often merged as [ɪ]. This [ɪ] occurs to the exclusion of [ɛ] in all environments except that of a following preconsonantal or final /r/, where [ɛ] is found to the exclusion of [ɪ] (i.e. in NEAR and SQUARE). Thus *bit* and *bet* are merged as [bɪt], while *beer, bear* and *bare* are [bɛr]. Since [ɪ] and [ɛ] are in complementary distribution in this accent, they are to be regarded as allophones of a single phoneme. The number of distinctive short vowels is thus reduced to five.

In certain words where the TRAP or BATH vowel is followed by a palato-alveolar consonant, /ɛɪ/ tends to be used rather than /æ ~ æː/, particularly in the 'mainland': thus *branch* and *dash* with /ɛɪ/ (but *snatch* with /æ/).

6.2.9 Newfoundland: consonants

As mentioned already, there are no dental fricatives in the consonant system of the broad accent. *Think* and *then* are pronounced [tɪŋk] and [dɛn] respectively, with initial plosives, alveolar or sometimes dental. But *bath*, for instance, may sometimes be [bæːf] rather than [bæːt]; there is apparently considerable idiolectal variation between /f, v/ and /t, d/ in words which in the reference accents have /θ, ð/. The possible sociolinguistic indexicality of this variation is not known. That of [θ, ð] is clear, though as yet not quantified: they are associated with higher levels of education and social status. In the Newfoundland regional standard, /θ/ and /ð/ are used just as in other standard accents, though there are many speakers with a broad-accent background who do not use them consistently. Dental plosives [t̪, d̪] are used for /θ, ð/ in the exclusively Irish settlements on the Southern Shore Line of the Avalon Peninsula.

Whilst most Newfoundland speech, whether broad or standard, is consistently rhotic, there are sporadic non-rhotic enclaves. For example, in the Bay Roberts area of the Avalon Peninsula, the local accent is non-rhotic: /r/ occurs only prevocalically and /ɜː/ is un-r-coloured. In this same enclave, there is no segmental phoneme /h/, though [h] is used in a manner which could be regarded as part of the prosodic system.

The sequence of vowel plus nasal is often realized as a nasalized vowel, especially in unstressed syllables: thus *Newfoundland* [nufɛ̃'læn]. This rule of nasalization also applies to a certain extent in the Newfoundland standard accent.

In much of the Avalon Peninsula, /h/ is contrastive and consistently used. In the broad speech of the rest of the island (as well as in the Bay Roberts enclave mentioned above), it is generally not a segmental phoneme (H Dropping, vol. 1, 3.4.1). This may well be an independent Newfoundland innovation rather than a British import; as far as is known, there are no other H Dropping accents in North America.

In *wh-* words /h/ is absent everywhere in both broad and standard speech, e.g. *whine* /wəin/; in words of the type *huge*, the broad accent has bare /j/, but standard speech /hj/.

As mentioned above, the broad accent has undergone a simplification of final consonant clusters (Cluster Reduction, cf. 7.1.4 below), e.g. *post* /pʌus/. In the regional standard accent, this simplification is avoided, and *post* is /pʌust/ (though with the preconsonantal variant [pʌus] as a consequence of optional and context-sensitive Elision). The conflict of broad and standard gives rise to various hypercorrect forms. Thus the plural of *post* may be ['pʌusɪz] or ['pʌustɪz] as well as the orthodox [pʌus(t)s].

Glottalling of /p, t, k/ occurs in the environment of a following syllabic nasal or lateral, as *button, chicken, little, captain* ['kæpʔm].

6.3 New York City

6.3.1 Introduction

New York and London are rivals for the title of the world's most populous English-speaking city. With its 7¾ million population, New York is also the largest city in the western hemisphere. It also has a distinctive accent, which differs from others more sharply than does any other North American regional accent. Americans in general are more aware of this accent than of any other local accent except possibly American southern accents (and in this they differ from the British, who are usually quite unaware that a New York accent is in any way different from other American accents).

New York is unique, too, in the sharp social stratification of its pronunciation patterns. In most parts of North America, particularly away from the east coast, social-class differences in accent are relatively unimportant – at least if we ignore the basically geographical and/or ethnic differences arising from the recent migration of blacks from the south to the northern cities. But in New York there are clear differences between social classes both in the basic vowel system and in many details of phonetic realization. As Hubbell (1950a) puts it, 'the pronunciation of two New Yorkers, both of them born and bred in the city, may exhibit far greater divergences than those that distinguish the speech of Wisconsin, let us say, from that of Oregon'. This variability provided the rich ground for Labov's pioneering study (1966).

A broader or more striking variety of the New York accent is sometimes referred to (usually disparagingly) as 'Brooklynese'. There is, however, no evidence for any geographical difference of accent within the New York metropolitan area: Brooklyn speech does not differ as such from that of Queens or the Bronx.

Now it is not unusual for the popular accent of a large city to be disparaged: in this respect New York is only in the same position as London, Birmingham, or Liverpool in England. But there is no other American city whose speech evokes such disapproval. Moreover, the New York accent lacks not only overt but also covert prestige. As Labov remarks, 'as far as language is concerned, New York City may be characterized as a great sink of negative prestige' (Labov 1966: 499) – with the exception of older blacks, almost all his New York informants had a very negative attitude towards the accent associated with their native city. This negative attitude is shared by other Americans, who express it not only in words but also by their failure to imitate New York's example. Unlike virtually all other large cities, New York does not act as a focus of linguistic innovation: there are no waves of sound changes and other phonological innovations radiating from it. Whereas most other variety boundaries reflect the extent of the expansion of prestige models, the one around New York City reflects rather the limits within which a stigmatized model has been confined. The New York accent extends only to the boroughs of the city itself, together with a sharply restricted area of adjacent New York State and New Jersey.

Among the salient characteristics of a New York accent are variable non-rhoticity, the quality of the TRAP–BATH, CLOTH–THOUGHT, and NURSE vowels, and the realizations of /t, d, θ, ð/.

6.3.2 The vowel system

The vowel system of the New York accent is shown in (231).

(231)	ɪ ʊ	i	(ɪu) u	ɪə	ʊə
	ɛ ʌ	eɪ ɔɪ		ɛə ɜ	ɔə
	æ ɑ	ɑɪ	aʊ	(æə) ɑə	

The phonetic realization of several of the vowels varies considerably among different sectors of the population and, to a lesser extent, in different phonological environments; this is discussed below. The lexical incidence of vowels is shown in (232).

(232)	KIT	ɪ	FLEECE	i	NEAR	ɪə(r)[1]
	DRESS	ɛ	FACE	eɪ	SQUARE	ɛə(r)[1]
	TRAP	æ, æə, ɛə[1]	PALM	ɑə	START	ɑə(r)[1], ɑr
	LOT	ɑ, ɑə[1]	THOUGHT	ɔə[1]	NORTH	ɔə(r)[1]
	STRUT	ʌ	GOAT	oʊ	FORCE	ɔə(r)[1]
	FOOT	ʊ	GOOSE	u, ɪu[1]	CURE	ʊə(r)[1]
	BATH	æə, ɛə[1]	PRICE	ɑɪ	happY	i
	CLOTH	ɔə[1]	CHOICE	ɔɪ[1]	lettER	ə(r)[1]
	NURSE	ɜ(r)[1]	MOUTH	aʊ	commA	ə

[1]discussed below.

There are thus mergers of the standard lexical sets CLOTH with THOUGHT and NORTH with FORCE as well as (subject to the reservations discussed below) of these two pairs with one another, and occasionally with CURE; of START with PALM; of lettER with commA; also, potentially, of BATH and certain TRAP words with SQUARE or even NEAR, and of certain LOT words with PALM(– START).

The vowels here written /i/ and /u/ are in fact very commonly diphthongal, and might alternatively have been symbolized /ɪi, ʊu/. The extent of the diphthongal movement tends to vary sociolinguistically, being smaller in middle-class speech and greater in working-class speech: in the latter the first elements of the two diphthongs may well be central, [ɨi] and [əu]. But another popular-speech variant of /u/ is monophthongal and very back, about cardinal 8. The rounding of /u/ is weak, without any lip protrusion.

The pronunciation of words like *tune, duke, new* raises the question: does a New York accent include a distinctive /ɪu/ in opposition to /u/ and /ju/? The answer is on the whole yes, although the evidence is not absolutely clear-cut for all speakers and styles. Potential minimal pairs are *yew* /jɪu/ vs. *you* /ju/, *dew* /dju ~ djɪu ~ dɪu/ vs. *do* /du/. However *do* can also be pronounced with the /ɪu/ diphthong, making it a possible homophone of *dew* /dɪu/. On the other hand *dew* is not normally pronounced /du/, so that the homophony works in one direction only (Labov 1966: 546). Pronunciations including /j/ after the alveolar stop are often perceived as affected. The most usual New York pronunciation for the three keywords mentioned is perhaps /tɪun, dɪuk, nɪu/.

The vowel here written /ɜ/ has a variety of phonetic realizations, as discussed below (6.3.4).

The centring diphthongs symbolized /ɪə, ɛə, ɑə, ɔə, ʊə/ are by no means restricted lexically to words which had historical postvocalic /r/. In fact /ɛə/ is found most frequently in certain BATH and TRAP words: the pronunciation /bɛəd/, while possible for *bared*, is more likely to stand for *bad*. And /ɑə/ and /ɔə/ regularly occur in PALM and CLOTH–THOUGHT respectively, where they correspond to GenAm /ɑ/ and /ɔ/; /ɑə/ is also used in certain LOT words (6.3.7 below). Hence *saw* is commonly a homophone of *sore–soar* /sɔə/, while *god* is usually /gɑəd/, making it a potential homophone of *guard*. The complicating factor here is the variability of the /r/ in such words (6.3.3): if *bared, sore*, and *guard* are pronounced /bɛərd, sɔər, gɑərd/ – as they often are – then they are no longer homophones of *bad, saw*, and *god* respectively.

All the centring diphthongs have monophthongal variants, of the type [ɪː, ɛː, ɑː, ɔː, ʊː] respectively. These occur most readily in the environment of a following intervocalic consonant within a word, as *hearing, dairy, Chicago, sausage, curious*. The degree of openness of /ɛə/ and /ɔə/ varies considerably, as discussed below (6.3.5 and

6.3.6). Short /ɑ/ is central, [ɑ₊], and the starting-point of /ɑə/ may either be similar to it or else considerably backer – fully back like cardinal 5. This latter type, [ɑːə], is associated with the use of a closer /ɔə/ variant ([ʊːə] etc.), the former with a relatively open one ([ɔ̈ː] etc.). Some speakers use the central quality in all LOT words, e.g. *god* [gɑ₊ːəd], but the back quality in START (with or without restored /r/), e.g. *guard* [gɑːə(r)d]. This is associated with intermediate variants of /ɔə/. Clearly, for those (predominantly middle-class) speakers who use central /ɑə/ and also restore historical /r/, the /ɑ–ɑə/ opposition is tenuous, being neutralized in most environments. See further, 6.3.7 below.

The starting-point of the diphthong /ɑɪ/ also tends to be rather back – particularly in working-class and lower-middle class speech. The New York pronunciation of a word such as *night-time* /ˈnɑɪttɑɪm/ can sound very like the Cockney of London.

The oppositions /i–ɪə, eɪ–ɛə/ tend to be neutralized in the environment of a following /l/, with /ɪə, ɛə/-like qualities being used in every case. Thus not only may *reel* and *real* fall together, but also pairs such as *Bailey* and *barely*; [ɛː ~ ɛə] is very commonly heard in words such as *bail, sailor, failure*.

The oppositions /ɪ–ɪə, ɛ–ɛə/ are usually preserved in New York speech, so that *mirror* does not rhyme with *nearer*, nor *ferry* with *Mary* (vol. 1, 3.3.1, Vowels before /r/). But speakers are not always entirely consistent, particularly in the case of /ɪ–ɪə/ before a non-morpheme-final /r/, as *serious* [ˈsɪ(ː)rɪəs].

Examples of oddities of lexical incidence of vowels particularly characteristic of New York include *Durham* /ˈdʊərəm/, *donkey* /ˈdʌŋki/, *won't* /wʊnt/, *forward* /ˈfoʊwəd/, *almost* /ˈoʊmoʊs(t)/, *always* /ˈoʊweɪz/; the last three are all regarded as non-standard, and all exist alongside alternatives with the expected /ˈdʌr-, ˈdɑŋ-, woʊnt, ˈfɔə-, ˈɔəl-/. (Philadelphians, too, say /dʌŋki/.)

6.3.3 Variable non-rhoticity and its consequences

New York has traditionally been regarded as having a non-rhotic accent. Historically, this reflects the loss of /r/ in all non-prevocalic environments (R Dropping, vol. 1, 3.2.2), yielding pronunciations such as *near* /nɪə/, *square* /skwɛə/, *start* /stɑət/, *north* /nɔəθ/, *force* /fɔəs/, *cure* /kjʊə/, *letter* /ˈlɛtə/, *nurse* /nɜs/ [nɜɪs]. Now, however, a process of restoring the lost historical /r/s is well under way; it is presumed to result from the pressure exerted by GenAm, which is now looked on as a standard and is of course fully rhotic. The resultant pronunciations of the same keywords are /nɪər, skwɛər, stɑərt, nɔərθ, fɔərs, kjʊər, lɛtər, nɜrs/. This R Restoration does not alter the fact that the New York vowel system is of the type characteristically found in non-rhotic accents, including as it does a set of centring diphthongs /ɪə, ɛə, ɑə, ɔə, ʊə/.

Non-prevocalic /r/ was the subject of Labov's famous investigation in New York department stores (1966: 63–89). For this he took three stores, one low-status, one intermediate, and one high-status. In them he proceeded to accost over 200 sales staff and elicited from each the utterance *fourth floor*. This provided him in each case with two instances of a potential non-prevocalic /r/ – one preconsonantal, one absolute-final, both morpheme-final – and so enabled him to construct (r) indices for each store and for various categories of employee (see (233)). One important finding was that variability in the use of non-prevocalic /r/ is the rule rather than the exception among New Yorkers. Another was that the kind of social stratification revealed was different for different age groups. In the lowest-status store (Klein's, where the sales staff were presumed to be of relatively low social class), a non-rhotic pronunciation was the norm for all age groups, although some rhotic pronunciations too were always present, particularly among the oldest and youngest employees. There were more rhotic pronunciations in the other two stores. But, while in the intermediate-status one (Macy's) rhoticity increased with age, in the highest-status store (Saks, where the social class of the employees, too, was assumed to be highest) it decreased with age.

(233)	Upper middle class (Saks)	Lower middle class (Macy's)	Working class (Klein's)
Estimated age			
15–30	67 (78)	21 (47)	10 (25)
35–50	26 (65)	26 (56)	0 (15)
55–70	13 (48)	39 (58)	4 (23)

Percentages of New York department-store employees using /r/ in both *fourth* and *floor*, by age and social class (in brackets, percentages using /r/ in at least one of the two words). Derived from Labov 1966: 349

The pattern of /r/ usage in Labov's wider survey, based on a random quota sample of dwellers in the Lower East Side, turned out to be identical. It was also found that in their subjective evaluation of recorded accents, New Yorkers aged under about forty (in the early 1960s) reacted favourably to rhoticity, and unfavourably to non-rhoticity, while the older respondents had mixed reactions. And in their most careful and deliberate style of pronunciation, when reading aloud potential minimal pairs such as *guard–god*, a rhotic pronunciation was used by a very large proportion of New Yorkers; the exceptions were the youngest and oldest members of the lower class and the working class.

As discussed in volume 1, 1.1.8, the New York use of non-prevocalic /r/ varies not only by socio-economic class and age but also by style. In casual style, all social groups use it in under 20 per cent of the cases where it would occur in a rhotic accent. This is the justification for regarding New York English as basically non-rhotic, even though in very careful and monitored styles the proportion of non-prevocalic /r/ used may reach almost 80 per cent.

As in other non-rhotic accents, a morpheme-final /r/ does nevertheless occur when the following segment is a vowel (/r/ sandhi, vol. 1, 3.2.3). Here New York speech conforms to the pattern found in England, the southern hemisphere, and eastern New England rather than the American south, since (i) /r/ sandhi occurs freely across word boundaries, and (ii) intrusive /r/ – that is, /r/ sandhi in cases where no historical /r/ occurred – is common. Thus the word *nearest* (*near#est*) is pronounced /ˈnɪɔrɔst/, even though *nearby* is most commonly /nɪəˈbaɪ/; *near Albany* is /ˈnɪər ˈɔəlbəni/, although *near* by itself is usually /ˈnɪə/; and *the idea is* may well be /ði ɑɪˈdɪər ˈɪz/. /r/ sandhi applies to all the centring diphthongs, as well as to /ɜ/ (insofar as final non-r-coloured variants occur) and to /ə/.

Pronunciations such as *idea* /ɑɪˈdɪər/, *law* /lɔər/ may also occur for another reason, namely through inaccurate attempts at restoring the statusful historical /r/ (see above). Once /fɪər/ comes to be perceived as more statusful than /fɪə/, and /stɔər/ than /stɔə/, then such pronunciations are naturally likely to arise through the application of an R-Insertion rule after any /ɪə, ɛə, ɑə, ɔə, ʊə, ɜ, ə/ indiscriminately. There are no statistics on the frequency of occurrence of forms of this type in New York, but they certainly occur. So (occasionally) do cases such as *cob* /kɑərb/, for the same reason.

In the case of a prevocalic intrusive /r/, as in *the idea*/r/ *is*, *law*/r/ *and order*, there is no way of knowing which of these two mechanisms is responsible in any given case; no doubt the one reinforces the other.

The actual realization of /r/ is usually post-alveolar, [ɹ]. It is often strongly labialized, particularly in syllable-initial positions; and there are quite a few New Yorkers who use a labiodental approximant, [ʋ], rather than a post-alveolar. Although sometimes thought of as typical of Brooklynese, this is probably a personal idiosyncrasy not associated with any particular social parameter.

6.3.4 NURSE and CHOICE

The caricature stereotype has it that the Brooklynese for *thirty-third* is *toity-toid*. Reality, as always, is more complicated. The traditional New York realization of the NURSE vowel is [ɜɪ], a closing diphthong with a mid central starting-point. This diphthong was also used in certain CHOICE words, so that *earl* and *oil* became homophones, though as [ɜɪl] rather than as [ɔɪl]. But this applies only preconsonantally: *stir* and *boy* never rhyme, even in the broadest Brooklynese. Furthermore, [ɜɪ] is in competition with a number of other possible realizations of the vowels in NURSE and CHOICE, and appears now to be sharply recessive in the face of competition from [ɝ] and [ɔɪ] respectively. By hypercorrection, *oil* is often [ɝl] and *toilet* ['tɝlət].

In NURSE words there are some New Yorkers who use a mid central monophthong, [ɜ], much as in British RP. Hubbell (1950a: 86) reports this as being restricted to 'cultivated' speakers and as commoner for women than for men. The influence of the new, midwestern, prestige model has now led to an increasing use of a monophthong which is similar, except for being r-coloured, [ɝ] (or more precisely [ɝ:]). This is found even in the speech of many who do not otherwise use much rhoticity – Hubbell reports his own usual pronunciation as being non-rhotic in *beard, cared, hard, court, cured,* but with [ɝ] (which he writes [ɾ]) in *turn* (1950a: 49). For New Yorkers born since about 1950, this r-coloured variant is the usual one for the NURSE vowel.

The other variants are restricted by phonological environment. The famous [ɜɪ] occurs only in the environment of a following consonant belonging to the same morpheme, as *turn, first, word.* Elsewhere – as *her, fir, furry,* or where the following consonant belongs to a suffix, as *stirs, occurred* – there is the possibility of [ʌ] or a lengthened version of it, [ʌ: ~ ʌɐ].

For an older generation, [ɜɪ] was not stigmatized in NURSE words of the first group just mentioned. Well over half of Labov's informants born before 1910 used it; it can be observed regularly in the speech of such sophisticated New Yorkers as Henry Miller and the late Groucho Marx, for whom *first* is [fɜɪst] and *third* is [θɜɪd]. There was perhaps a tendency for the extent of the diphthongal glide to be smaller in middle-class speech than in rougher accents, where the realization might be rather [ʌɪ]. Suddenly, however, the [ɜɪ] type became stigmatized – indeed, it can now be described as 'the most well known example of a stigmatized New York City trait', and has come to symbolize 'Brooklynese' (Labov 1966: 337). In the speech of those born between about 1925 and 1945 its use exhibits sharp social stratification, as it receded down the social scale; for those born since the Second World War it is now a highly stigmatized mark of lower-class speech.

There is also a compromise pronunciation sometimes encountered, namely a closing diphthong in which the first element is r-coloured, namely [ɚɪ].

The diphthong [ɜɪ] is also sometimes found in CHOICE words, but again only in the environment of a following consonant belonging to the same morpheme, as in *voice*, [vɜɪs], or *join* [dʒɜɪn]. This can result in homophony with NURSE words where they too have [ɜɪ], as *learn–loin, curl–coil*. Labov reports a few of his working-class or lower-class informants as having *oil* and *earl*, *voice* and *verse* identical. In other environments an [ɔɪ]-type diphthong is always used, though with the first element varying in backness, rounding, and protrusion somewhat as /ɔə/ does: e.g. *boy, enjoy, annoys*. Exceptionally, *noise* seems always to have [ɔɪ], never [ɜɪ].

It seems likely that for speakers who have *oil* and *earl*, etc., as homophones [ɜɪ] should be considered an allophone of /ɔɪ/. Indeed, this is probably the case for many who use [ɚ] in *earl* but [ɜɪ] in *oil*; Hubbell (1950a: 70) reports that he has had many New York college students who would say [bɔɪ] for *boy* and [bɜɪl] for *boil* and think that they were pronouncing the same diphthong in both words. It is for this reason that I have not included any putative phoneme /ɜɪ/ in the vowel system displayed in 6.3.2 above. The switch from earlier [bɚd] to [bɜɪd] was presumably a question of rephonemicization, as the [ɜɪ] allophone came to be associated with the /ɔɪ/ phoneme; but the switch back to [bɚd] can be seen as a relexification, a change in phoneme incidence from /ɔɪ/ to /ɜr/ – a view supported by the attested occurrence of various hypercorrections such as [ɜˑl] *oil* and [dʒɝn] *join* (Hubbell 1950a: 69).

In NURSE words where there is no following tautomorphemic consonant, there is – as mentioned above – the possibility of [ʌ] or [ʌː ~ ʌɐ]. The former implies that the phonetic distinction between pairs such as *stirred–stud* is lost, the second that it is retained. There are also closer qualities possible, [ə ~ ɪ]. Although these non-rhotic pronunciations are not as common as the standard [ɝ], there is no clear correlation between their use and social class or age. They are not – or not yet – stigmatized in New York in the way that [ɜɪ] is. Stressed *her* fluctuates between [hɝ] and [hʌ ~ hʌː] in a way we do not altogether understand. Perhaps it is a case of genuine free variation.

6.3.5 BATH Raising

We have discussed above (6.1.4) the sound change currently in progress in North America, whereby [æ] is giving way to closer, longer, diphthongal qualities in an increasing number of TRAP and BATH words. In New York this process of BATH Raising is of particular interest: (i) because the local accent, unlike GenAm, includes /ɛə/ and /ɪə/ phonemes with which the raised BATH collides, and (ii) because it was chosen as one of the variables to be studied and quantified by Labov (1966), and was shown to be linked to socioeconomic class and other social parameters.

New York speech regularly retains /æ/ in the environment of a following voiceless plosive or affricate, as *cap, hat, back, match*, and also before /l/, as *pal, shallow*. Lengthening, and usually raising (and what many consider to be tensing) is general in the environment of a following final voiced stop (*cab, bad, rag, badge*), voiceless fricative (*laugh, bath, grass, cash*), or /m, n/ (*ham, man*). It also applies when one of these consonants is followed by an inflectional boundary (*stabs, grassy, manly*) or an obstruent (*camp, dance, candy, branch*), but not if it is followed by a vowel or liquid. Thus there is typically a phonemic contrast between /æ/ in *dragon* and something else in *dragging*. Modals and auxiliaries are exceptions, so that *had* and *can* retain /æ/ (in their strong form); thus *had* /hæd/ contrasts with *bad* and *can* 'be able' with *can* 'container'. There is inconsistency in the environment of a following final voiced fricative or /ŋ/, as *salve, jazz, bang*; some speakers use /æ/, some the lengthened vowel.

As his phonological variable '(eh)' Labov considered the words in which lengthening is usual, i.e. those exemplified by *cab* to *branch* above. These are words which in New York do not have the /æ/ of *fat*. The question is, what vowel do they have?

Hubbell sets up two phonemes, /æə̄/ and /aə̄/, to cater for the middle-class and elegant New York pronunciations of these words with [æ: ~ æə] and [a: ~ aə] respectively. Otherwise he considers them as having the same /ɛə/ as in the non-rhotic pronunciation of SQUARE words. In the latter case *bad* becomes a homophone of *bared*, [bɛ:əd]. Many speakers, though (he reports), deliberately avoid this pronunciation; but there is 'a great deal of variation in successive utterances of the same word', and usage seems 'extremely haphazard' (Hubbell 1950a: 75–8).

Labov has now shown that the range of vowel qualities used is in fact even greater, extending from the [a:] and [æ:] mentioned above through intermediate [æ⁺:] and [ɛ:ə] to half-close or even closer qualities, [e⁺:ə] or [ɪ+:ə]. Thus *bad* overlaps not only with non-rhotic *bared* but also with *beard* /bɪəd/.

Labov's findings for (eh) can be summarized as shown in (234). The height of the vowel in the words in question increases as we travel down the social scale and as we move from formal to casual style. In the casual speech of the lower class, the average quality is [ɛ:ə] – more precisely, one-third of the way from [ɛ:ə] to [æ:]. In the same socio-economic class's word-list style, the average quality is just beyond [æ:] in the direction of [æ:]. For the working class (between the lower class and the middle class), the average quality in casual speech is half-way between [ɛ:ə] and [æ:], while for the middle class it is two-thirds of the distance from [ɛ:ə] to [æ:]. In the reading-passage style, the working class are like the lower class, while the middle class are just half-way between [æ:] and [æ:]. In figures, the full scores for (eh) by social class and contextual style are as shown in (234). These averages are calculated on the basis that [ɪ:ə ~ e:ə] (like NYC *beard*) is scored 10, [ɛ:ə] (like NYC *bare*) 20, [æ:] 30, [æ:] (qualitatively like NYC *bat*) 40, and [a:] 50.

(234)	Casual style	Interview style	Reading style	Word-list style
Lower class	23	27	29	32
Working class	25	28	30	32
Middle class	27	30	34	35

(derived from Labov 1966: 221)

These average scores conceal not only considerable variation between individuals, but also – for example – the fact that while only 2 per cent of Jews in the sample scored 18 or under in casual-speech style, 38 per cent of the Italian-Americans did so: that is, they had an average quality closer than [ɛːə]. This is seen as a reaction against the first-generation Italian immigrants who used a very open [a] for [æ], perceived by Americans as 'foreign'.

Another interesting fact is revealed when we split the middle class into lower middle and upper middle, and compare the vowel respondents reported they used with the vowel they actually used. Lower-middle-class speakers in New York showed a strong tendency to report themselves as using [æː] in the word *pass*, although as objectively observed they tended to use the pronunciation with [ɛːə]. And in the most formal style (word lists) they produced on average an opener quality than the upper-middle-class speakers – an example of Labov-hypercorrection (vol. 1, 1.1.8).

Quite apart from the degree of raising in TRAP and BATH words, it turns out that there are New Yorkers who merge the NEAR and SQUARE vowels. A group of white working-class Manhattan teenagers studied by Labov *et al.* (1968) had an (eh) average scarcely closer than [æː], and did not merge *bad* and non-rhotic *bared*; but they had a complete merger of NEAR and SQUARE, with *bared–beard*, *bear–beer* as homophones.

The general trend, then, is to reduce the number of front centring diphthongs. Some New Yorkers have three surface phonemes of this type (assuming a non-rhotic pronunciation as basic): /æə/ in *bad*, /ɛə/ in *bared*, and /ɪə/ in *beard*. The first two tend to merge because of BATH Raising, giving a pattern of /ɛə/ in *bad–bared*, /ɪə/ in *beard*. The latter two may merge as just mentioned, giving a pattern /æə/ in *bad*, /ɪə/ in *bared–beard*. Eventually we get a three-way merger, with /ɪə/ in *bad–bared–beard*. Three phonemes are reduced to one.

6.3.6 CLOTH–THOUGHT Raising

For the /ɔə/ vowel in CLOTH and THOUGHT the standard and upper-middle-class New York pronunciation is [ɔ:ə] or [ɔ:]. The quality of the first part of the diphthong, or of the whole in the case of the monophthongal variant, is identical with that of GenAm /ɔ/ in NORTH words, i.e. slightly closer than cardinal 6. The monophthongal variant is found before intervocalic consonants in polysyllables, as *water, sausage*, and quite often in other preconsonantal environments. The same vowel is used in the non-rhotic pronunciation of NORTH and FORCE words: *law* and non-rhotic *lore* are homophonous, /lɔə/.

Often, though, a closer quality is used, together with a more prominent centring glide. This gives a diphthong of the [o:ə] type, thus *loss* [lo:əs], *law* [lo:ə]. This is common in the casual style of speech of the middle class and also in the careful reading style of the lower class; unlike the closer varieties of the TRAP–BATH vowel, it is not perceived as socially significant by the general New York public. Some speakers use a closer vowel still, with more intense rounding, [u:ə]; Labov suggests that women tend to purse their lips when articulating this closest variant, but men to use some kind of 'hollowing of the tongue' or inner rounding. This leads to a potential loss of phonemic opposition between /ɔə/ and /uə/, with *sure* and *shore* merging.

Scoring [u:ə] as 10, [o:ə] as 20, [ɔ:(ə)] as 30, cardinal-type [ɔ:] as 40, and occasional opener types [ɒ] and [ɑ+] as 50 and 60 respectively, Labov derived averaged '(oh) scores', tabulated in (235) by style and socio-economic class.

(235)

	Casual style	Interview style	Reading style	Word-list style
Lower class	23	24	24	21
Working class	20	22	23	24
Middle class	20	24	27	30

(derived from Labov 1966: 221)

Analysis by ethnic group revealed that in this case it is the Jewish New Yorkers who are spearheading the trend towards a closer /ɔə/ quality: almost 20 per cent of Jews in the sample scored 13 or under in casual-speech style (i.e. predominantly used [u:ə], the closest variant, implying a merger of /ɔə–ʊə/), while none of the Italians did.

6.3.7 LOT Lengthening

As discussed above (6.3.2), there may or may not be an /r/ in the New York pronunciation of *cart*. If there is none, *cart* and *cot* are distinguished by the backer quality and/or longer duration of the vowel of *cart* /kɑət/ compared with that of *cot* /kɑt/. If /r/ is present, these vowel differences may remain; or, being now redundant, they may be lost as in GenAm, giving [kɑrt] vs. [kɑt] (with centralized [ɑ]). But in no case do the two words become homophonous. The same applies before other voiceless stops: *lock* remains distinct from *lark* and *shop* from *sharp*, while *scotch* does not rhyme with *starch*. However, in certain other phonetic environments there is no such opposition between words of the LOT and START sets. In New York there has evidently been a historical sound change we may call LOT Lengthening. This consisted in the lengthening and diphthonging of earlier /ɑ/ (from Middle English /ɔ/) in the environment of a following word-final voiced stop, /b, d, dʒ, g/, as shown in (236).

(236) ɑ → ɑə / __ {b, d, dʒ, g, m} #

Thus *bob, cod, lodge*, and *cog* are now /bɑəb, kɑəd, lɑədʒ, kɑəg/. The first three are homophonous with the non-rhotic pronunciations of *barb, card*, and *large* respectively. This LOT Lengthening also applied before /m/, but not before other sonorants. Thus *bomb* is usually /bɑəm/, homophonous with *balm* and rhyming with non-rhotic *harm* /hɑəm/; but *swan, loll* retain /ɑ/ and consequently do not rhyme with *barn, snarl*. Exceptionally, *on, John*, and *doll* may have /ɑə/; there are also sporadic instances of LOT Lengthening before /ʃ/ and voiced fricatives, as *wash* /wɑəʃ/, *bother* /'bɑəðə(r)/.

Before non-final consonants, LOT Lengthening does not apply. Thus *gobble* has /ɑ/, and does not rhyme with *garble*; similarly, *toddy* vs. *tardy*, *goggles* vs. *gargles*, *hominy* vs. *harmony*. When the following consonant is morpheme-final but not word-final, there is some variability and inconsistency. Whereas *rob* is definitely /rɑəb/ and *robin* definitely /'rɑbən/, *robbing* and *robber* may have either vowel. Although *Bob* and *John* are /bɑəb, dʒɑən/, *Bobbie* and *Johnnie* are usually /'bɑbi, 'dʒɑni/. The *Dodgers* may rhyme either with *Rogers* or with non-rhotic *enlargers*. Here, too, there are occasional anomalies: *toboggan*, which contains no morpheme boundary, is nevertheless reported to be /təˈbaəgən/, homophonous with non-rhotic *to bargain*.

6.3.8 Alveolars and dentals

Many New Yorkers pronounce the alveolar consonants /t, d, n, l/ with the blade of the tongue rather than with the tip. The articulation is made by the blade forming a closure against the alveolar ridge, while the tip of the tongue stays down, usually in contact with the lower teeth. With /t/ and /d/ a secondary articulation (velarization or pharyngealization) may be present. A characteristic auditory effect is noticeable, particularly with /t/ and /d/ at the beginning of a stressed syllable. This blade articulation may even be used for the cluster /tr/, as in *try*, where the tongue tip may remain against the lower teeth throughout.

In syllable-initial position, and sometimes also utterance-finally, the special character of the blade-alveolar realization is enhanced by its being particularly heavily aspirated, or indeed affricated. Thus *tin*, *din*, may be [tʰɪn ∼ t̪ˢɪn, d̪ᶻɪn] (where [t̪, d̪] denote blade articulations).

The other respect in which New York /t/ differs from GenAm norms is in the prevalence of the glottal allophone [ʔ] in a wider range of syllable-final environments. Although there is never anything approaching British-style glottalling, lower-status New York speech is known for pronunciations such as ['baʔl] *bottle*, ['ʃʌʔl] *shuttle*. It does not occur as a realization of intervocalic /t/ except very occasionally across a word boundary, as *not only*; although reports from the nineteenth century mention pronunciations like ['lɛʔə] *letter*, they are not to be found in current New York speech.

Of the phonological variables studied in detail by Labov, the two we have not so far discussed are those he labels (th) and (dh), namely the realization of /θ/ and /ð/. In popular New York speech these are frequently pronounced as affricates or stops, rather than as fricatives. Usually they remain dental, so that the oppositions /t–θ/ and /d–ð/ are not lost. Thus *thanks* may be [θæŋks], [t̪θæŋks], or [t̪æŋks], in decreasing order of statusfulness; all are distinct from *tanks* [tʰæŋks ~ tˢæŋks]. The [ʇ] variant has a weakish articulation. The /t–θ/ opposition may be lost, exceptionally, in the environment of a following /r/ (*three* = *tree*), and in the case of the word *with* (so that *with a* may rhyme with *bitter–bidder*; *with you* may be [wɪtʃu], following the same Yod Coalescence rule as *hit you*). These pronunciations are all stigmatized.

The /d–ð/ opposition seems to be lost rather more readily, though not as readily as the Brooklynese stereotype might lead one to believe. As in many other places, initial /ð/ is subject to assimilation or deletion in a range of environments in relatively informal and/or popular speech, e.g. *who's there?* ['huz‿(z)ɛə]; as in many other places, it is also subject to stopping, e.g. *there* [dɛə]. This option extends to one or two words in which the /ð/ is not initial, e.g. *other* /'ʌðə(r)/, which can thus become a homophone of *utter– udder*. But it would not be usual for *southern* to be pronounced identically with *sudden*, or *breathe* with *breed*.

Labov's scoring procedure for (th) and (dh) is such that consistent use of fricative realizations for /θ/ and /ð/ scores zero, while consistent plosives would score 200. Affricates are scored as intermediate between fricative and stop; so, too, is the zero realization (deletion) of /ð/. The two tables (237, 238) summarize his scorings for the (th) and (dh) variables respectively, by style and socioeconomic class.

(237)

	(th)		
	Casual style	Interview style	Reading style
Lower class	78	65	44
Working class	68	54	27
Middle class	26	17	10

(238)

	(dh)		
	Casual style	Interview style	Reading style
Lower class	79	56	49
Working class	64	45	34
Middle class	30	17	13

(derived from Labov 1966: 221)

These figures are again averages; individual scores ranged from a working-class woman with around 150 (stop or affricate in most occurrences of /θ, ð/) down to several respondents with zero (all /θ, ð/ fricative). The middle-class figures are biased because of one anomalous respondent who had, as he acknowledged, 'a speech problem with *ths*'. Excluding him, the middle-class scores are lower; the casual-speech score of the upper middle class is then as low as 12 for (th), 21 for (dh).

One can conclude that any New Yorker who uses no plosives or affricates for /θ/ or /ð/ in careful conversation has been to high school and is not a manual worker – quite likely he is a professional. If he uses plosives or affricates sporadically, he has probably been to high school, but is not a professional; if he uses them a lot, he has probably had no high school education. Thus the great majority of New Yorkers use at least some plosives or affricates for /θ, ð/. Furthermore, men use many more than women, and Italians use more than Jews.

As in other accents where plosive realizations of /θ/ and /ð/ are frequent, the clusters /tθ/ and /dθ/ are ruled out by the phonotactics. In consequence *eighth* rhymes with *faith* and *width* with *myth*: in a broad New York accent they are [eɪt̪] and [wɪt̪].

6.3.9 Other consonants

As in RP, Glide Cluster Reduction (vol. 1, 3.2.4) is usual in New York speech. Thus *white* and *when* are /waɪt, wɛn/; pronunciations such as /hwaɪt/ and /hwɛn/ are used inconsistently if at all, and only as a result of a conscious attempt to adopt them.

Morpheme-final [ŋg] for [ŋ] is sometimes to be observed with New Yorkers, as *singer* ['sɪŋgə(r)], *Long Island* [lɔːŋg'aɪlənd]. Some claim this is restricted to the speech of those whose parents were first-generation immigrants to the United States, so that it is to be seen as a residual foreignism rather than as a continuation of the pattern to be found in parts of the American south and the midlands and north of England (vol. 2, 4.4.6); I am not so sure.

L Vocalization is quite common in New York, though not on the scale found in the English or the American south. It is found in the non-prevocalic environments (*sell, sells, sold*; but not *selling*, although this intervocalic position has a lateral which is definitely 'dark' by British standards). Hubbell describes the vocalized /l/ as involving some raising of the tip and blade of the tongue, though not to the point of any contact with the alveolar ridge; 'sometimes the back of the tongue seems to articulate against the velum'. I find the auditory result of this articulatory configuration less striking than the entirely vowel-like sounds to be observed in London speech; and unlike in London vocalized /l/ does not, for instance, occur in words such as *little, middle* in such a way as to change the alveolar release from lateral to median (as far as I am aware). Bronstein (1960: 128) characterizes it as 'careless' (quotation marks his), and as a faulty variation associated with substandard speech. Hubbell, though (1950a: 51), explicitly asserts that it is not confined to uncultivated speech, and this is my impression too.

6.4 New England

6.4.1 Introduction

New England comprises the states of Connecticut, Maine, Massachusetts, New Hampshire, Rhode Island, and Vermont. It falls within the northern speech area of the United States (see 6.1.1 above); the western part of New England (Connecticut, Vermont, western Massachusetts) falls under the 'GenAm' category and is covered in the section so entitled (6.1 above). The eastern part, however, has certain special pronunciation characteristics, and it is to **eastern New England** that this section is particularly devoted.

The principal city of eastern New England is Boston, Mass. As a leading seaport, Boston has throughout its history been a centre through which European influences (particularly those from England) have spread. In pronunciation, too, it is clear that some of the characteristic eastern New England traits represent the importation of innovations originating in the south of England: non-rhoticity (loss of historical /r/ except before vowels), BATH Broadening ([ɑː ∼ ɑ:] rather than [æ] in words of the lexical set BATH), and others. North-eastern New England is an area of rather difficult communications (mountains, a deeply indented coastline), and there is a considerable amount of geographical variation between the various settlements; but it is reasonable to regard Maine, New Hampshire, eastern Massachusetts, Rhode Island, and the eastern-most corner of Connecticut as constituting a single speech area, corresponding to the popular American perception of a Bostonian, New England, or vaguely 'eastern' accent (though the latter may also refer to the speech of New York City). The western boundary of eastern New England runs from the mouth of the Connecticut River opposite the end of Long Island, east of Hartford and Springfield, Mass., then through Vermont to the Canadian border.

Under present-day circumstances the distinctive characteristics of eastern New England pronunciation are steadily being eroded by the influence of GenAm speech patterns. This homogenization will doubtless continue; New England is no longer the centre of fashion and innovation which it once was, and Boston no longer sets the tone for unsophisticated hinterlands. On the contrary, the mid west and the far west now influence Boston, which in any case is now not so much a special city apart as the northern end of the Boston–Washington conurbational corridor.

On the basis of the *PEAS* findings, the eastern New England vowel system is as shown in (239).

(239)

ɪ	ʊ	i		(ɪu)	u	iə		uə
ɛ	(ɵ)	eɪ			o	æə	3	oə
æ	ʌ	aɪ	ɔɪ	aʊ		ɑ		ɒ

From a systemic point of view, /a/ could equally well be written as /ɑ/, /ɒ/ as /ɔ/, and /æə/ as /ɛə/ or /eə/. Length-marks could well be used for the monophthongs in part-systems B, C, and D, too, as in the structurally similar RP. That /ɒ/ is a long vowel is clearly heard in the pronunciation of the name *Boston* /ˈbɒstən/ [ˈbɒːstən] (compare the English [ˈbɒstən]).

The lexical incidence of these vowels is shown in (240)

(240)

KIT	ɪ	FLEECE	i	NEAR	iə
DRESS	ɛ	FACE	eɪ	SQUARE	æə
TRAP	æ	PALM	a	START	a
LOT	ɒ	THOUGHT	ɒ	NORTH	ɒ
STRUT	ʌ	GOAT	o	FORCE	oə
FOOT	ʊ	GOOSE	u	CURE	uə
BATH	a, æ	PRICE	aɪ	*happ*Y	ɪ, i
CLOTH	ɒ	CHOICE	ɔɪ	*lett*ER	ə
NURSE	3	MOUTH	aʊ	*comm*A	ə

We may further note that New England is well-known for the traditional tendency to use /ɪ/ rather than /ə/ in the weak syllables of *waited* /'weɪtɪd/, *horses* /'hɒsɪz/, *ticket* /'tɪkɪt/, etc.

6.4.2 Non-rhoticity

In the early part of the twentieth century, Boston speech was well-known for its non-rhoticity. The speech of eastern New England, like that of eastern England, evidently underwent the innovation of R Dropping (vol. 3.2.2). It is the great impact on the vowel system which this development inevitably entails which furnishes one reason for treating this accent separately from the rest of the north of the United States. In the country as a whole, however, this century has seen the rhotic GenAm norm become established to such an extent that eastern New England is now undergoing a return to rhoticity.

The Linguistic Atlas records, dating from the early 1930s, show forms such as [iə] *ear*, [kæə] *care*, [baˑn] *barn*, [kɒˑn] *corn*, [doə] *door*, [pʊə] *poor*, all without any consonantal /r/-type articulation, throughout eastern New England. (But conservative enclaves of rhoticity were found at Cape Ann, Marblehead, and Martha's Vineyard: see map, fig. 21.) As in England, 'linking /r/' is used in phrases such as *far out, your aunt*. Popular speech, though not always cultivated speech, also uses 'intrusive /r/' in phrases such as *Ma and I, law and order*; this is good evidence for rule inversion resulting in a synchronic rule of R Insertion (vol. 1, 3.2.3).

In NURSE words, /r/ is retained somewhat more widely. The Linguistic Atlas records show the /nɜrs/ type as found not only in Cape Ann, Marblehead, and Martha's Vineyard, but also in Nantucket (like Martha's Vineyard, an island off the Massachusetts coast) and sporadically elsewhere; 'only in the immediate neighbourhood of Boston and in the greater part of New Hampshire and Maine is the so-called Eastern pronunciation universal', reported Bloch (1939, based on his dissertation of 1935); though he also demonstrated that the non-rhotic /nɜs/ type was spreading along the coast, northwards into northern Maine and southwestwards into Rhode Island and Connecticut, as shown by the fact that younger informants had less r-colouring than older informants; this applied also to the hitherto rhotic enclaves ('in nearly all

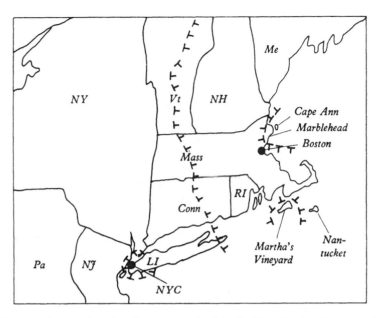

Fig. 21   Areas of predominant non-rhoticity in New England, as noted
in the early 1930s

the speech islands along the New England coast where the pronunciation with *r* has been preserved until the present day, retroflection
is now giving way to the prevailing type'). But a countervailing
pressure from eastern Connecticut and the Hudson Valley meant
that away from the New England coastline it was the /nɜrs/ type
which was winning out. Everywhere the usage of many individual
speakers was 'inconsistent'.

The picture seems rather different now. Only thirty years or so
later, Parslow found that 'of all present phonological developments
in the Boston dialect the most apparent is the re-introduction of
r-timbre in vocalic nuclei' (1967: 127). Boston, far from continuing
as a centre for the dissemination of non-rhotic pronunciation, is
itself becoming rhotic. Nearly half of Parslow's Boston informants
had 'some degree of *r*-timbre' in NURSE words, and they were all in
the younger age groups; the percentage of /r/ in NURSE rose from
zero among his oldest informants to 60 per cent among his youngest.
Final /r/ in *lett*ER words, where the following word began with a
consonant, rose from 15 per cent among the elderly to 33 per cent

among the young. On the other hand, intrusive /r/ in the phrases *law and order, vanilla ice,* and *Nevada and Colorado,* usually a characteristic only of non-rhotic accents, rose from 19 per cent among the elderly to 44 per cent among the middle-aged (and then fell somewhat to 33 per cent among the young).

Not surprisingly, R Restoration leads to a number of unhistorical instances of /r/. Not only did one-third of Parslow's informants have /r/ in *law*, some of them had it in *dog* and *cough* too, no doubt by analogy with words such as *wharf*, as shown in (241).

(241)		*for*	*law*	*north*	*cloth*	*wharf*	*cough*
	Older Boston pronunciation	fɒ	lɒ	nɒθ	klɒθ	wɒf	kɒf
	R restoration, Ø → r/ɒ—	fɒr	lɒr	nɒrθ	klɒrθ	wɒrf	kɒrf

Since hyper-rhotic pronunciations such as /kɒrf/ are even more ludicrous in the eyes of the American majority than traditional Boston non-rhoticity, they are unlikely to become established.

6.4.3 The open front vowel area

The distinctively Bostonian pronunciation of START words involves a long open front vowel /a/ [aː], as in the stereotype example *Park your car in Harvard Yard* /ˈpak jəˈka(r) ɪn ˈhavəd ˈjad/. This vowel is also used in certain words of the lexical set BATH, e.g. *half* /haf/, potentially rhyming with *scarf* /skaf/, and in PALM words (*farther = father* /ˈfaðə/). In this respect eastern New England is like, say, Australian English.

In phonetic quality, /a/ ranges from front [a] to a central [ɑ+] similar to GenAm LOT. (It is usually distinct, however, from the local pronunciation of LOT with /ɒ/, as well as from that of TRAP with /æ/.) The main effects of pressure from the GenAm now perceived as a norm are (i) to reintroduce /r/ in START words, and (ii) to replace /a/ with a vowel of the /æ/ type in BATH words. In current Boston speech, START words are pronounced with a variety of front and central qualities, with or without /r/; as might be predicted, occasional hypercorrections occur, with /r/ being added to PALM words (e.g. *calm* /karm/, reported by Parslow 1967). There is a great deal of variation in BATH words, which are subject not only to the competition between traditional local /a/ and GenAm /æ/ but also to the newer possibility of [eə] (etc.) rather than [æ] (BATH Raising, 6.1.4 above).

The use of /a/, the START vowel, in BATH words, is in very sharp
decline in New England; and the details of its use or non-use vary
very much from word to word. With reference to *calf, glass*, and
dance in eastern New England, *PEAS* comments, 'many speakers
freely shift from /a/ to /æ/ and back again in one and the same word.
Some regard /a/ as refined, others as rustic' (p. 136). In a survey of
the pronunciation of some fifty-odd BATH words by New
Englanders, Miller (1953) found a preference for [ɑ ~ a] only in the
items *aunt, bath, laugh, half, pajamas*, and *path*; there was preference
of over 95 per cent for /æ/ in *cast, nasty, castle, advantage, mast, gasp,
rasp, clasp, mask*, and *command*. Among the respondents from
eastern Massachusetts, *ask* had /æ/ for 84 per cent of the men, but
only 27 per cent of the women (and 41 per cent of the children),
which suggests that [ask ~ ɑsk] is still perceived as more elegant.
Some years later, Thomas (1961) reports a proportion in 'the so-
called broad-*a* words' of 85 per cent [æ], 12 per cent [a], and 3 per
cent [ɑ]; he notes that *aunt* is more likely to have the broad *a* than
after, answer, ask, basket, baths, blast, glass, pass, or *past*. In Boston,
Parslow (1967) found /æ/ predominant in *ask* and *glass*, but not in
past, aunts, and *half*.

In an interesting article, based on a small survey of fourteen
Boston informants, Laferriere (1977) demonstrates the impact of
the new tendency towards Raising. Her older informants have /a/ in
half, path, ask, and *can't*, as against /æ/ in *craft, math, gas*, and *bad*; in
hand they have the first signs of Raising, with [æ ~ ɛə] rather than
[æ]. (Boston does not have the closer [eə], etc., types found in New
York City.) The informants aged between twenty-five and forty-
nine are reported to keep /a/ in *half* and *path*, but a neutral or raised
/æ/ in *ask* and *can't*; they may vary stylistically, casual /a/ competing
with careful /æ/. They use raised allophones of /æ/ in words belonging to both our lexical sets BATH and TRAP, e.g. *ask, can't, hand*,
and sometimes *gas* and *bad*. The youngest group have consistent
Raising in *craft, math, gas, hand*, and *bad*, while in *half, path, ask*,
and *can't* they may have raised /æ/ as an alternative to the traditional
Bostonian /a/ of their parents and grandparents. Thus BATH
Raising is invading territory once the domain of BATH Broadening;
as the older [a] declines, the new [ɛə] takes over, often without a stop
at the hitherto standard GenAm [æ] type. Two processes are at
work: the lexical restructuring of BATH words so as to have the /æ/ of

TRAP rather than the /a/ of START, and the change in the realization of /æ/ in specified environments. (This set of environments, as it happens, includes all those in which BATH Broadening took place, as well as others such as /__b, d, g, ʃ, v/.)

Unlike some New Yorkers, New Englanders do not have [a] as an elegant variant in TRAP words such as *man*.

6.4.4 The open back vowel area

In eastern New England LOT is commonly merged with THOUGHT–CLOTH as /ɒ/, phonetically a back and usually rounded vowel in the [ɒ ~ ɔ] area. The same vowel phoneme is also used in the lexical set NORTH, though not in FORCE.

That, at any rate, is the picture presented by the Linguistic Atlas data in *PEAS*. Here is a major point of difference between the eastern New England and New York City varieties of 'eastern' pronunciation: where Manhattan has LOT /a/ less back than START /ɑə/ and both sharply distinct from THOUGHT /ɔə/, Maine has START /a/ fronter than, and sharply distinct from, LOT–THOUGHT /ɒ/.

Other reports offer a more complicated pattern. It appears that some eastern New Englanders do distinguish *cot* from *caught*; but the phonetic realizations of both LOT and THOUGHT–CLOTH are so variable that it is often very difficult to be certain of the underlying phonemic categories. Thomas (1961) puts it as follows: '*cot* and *caught* overlap, but *cot* varies in the direction of [ɑ] (sc. central [ɑ+]), and *caught* in the direction of [ɔ]. It seems fair, therefore, to set up the phonemes /ɒ/ for *cot*, *box*, and *boss*, and /ɔ/ for *caught*, *bought*, and *born*. Granted that *bought* and *caught* may, in some idiolects, fall in the /ɒ/ category, we cannot deny the contrast in other idiolects ...'. If phonological analysis is an attempt to model the way pronunciation is represented in the speaker's mind, it is no doubt right to distinguish /ɒ/ from /ɔ/, in the case of some speakers, but not for others. Parslow's report (1967) suggests that not only LOT words but also THOUGHT–CLOTH words readily turn up with [ɑ]; one middle-aged man in his survey evidently has a centralized front vowel in *cough*. The same speaker is shown as having [ɒ+] in *horse*, the only NORTH word analysed, which leaves one quite uncertain what the appropriate phonemic categories for this speaker are; the unusual phone [ɒ+] does suggest some confusion.

In the environment __rV, Thomas reports [ɑ] as predominating throughout eastern New England in words such as *borrow, forest, orange, sorry, tomorrow*; according to *PEAS* (p. 126), *tomorrow* 'clearly has /ɒ/'. In western New England, where the LOT vs. THOUGHT opposition is clearly present, these words have /ɔ/ except where New York City influence has displaced it by /ɑ/. The northernmost part of Maine (Aroostook County) also has [ɔ]. In Boston, Parslow's data suggests an ongoing trend away from rounded [ɒ] towards unrounded [ɑ] in words of this category.

The distinction between the NORTH and FORCE lexical categories used to be well preserved everywhere in eastern New England, although now it is becoming lost in many places. *PEAS* comments (p. 120) that their vowels are 'strikingly different', with /ɒ/ in *forty, horse*, and /oə/ in *four, hoarse*. Parslow's report confirms the distinction in Boston speech on the whole, though not necessarily with strikingly different vowel qualities. R Restoration means that *corn* will no longer necessarily rhyme with *lawn* as /kɒn, lɒn/, nor *horse* with *loss* as /hɒs, lɒs/.

Where /oə/ occurs in free position, in words such as *shore, four*, a disyllabic pronunciation is sometimes used when the syllable is prosodically salient, thus [ʃɔˑ(w)ə] etc. Presumably this makes *more* a variable homophone of *mower*.

6.4.5 The New England 'short *o*'

In certain words of the standard lexical set GOAT some New Englanders use not the /o/ of most GOAT words but a short vowel usually represented as /ɵ/. They may, for example, distinguish between *rode* /rod/ and *road* /rɵd/; *home* /hɵm/ may not rhyme with *gnome* /nom/.

Phonetically, /ɵ/ is usually a centralized mid back [ɵ̈], thus *whole* [hɵ̈l], *most* [mɵ̈st]. In the environment of a following /t, d, n/, however, it is realized as a centring diphthong from this starting-point, thus *coat* [kɵ̈ət], *road* [rɵ̈əd], *stone* [stɵ̈ən]. Thus [ɵ̈] and [ɵ̈ə] are co-allophones of /ɵ/; in the speech of those who use this phoneme, they contrast with the [oʊ] of /o/ and also with /ʊ/ and /ʌ/.

As well as those quoted already, words in which /ɵ/ may occur include *smoke, hold* (n.) /hɵlt/, *yolk, toad, folks*, and *bone*.

Even in the early 1930s, when the fieldwork for the Linguistic

Atlas was carried out, /ɵ/ was clearly sharply recessive. It tended to be avoided by educated speakers; and those who did use it used it more readily in words associated with the home or the farm, and therefore less subject to school influence. It is gradually being replaced by ordinary /o/, making *road* a homophone of *rode* as in most other accents of English. In *whole* and *gonna* it may be replaced rather by /ʌ/ (or /ə/?); many speakers who otherwise do not use /ɵ/ at all have some relic of it in these items: this is true in some inland New England settlement areas, too. Otherwise, /ɵ/ must by now be very rare. New Hampshire and Maine, i.e. northeastern New England, is the area where *PEAS* and Avis (1961) find it to be most persistent. Most Bostonians entirely lack the phoneme; though Parslow (1967) does surprisingly report one young Boston informant with /ɵ/ in *ago, coat,* and *home.*

The New England /ɵ/ is no doubt related to the East Anglian use of /ʊ/ in certain GOAT words (vol. 2, 4.3.2). Since /ɵ/ in the United States and /ʊ/ for GOAT in England are both restricted to the east of the respective country, one is tempted to group them together under the title 'Eastern GOAT Shortening'.

6.4.6 PRICE and MOUTH

The wide diphthongs /aɪ/ and /aʊ/, PRICE and MOUTH respectively, are generally pronounced in New England with an open first element somewhere between front [a] and central-back [ɑ+], thus [aɪ, aʊ]. But in many places there are also variants with raised first elements, [ɐɪ] and [ɐʊ]; these are more likely to be found in folk speech than in that of educated people, and more characteristic of rural than of urban areas. In the case of MOUTH there are also rural variants [æʊ, ɛʊ, ɜʊ].

A careful study of the sociolinguistic variables represented by these diphthongs in the island of Martha's Vineyard was carried out by Labov (1963). He found that raising of the first element of /aɪ, aʊ/ to [ɐ], or further to [ə], was favoured by various factors: the phonetic environment (in which the most favourable condition was a following /t/ or /s/, then in order /p, f; d, v, z; k, θ, ð; #; l, r; n, m/); strong stress; age thirty-one to forty-five; rural (up-island) location; occupation (fisherman more than farmer). But the most important factor favouring a raised starting-point to the diphthongs was found to be self-identification as a Vineyarder, with the resistance to mainland influence which this implies: 'when a man says [reit] or [hɐʊs], he is unconsciously establishing the fact that he belongs to the island: that he is one of the natives to whom the island really belongs'.

6.5 The south

6.5.1 Introduction

The linguistic south of the United States comprises in the first instance Virginia, the Carolinas, and Georgia, extending inland to Alabama and Mississippi; then also the more recently settled Florida and, across the Mississippi, Arkansas, Louisiana, and Texas (the latter two states having many speakers of French and Spanish respectively, which languages may have exerted some influence on the local English). The upland states of West Virginia, Kentucky and Tennessee, together with the westernmost parts of Virginia and the Carolinas and the northernmost parts of Georgia and Alabama, form a transition zone between the south and midland dialect areas; their southern mountain speech is classified as south midland by Kurath, but popularly regarded as a variety of southern accent.

Bailey (1969b) classifies southern accents into three types: the **tidewater** of eastern Virginia and the eastern Carolinas, the **inner southern** of the deeper south and in particularly its older aristocracy, extending 'as far north as central Kentucky' and being typically non-rhotic, and the **outer southern** of the upper south and the south-west, including southern mountain, typically rhotic.

A rival, lexically based, classification of southern accents, is that of Wood (1972), shown in fig. 22.

It is difficult to fix the western limits of the linguistic south. In Arizona and Nevada, for example, one notices such characteristic southernisms as the merging of the vowels of *pin* and *pen*; [i] for [ɪ] in *string* reaches as far as the Pacific north-west; but these would hardly be considered southern accents.

'The uniformity of Southern speech is grossly exaggerated',

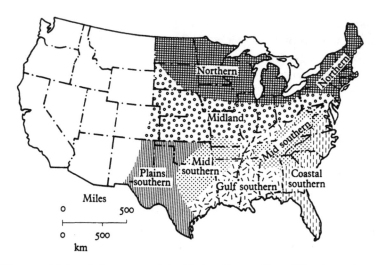

Fig. 22   Major dialect areas of the United States (from Wood 1972)

complains McDavid (1970), and warns against speaking of the southern accent as if it were something monolithic.

Within the territory where Southern traditions are important, there is evidence of at least three major speech types: 1) Southern proper, the speech of the old plantation country; 2) South Midland, the speech of the Southern Uplands, ultimately affiliated with that of western Pennsylvania; and 3) North Midland, the speech of Pennsylvania and its immediate dependencies. Within these regional patterns one finds at least nine clearly marked areas of consequence in the pre-Revolutionary South alone...; when the [Linguistic Atlas] returns are in we can expect to find at least thirty important subvarieties of Southern speech.

(The whole of the article from which this quotation is taken is warmly recommended.)

There is on the whole little to distinguish the speech of southern blacks from that of southern whites with comparable social advantages or disadvantages, except in the Gullah country: we discuss this question further in section 6.6, Black English.

The south lagged behind the north both in industrialization and in education. Its predominantly rural nature and the relative absence of schoolteacher influence are no doubt the principal factors which have led northerners to look on southern speech as something quaint. (English people, on the other hand, may well find it less abrasive and more in tune with the implicit standards of England than is GenAm.) They are reflected in the relatively high proportion of lexical-incidential deviations from the RP–GenAm norm – pronunciations which in Britain we might well classify as 'traditional-dialect', e.g. /dif/ for *deaf*, /'waʊndɪd/ for *wounded*. Even educated Charlestonians make liberal use of *ain't* (which seems to shock other Americans much more than it would the British). And *catch* is in some parts so widely pronounced /kɛtʃ/ that to use the (elsewhere standard) pronunciation /kætʃ/ risks incurring the charge of social climbing.

The best-known characteristic of southern pronunciation is the so-called southern drawl. Easy to recognize but difficult to describe satisfyingly, it involves relatively greater length in stressed, accented syllables as compared to unstressed; this is accompanied by diphthongization and other modifications of some accented syllables (6.5.3 below), together with a wider weakening of unstressed syllables than in other accents, but **not** necessarily an overall slow rate of delivery. Note also stressings such as '*hotel*, '*insurance*, '*Detroit*.

Of southern vowel qualities, the one which attracts most attention from the layman is the monophthongal [aˑ] in PRICE. But it is interesting to see the very different preoccupations of an American northerner and an Englishman in caricaturing a southern accent through eye-dialect:

Most of yew religious leaders ah haven't seen in many yeuhs. Ah jus wus tawkin to Billi this aftuhnoon... Ah, the greyaph heah tells the stawry... Faw the fust time in twelve yeuhs, ... (Lenny Bruce 1975: 21)

Ah, Apollo jars. Arcane standard, Hannah More. Armageddon pier staff. (Kingsley Amis 1968: 61)

(I imagine that Kingsley Amis's version would be rather impenetrable for an American audience. Orthographically it reads *I apologize. I can't stand it any more. I'm a-gettin' pissed off.* Amis has correctly noticed [ɪə] in *pissed* and the less than close final vowel in *any*.)

The attitude of southerners towards their accent, in the face of the unfavourable comment passed by northerners, ranges from a patriotic indifference or defiance to a self-oppressive determination to extirpate all southern features. White (1980: 153) writes:

No state has been more satirized than Texas, and Texans, accordingly, have become wary of outsiders. Even their own accent troubles them. [. . .] In some contexts Texans think of their accent as the way people should talk; it is the sound of sociability and sincerity. But they also know it is considered comical, substandard. Many educated Texans speak like Yankees at work and like Southerners at home with friends.

The present flow of population and industry from the north to the sunbelt states, reversing the trend of a century, may be expected to increase the pressures tending to make southern speech more like that of the rest of the country. Or will the incoming northerners adopt at least some southernisms?

6.5.2 The vowel system

It proves to be quite difficult to establish the vowel system of a southern accent in taxonomic-phonemic terms. The principal complications arise from the possibility of vocalization and/or loss of /r/ and /l/; but there is also particularly extensive phonetic variation in vowels as a result of certain late phonological rules. We discuss these effects below (6.5.3 Umlauting and Breaking, 6.5.7–9 vocalization of liquids).

Excluding those vowels which arise only or mainly as decay products of historical /Vr/ and /Vl/, we have the typical vowel system shown in (242) (part-systems A,B,C only):

(242)	ɪ	ʊ	i		ɪu	u
	ɛ	ʌ	eɪ			oʊ
	æ	ɑ	(æɪ)	aɪ ɔɪ	æʊ	ɔ

Because of the extent of allophonic variation, it can be difficult to select an appropriate notation for some phonemes. For example, the /aɪ/ of PRICE has the well-known southern monophthong [a(ː)] as one of its possible realizations, which suggests the notation /a/. But since most speakers also have a diphthongal [aɪ] realization for this vowel in certain phonetic environments or under particular stylistic conditions, we retain the familiar notation /aɪ/. In discussing GenAm, we wrote the vowels of FACE and GOAT as /eɪ/ and /o/ respectively, even though both are usually diphthongal in realization. For southern accents we write them /eɪ/ and /oʊ/, making their diphthongal nature explicit; partly this is to emphasize that in southern speech they are more firmly diphthongal than in northern, although it could be argued that on identical grounds we ought to write /ɔʊ/ for THOUGHT, rather than /ɔ/.

The parenthesized item in the system as set out, namely /æɪ/, may be variable or absent, and in any case of doubtful phonemic status. See further below.

There are several other phonetic diphthongs which could be considered as candidates for inclusion as distinctive items in the vowel system. In particular, there are diphthongs [ʊɪ] in *fluid* and [oɪ] in *poet*; although phonetically these are comparable to the [ɔɪ] of CHOICE, which we take as a separate phoneme /ɔɪ/, we interpret them here as realizations of the phonological sequences /u/ plus /ɪ/ and /oʊ/ plus /ɪ/ respectively. (Cf. vol. 1, 3.2.9, Smoothing.)

On this basis the partial table of lexical incidence is as shown in (243).

(243)	KIT	ɪ	FACE	eɪ
	DRESS	ɛ	PALM	ɑ
	TRAP	æ, æɪ	THOUGHT	ɔ
	LOT	ɑ	GOAT	oʊ
	STRUT	ʌ	GOOSE	u, ɪu
	FOOT	ʊ	PRICE	aɪ
	BATH	æ, æɪ	VOICE	ɔɪ
	CLOTH	ɔ	MOUTH	æʊ
	FLEECE	i	*happ*ʏ	ɪ

Special considerations apply to short front vowels in the environment of a following velar. In words such as *sing*, *thing*, where most accents have /ɪŋ/, careful southern speech usually has /iŋ/; in more casual or rapid speech, the quality is that of /eɪ/ or even /æɪ/ plus /ŋ/ (the latter possibility making *ring* a homophone of *rang*). Before /g/, /eɪ/ tends to occur to the exclusion of /ɛ/ in words such as *egg*, *leg* [leɪg]. This may also apply in the environment of a following palato-alveolar fricative, as *measure* /ˈmeɪʒə(r)/.

There remains the question of the putative /æɪ/. The diphthong [æɪ] has developed from historical /æ/ in certain words, splitting the TRAP-BATH sets in a manner reminiscent of the BATH Raising of other American accents (6.1.4 above). In southern accents, however, the raised/tensed variant is affected in its offglide rather than its first element. Its status is marginally phonemic vis-à-vis [æ] in

531

much the same way as that of GenAm [eə]; there are a small number
of minimal pairs such as [kæɪn] *can* 'container' vs. [kæn] *can* 'be
able', [hæɪv ∼ hæɪəv] *halve* vs. [hæv ∼ hæəv] *have*. (Both variants
are subject to the possibility of a schwa offglide.) On these grounds
some would recognize two distinct phonemes, /æɪ/ vs. /æ/. The
opposition is nonetheless pretty tenuous. As described by McMillan
(1946), the complex [æɪ] type occurs before a following /g/, voiceless
fricative /f, θ, s, ʃ/, /v/, or /n/, as in *bag, sag, wagon, dagger*; *half,
laugh, staff*; *path, bath*; *pass, grasp, blast, mask, passel*; *cash, ashes,
fashion, national*; *halve, calve, savage, lavender*; *fan, man, sand, bank,
ant, dance, branch*. It is usually restricted to monosyllables (but note
the disyllabic examples quoted). In the complementary environments, simple [æ] occurs (or, through the operation of processes
discussed in 6.5.3 below, [ä] or [æə]). Before /d/, [æɪ] may be a
possibility (*bad, sad*). Note that in the Alabaman accent described
by McMillan simple [æ] is used before /dʒ/ (*badge, pageant*) and also
before /m/ (*ram, damage*), environments where northerners often
have raised [eə] (etc.). McMillan gives no examples involving a
following velar nasal, but it is clear that this is an environment
favouring [æɪ], thus *sang* [sæɪŋ], *sank* [sæ̈ɪk] (but compare *sack* [sæk],
where voiceless /k/ favours simple [æ]). This is an environment
where /æ/ tends not to be raised in northern speech.

Some southern accents, particularly tidewater ones, have no [æɪ],
only simple [æ ∼ æə]. In Louisville, Kentucky, [æɪ] is reportedly
found only in the speech of some whites, never in that of blacks
(Howren 1958). There are others again with a **three**-way opposition, e.g. *had* [æ] vs. *sad* [æ·] vs. *bad* [æ ɪ] (McDavid 1979: 384); I
have not worked out the phonological implications of this.

For those southerners who do have the [æ ∼ æɪ] alternation, the
details of the factors governing it clearly vary regionally and socially. Although a following /m/ was included by McMillan as one
of the environments favouring simple [æ] in Alabama, in Louisville
it is listed by Howren as one favouring the complex variant, thus
(with nuclear accent) [ræɪəm]'*ram* (actually written by Howren, no
doubt more accurately, as [ræɛæm]). There are also many southerners who pronounce *damp* as [dæ̈ɪp].

Those who do use [æɪ] apparently always keep it well distinct
from /aɪ/, e.g. *mass* [mæɪ(ə)s] vs. *mice* [maɪs], *laugh* vs. *life*. Where
[æɪ] does occur, it seems that it is often intuitively real as a phoneme

distinct from /æ/ for many people, notwithstanding the weakness of the phonological arguments for its recognition as /æɪ/.

6.5.3 The lax vowels

It seems best to classify the vowels /ɪ, ɛ, æ, ʊ, ʌ, ɑ/ in southern speech as 'lax'. These checked vowels, part-system A, cannot be called 'short' in any synchronic sense, since their duration is not appreciably shorter than that of the free and traditionally long vowels of part-systems B and C. Indeed, it is this absence of a sharp cut-off in their duration which presumably encouraged the development of the assorted offglides characteristic of the lax vowels, the closing or centring diphthongization which is so striking a feature of a southern accent. This **southern Breaking** occurs most readily in a lax vowel in a stressed monosyllable. Before attempting to analyse Breaking, though, we must take note of two other characteristic processes affecting southern lax vowels: Umlaut and Shading.

The term **Umlaut** was suggested by Sledd (1966) as a name for a process reminiscent of the historical umlaut responsible many hundreds of years ago for the difference reflected in present-day alternations such as *goose–geese*, *mouse–mice*, German *Bruder–Brüder*. Namely, in a southern accent one can usually hear a difference in the quality of the stressed vowels in pairs such as *jelly–cellar*, *horrid–horror*. In each case the first word has a fronter vowel, the second a more retracted one. The difference is conditioned by the differing vowels of the second, weak syllable: in /ˈdʒɛlɪ/ and /ˈhɑrɪd/ it is /ɪ/, in /ˈsɛlə(r)/ and /ˈhɑrə(r)/ it is /ə/. The /ɪ/ exerts an effect extending back into the first syllable, keeping the strong /ɛ/ of *jelly* fully front and causing the /ɑ/ of *horrid* to be somewhat advanced: [ˈdʒɛlɪ, ˈhɑ+rɪd]. A following /ə/, on the other hand, causes the /ɛ/ of *cellar* to be centralized, while preserving the backness of the /ɑ/ of *horror*: [ˈsël̈ə, ˈhɑrə].

The Umlaut effect is most noticeable across an intervening /r/ or /l/, though it can also operate across other intersyllabic consonants. It applies only to stressed lax vowels.

The series *picket* /ˈpɪkɪt/, *pick* /pɪk/, *picker* /ˈpɪkə(r)/ exhibits three perceptibly different allophones of stressed /ɪ/. The frontest is that of *picket*, due to the Umlauting triggered by the following weak /ɪ/.

The least front is that of *picker*, because of the /ə/. The /ɪ/ of *pick* is intermediate.

Other examples of the effects of Umlauting include the following (all from Sledd 1966): /ɪ/ fronter in *cereal* than in *mirror*; /ɛ/ fronter in *herring* than in *heron*; /æ/ fronter in *parry* than in *parrot*; /ɑ/ fronter in *hopping* than in *hopper*; /ʌ/ fronter in *putty* than in *butter*; /ʊ/ fronter in *bushy* than in *pusher*.

Umlauting is blocked not only by a word boundary but also, for some speakers at least, by an inflectional morpheme boundary. Hence *sister*, with umlauted [ï], fails to rhyme with *resist # er*, which has non-umlauted [ɪ]; similarly, *d*[ï]*nner* but *th*[ɪ]*n # ner*. In the days when the Trager & Smith analysis of English vowels was in fashion, such pairs were frequently used as evidence for a phoneme /ɨ/.

The /ɪ/ allophones in *ripping*, *rip*, *ripper*, are affected by Umlaut in the way we have described, and are successively less and less front. But it is also noticeable that all are somewhat backer (more [ɯ]-like) than those of the corresponding series *picket*, *pick*, *picker*: and this is where what we may call **Shading** comes into play. This is the effect upon vowel timbre of the nature of a following consonant. In southern speech it applies very noticeably to /ɪ/, and to some extent to other lax vowels.

Because of Shading, /ɪ/ is firmly front only when followed by a velar consonant (*stick*, *big*). Before a labial, it is qualitatively central [ɪ̈]. Palato-alveolars, alveolars, and dentals may or may not constitute environments which trigger [ɪ̈]. The liquids, /l/ (except when prevocalic and therefore 'clear') and /r/ also condition [ɪ̈], as in *milk* and perhaps in *spirit*.

The interaction of Umlaut and Shading produces a considerable number of perceptibly different realizations of /ɪ/, even without considering the diphthongal variants resulting from Breaking (discussed below). Thus *ticket* is ['tɪkɪt], with a quality of /ɪ/ kept forward both by the following /k/ and by the subsequent weak /ɪ/. In *ripping* ['rɪpɪn ~ 'rɪpɪŋ], the stressed /ɪ/ is slightly retracted by the labiality of the /p/; in *ticker* rather more so by the /ə/ of the following syllable. In *dipper* and *ribbon* both factors combine to give a definitely central [ɪ̈]. (The multiplicity of these subtly different qualities is one of the arguments against the phoneme /ɨ/ of Trager & Smith's analysis.)

In southern accents the /ʊ/ of FOOT is often not rounded; in fact

an unrounded, central [ɪ]-type quality for /ʊ/ is particularly characteristic of inland southern speech. This means that there is often
considerable phonetic overlap between /ɪ/ and /ʊ/. It has been
shown experimentally (Bailey 1969a) that as many as eleven degrees
of fronting may be identified spectrographically for /ɪ/ and /ʊ/ in
some southern speech, depending on the factors we identify here as
Shading and Umlaut.

In tidewater southern /ʊ/ is however rounded if adjacent to a
labial, as in the word [fʊt] itself.

The last process to be discussed in connection with the lax vowels
is the development of an offglide or offglides, the Breaking which
gives /V/ the realization [Və] or [Vɪ] in specified phonological environments. It must be acknowledged straight away that the facts of
Breaking are variable and intricate, and the following discussion
cannot be considered exhaustive.

The lax front vowels, /ɪ, ɛ, æ/, all receive a prominent schwa
offglide in a stressed monosyllable ending in a labial. Thus *lip* /lɪp/
is phonetically [lɪəp] (more accurately, because of Shading, [lɪəp]);
web /wɛb/ is [wëəb]; and *rap* /ræp/ is [rǽəp]. In a stressed monosyllable not ending in a labial, there may be no offglide, merely
added length ([ɪː, ɛː, æː]); though here, too, offglides may be heard
when the vowel is strongly accented, particularly if the consonant is
dental or alveolar: *bid* [bɪəd], *bed* [bëəd], *bad* [bæ̈əd] (or [bæɪd]). In
fact the environments favouring a schwa offglide are identical with
those in which Shading causes retraction (which leads Sledd (1966)
to explain the latter as resulting from the absorption of a schwa
offglide).

If the following consonant is one of /ʃ, ʒ, g, ŋ/, there may be a
different kind of offglide, namely a palatal [ï], so that *special* becomes
homophonous with *spatial* and *egg* rhymes with *vague* (as discussed
above, 6.5.2). The use of [i] (identified as phonemic /i/) rather than
[ɪ] (/ɪ/) before a velar nasal, as in *thing* /θiŋ/, reflects the same
tendency ([ɪ] plus palatal offglide → [i]).

Palatal offglides are most noticeable when a lax back vowel pre-
cedes a palato-alveolar, as in *push* /pʊʃ/ [pöïʃ], *much* /mʌtʃ/ [mʌɪtʃ],
dodge /dɑdʒ/ [dɑɪdʒ]. These glides tend to be socially stigmatized
(considered substandard), as do the [ɚ] glides sometimes used in
this environment by speakers of rhotic southern mountain accents,
thus *push* [pöɚʃ].

A similar distribution of allophonic off-glides is described by Cearley (1974) for his West Texas speech. This involves a schwa-type offglide [ə] where one of /ɪ, ɛ, æ/ is the last vowel in a word ending in an anterior consonant (a labial, dental, or alveolar), and a palatal offglide where /æ/ is followed by a non-anterior consonant (palato-alveolar or velar): thus [kɪət] *kit*, [æəd] *add*, [læɪk] *lack*, also /θæŋ/ [θæɪŋ] *thing*.

One reason why the analysis of [æɪ] as a separate phoneme /æɪ/ is attractive is that the palatal offglide it includes occurs in environments where palatal offglides are otherwise quite unexpected, such as before labials, as *half* [hæɪf]. Here, in fact, one can sometimes hear a schwa offglide to the whole diphthong, thus [hæɪəf]; so also *glass*, /glæɪs/, [glæɪəs] (a pronunciation that surprised me considerably the first time I heard it).

Aside from the processes operating upon vowels (Umlaut, Shading, Breaking), the basic qualities of the lax back vowels also call for comment.

The /ʊ/ of FOOT, as we have seen, is often central and unrounded, [ɨ]; though in tidewater accents it is back, [ɯ ∼ ʊ].

Several different qualities may be encountered for the /ʌ/ of STRUT. A mid central quality, [ɜ], is perhaps the most typically southern; it is this that gives rise to the British stereotype view that American southerners, at least as represented by Country-and-Western singers, say 'lerve' instead of *love* ('Please don't starp lervin me'). Perceptually very similar is the centralized-back mid [ɤ+]. In the tidewater area an opener and backer [ʌ] is usual. The circumstances surrounding the use of a front rounded variant, [œ], are not clear. Some speakers have an allophonic (Shading) alternation between the [ɜ] and [ʌ] types, with [ʌ] used before a labial and [ɜ] elsewhere: thus *cup* [kʌp], but *cut* [kɜt].

Open /ɑ/, the LOT vowel, is anywhere from central to back, [ɑ+ ∼ ɑ]. Usually it is unrounded, although along the coast from South Carolina southwards it may be rounded, [ɒ]. For the central variant, Bailey (1969b) writes [ɐ], with the implication that the quality is not fully open; he further characterizes it as being pronounced with an expanded pharynx. Suspending judgment on these claims, I will write it [ɑ+]. Many southerners have an allophonic (Shading) alternation between the central [ɑ+] and back [ɑ] types, the [ɑ] allophone being used before velars and after /w/, as *lock*, *swan*, and the central [ɑ+] allophone elsewhere, as *lot, top*. (Before /l/, as in *doll*, the back allophone is used, appropriately, since /l/ in this environment is characteristically velar, [dɑ+ʟ].) Some speakers also use the back allophone before labials, as *top* [tɑp] (otherwise [tɑ+p]). West of the Mississippi, LOT and THOUGHT are usually merged as [ɒ ~ ɔ].

6.5.4 PRICE and MOUTH

American southern /aɪ/, the PRICE vowel, is well-known for the readiness with which it is given a monophthongal or near-monophthongal realization, [a(:) ~ aɛ]. In the more stigmatized varieties in the deep south, monophthongal [a] can be found in all phonetic environments, e.g. *night-time* ['nattam]. In a southern accent of higher prestige, a wide-diphthongal allophone [ae ~ aɪ] is used in the environment of a following voiceless consonant within the same syllable, e.g. *bite* [baɪt], *rice* [raɪs]; the monophthong or near-monophthong occurs in other environments, e.g. *rise* [ra:z], *buy* [ba:]. In this standard southern pronunciation, *night-time* is thus ['naɪttam].

As in the parallel case of Canadian /aɪ/ (6.2.4 above), various interesting questions of syllabification arise. Bailey (1968b), mentions the cases of *psychic, icicle*, and *cycle* with [aɪ], as against *cyclone* and *bicycle* with [a], thus ['sakloʊn, 'basɪkʟ]. It can be inferred that the first /k/ in *psychic*, the /s/ in *icicle*, and the /k/ in *cycle* check the /aɪ/ by being in the same syllable with it, which triggers the diphthongal allophone; thus ['saɪk.ɪk, 'aɪs.ɪkʟ, 'saɪk.ʟ]; whilst in *cyclone* and *bicycle* there is a syllable boundary immediately after the /aɪ/, which in consequence is realized as a monophthong. (It is obscure why the /s/ of a Canadian *bicycle* should be in the first syllable, but that of an American southern one in the second.)

At one time it was de rigueur in prestigious southern speech to avoid the monophthongal allophone in the environment of a following voiceless consonant. But this proscription is now evidently breaking down. Writing in 1967, McDavid confirms that forty years previously there was a sharp social distinction in /aɪ/ allophones: although [a(:)] was used by all classes finally or before a voiced consonant, before voiceless consonants there was a social distinction in that educated speakers had a diphthong but many uneducated speakers a monophthong. Thus *nice white rice* was 'a well known social shibboleth'. Recently, though, he continues, 'the shibboleth has ceased to operate, and many educated Southerners now have the monophthong in all positions, and their numbers are increasing' (McDavid 1967b: 7).

In much of the tidewater area, the PRICE situation is somewhat different; though here too it is a question of allophonic variation within the /aɪ/ phoneme. In the coastal south, as in Canada, a diphthong with a raised starting-point, [əɪ], is typically used before a voiceless consonant, as *rice* [rəɪs]. In other phonological environments there is a longer ('slower') diphthong (sometimes with a rather front starting-point), or else a near-monophthong, thus *rise* [rɑ+ːɪz ~ raː(ə)z].

These pre-fortis raised-diphthong allophones are geographically restricted to two areas of the south: (i) Virginia and adjoining parts of Maryland and North Carolina, and (ii) the coastal belt of South Carolina, Georgia, and Florida. The allophonic variation is particularly striking in Virginia, where *rice* is [rəɪs] and *rise* [raːəz ~ raːɛz]. In South Carolina it is more moderate, usually [rɐɪs] and *rise* [rɑ+ːɪz]. Southerners from these parts are thus spared the embarrassment which some other southerners may encounter when referring to *ice* in northern settings.

The Outer Banks, a string of islands off the coast of North Carolina, have a quality for PRICE which seems to be unique in North America, namely [ɒɪ], thus [tɒɪt] *tight*, [tɒɪd] *tide*, ['ɒɪlənt] *island* (Howren 1962). The residents of the Outer Banks are sometimes called the Hoy Toiders.

The most usual southern quality for the vowel of MOUTH is [æʊ] (hence the phonemic symbolization /æʊ/ used above). The starting-point of the diphthong is thus considerably fronter than that used by most northerners. In South Carolina, however, and to some extent elsewhere, the [aʊ ~ ɑʊ] type prevails.

The two sub-areas of the south which have special pre-fortis allophones of PRICE also have them for MOUTH. In and around Virginia, *out* has [əu ~ ɐʊ] but *loud* [æ·ʊ]. In coastal South Carolina, Georgia, and Florida, *out* has [ɐʊ] but *loud* [ɑ+·ʊ]. In some parts of North Carolina, [aɪ] appears as an (optional?) variant for MOUTH, thus [daɪn taɪn] *down town* (Morgan 1969).

In the deep south, /æʊ/ may be subject to Breaking. I have heard a white woman from Biloxi, Mississippi, pronounce *brown* (with nuclear accent) as [bræɪæ̈ʊn]. (If the word remains authentically monosyllabic, this would appear to constitute that phonetic rarity, a tetraphthong.)

6.5.5 Other vowels

The FLEECE vowel, /i/, is usually monophthongal, [i ∼ iˑ]; in less standard speech diphthongs [ɪi, ɨi] also occur. The GOOSE vowel, /u/, on the other hand, is generally diphthongal and not fully back, thus [ʉu] or [ʉˑ]. Here tidewater speech may be an exception, with back [u].

Although *PEAS* declares that the falling diphthong /iu/ (or /ɪu/), as in *music, cute, tune*, 'is confined to the New England settlement area' and unknown in the south, Bailey (1969b), himself from Alabama, describes just such a diphthong as usual in southern speech. Its realization varies somewhat according to the nature of the preceding consonant, being rounded throughout after a labial, but otherwise having rounding only in the second element. Thus it is [yu] in *abuse, feud, view*, but [iy] in *cute, tune, duke, nude*. After palato-alveolars the opposition is neutralized, but the quality used may well be [iy] (= /iu/) rather than [ʉu] etc. (= /u/), thus *shoot* [ʃiyt], *choose* [tʃiyz]. After /t, d, n/, of course, some use plain /u/ rather than /iu/; some use /j/ plus /u/. Hence *tune* may be /tiun/, /tun/, or /tjun/.

The FACE vowel, /eɪ/, has a mid rather than a half-close starting-point, thus [ɛɪ]. Some speakers use opener qualities for the first element, thus [ɛ̈ɪ] and even (southern mountain) [æɪ]; these are generally stigmatized. The tidewater accent of coastal South Carolina, Georgia, and Florida, stands apart, using a monophthongal [e], thus *day* [deˑ], or (in checked position) a centring diphthong [eə], thus *face* [feəs].

Similar regional variation affects the /oʊ/ of GOAT. Most parts of the south have [oʊ], sometimes with some degree of centralization of the first element (a central starting-point is particularly characteristic of north-eastern North Carolina and the Outer Banks, where the GOAT vowel is like that of Philadelphia). A very rounded first element is typical of the deep south. Tidewater South Carolina has monophthongal [o], thus *go* [goˑ], and in checked position the centring diphthong [oə], thus *goat* [goət].

The vowel in PALM words may be either that of LOT, /ɑ/, or that of non-rhotic START (see 6.5.7 below). Thus *father* may rhyme with *bother* or, alternatively, be a homophone of *farther* /ˈfɑːðə/. Many PALM words also have old-fashioned or rural variants with /æ/, thus *calm* [kæəm] /kæm/ (otherwise /kɑːm/, /kɑm/). In Virginia an old-fashioned, upper-class, nowadays recessive pronunciation has an RP-style /ɑː/ in many BATH words rather than the usual /æɪ ~ æ/, thus *dance* /dɑːns/; *PEAS* shows *pasture* as /ˈpɑːstə/ (in *PEAS* notation, /pɑstə/) very widely in Virginia.

The THOUGHT vowel may be monophthongal [ɔ ~ ɒ]; but the most stereotypically southern realization is a closing diphthong of the [ɒʊ] type. *PEAS* (p. 107) writes it [ɒɔ] and describes it as 'common in the South from the Potomac to the Pee Dee in South Carolina, in the southern Appalachians, in the Upcountry of South Carolina, and the greater part of Georgia'. One can hear this diphthongal variant in both checked and free position: *lawn* [lɒʊn], *law* [lɒʊ]. In the coastal areas of the south, though, and from western Alabama westwards, monophthongal /ɔ/ is usual.

In most of Virginia and eastern North Carolina, the word *long* is pronounced /lɑŋ/, with the vowel of LOT, rather than /lɔŋ/, with the vowel of THOUGHT, which is what is used in all other American accents that have not merged LOT and THOUGHT. (There is a map of this in Atwood 1951.)

The /ɔɪ/ of CHOICE may have two distinct allophones, positionally determined, for those many southerners who have an [ɪ]-type vowel in *happY*. Word-finally, it tends to be [ɔɛ̈], with a relatively open endpoint; elsewhere, [ɔɪ] or [ɔe].

6.5.6 Vowel plus nasal

Two phenomena relating to the sequence vowel-plus-nasal are prevalent in southern speech: the neutralization of the opposition between /ɪ/ and /ɛ/ when preceding a nasal, and the coalescence of vowel and nasal into a nasalized vowel in certain environments.

The best-known example of the neutralization of /ɪ/ and /ɛ/ is the homophony of *pin* and *pen*. These two items are pronounced identically, as [pɪn], by most southerners. To relieve the possible confusion this may cause, lexical expansions such as *straight-pin*, *fountain-pen* are frequently employed. Other pairs which become homophonous by the same process are *hymn* and *hem*, *mint* and *meant*, and (usually) *sinner* and *center*.

The process can be viewed as the raising of historical or underlying /ɛ/ to [ɪ] in the environment of a following nasal. Further examples are *many* ['mɪnɪ], *defendant* [dəˈfɪndənt], *identify* [aˈdɪnəfa], *Memphis* ['mɪmfɪs], *condemn* [kənˈdɪəm]. The following nasal is necessarily almost always /m/ or /n/; but it can be /ŋ/, as in *strength* ['strɪŋθ ~ 'striŋθ].

Some speakers consider [ɪ] before /m, n/ incorrect, and endeavour to avoid it in careful speech; hypercorrections such as [sëəns] *since* are by no means unknown. On the other hand, McMillan (1946) claims that any [ɛ] before a nasal is substandard, and that cultivated speech always has the neutralization to [ɪ].

The suffix *-ing* is pronounced with /n/ considerably further up the social scale in the south than in most parts of the English-speaking world. We have seen that [ɛ(ɪ)ŋ ~ æ(ɪ)ŋ] in *thing* is stigmatized; it is logical, therefore, that the /ŋ/ variant of *-ing*, where it occurs in careful or high-social-group speech, is always [ɪŋ] or perhaps [ɪŋ], never [æɪŋ] etc. *Running* is generally /ˈrʌnɪn/, less commonly /ˈrʌnɪŋ/.

The rule of Nasal Coalescence takes as its input a vowel followed by a nasal; it converts it into the corresponding nasalized vowel in the environment of a following voiceless consonant within the same syllable, as shown in (244).

(244) V Nasal → Ṽ/—$\begin{bmatrix} C \\ -\text{voi} \end{bmatrix}$ $

Examples include *lump* /lʌmp/ [lʌ̃p], *pint* /paint/ [pãit], *drink* /driŋk/ [drĩk], *tint-tent* /tint/ [tĩət], *glance* /glæins/ [glæ̃is], *can't* /kænt ~ keint/ [kæ̃ət ~ kẽit], *constant* /ˈkɑnstənt/ [ˈkɑ̃stət] (compare *consent* /kənˈsint/ [kənˈsĩət], where the first /n/ and the /s/ are in different syllables). It would be an exaggeration to claim that Nasal Coalescence is an absolutely categorical rule in southern speech; but it often comes close to it. (See discussion by McMillan 1939.)

Gonna, the contracted form of the modal *going to*, has a special southern form [gõ] (alongside the usual [gonə ~ gʌnə]). *I'm going to* can therefore be [amgõ]; it can also be further contracted to [amõ]. *Don't* is [dõʔ] etc., sometimes losing its initial or final consonant, [õʔ ~ dõ] etc.

6.5.7 Is southern speech non-rhotic?

Southern speech tends to be stereotypically thought of as non-rhotic. Some of it is. But southern mountain speech, the speech of the outer south, is firmly rhotic, indeed often hyper-rhotic (*window* ['wɪndɚ] etc.). And those southern accents which are non-rhotic are often only variably non-rhotic.

Non-rhoticity is associated with two quite distinct social groups in the south: upper-class whites, and blacks. Rhoticity is in many places associated with lower-class whites.

'The conventional statement about the Southern postvocalic /-r/ is that it does not occur as constriction in words of the type [*thirty, Thursday, worm, barn, beard, father*]. The fact that in every Southern state one may find locally-rooted native speakers with constriction in at least some of these words has been either overlooked or deliberately ignored', complains McDavid (1948), in an article reporting his investigations into rhoticity and non-rhoticity in South Carolina. He found that R Dropping in up-country (inland) South Carolina represents the adoption of a prestige model associated with the old plantation caste and the political ascendancy of Charleston. 'The trend toward the loss of constriction continues. It even serves to reinforce Southern xenophobia, for among the phonetically sophisticated the lack of constriction has become a point of caste and local pride.' Rhoticity was perceived as characteristic of northerners and 'crackers' (poor whites).

But times change: already in 1948 McDavid commented that 'indications already exist that constriction of postvocalic /r/ may some day become respectable in South Carolina. [...] Even in the heart of the Low-Country, a number of girls in their late teens or early twenties are ... speaking with a newly acquired constriction of postvocalic /-r/', allegedly due to the influence of servicemen from other parts of the United States stationed in the south.

In an impressive and statistically sophisticated sociolinguistic survey of a community in neighbouring North Carolina, Levine & Crockett (1966) found very great variability in the r-variable. They took as their sample 275 white residents of a community which they do not name (according to McDavid (1979: 142), it was Hillsboro, NC). They found rhoticity scores ranging from less than 10 per cent to a full 100 per cent (i.e. from nearly non-rhotic to fully rhotic); in words of the NURSE set almost all speakers had consistent r-colouring, so they are excluded from the scoring. A high degree of education was associated with either a very high or a very low r-score, low education with an intermediate score; thus it was consistency ('R-norm clarity') rather than r-score as such which was linked to social position. It was found that a high r-score was most characteristic of women, young people, short-term residents of the community, and 'those who are near but not quite at the top of the "white-collar" class'. Levine & Crockett conclude that these groups are more ready to accept the national pronunciation norm (the rhotic norm) as their model, while males, older people, long-term residents, and blue-collar workers hold more firmly to the non-rhotic southern prestige norm of the coastal plain. Thus they believe that the white community is moving towards a position where rhoticity will be straightforwardly associated with high social status – just the opposite of the traditional situation described by McDavid.

In a separate survey of the speech of blacks in Hillsboro, Anshen (1970) found them, too, moving from an older non-rhotic to a newer rhotic norm: their r-scores increased with education, youth, and carefulness.

McDavid (1979: 142) doubts that increasing rhoticity among southerners represents a triumph of national norms over regional ones. 'A far simpler explanation is that increasing affluence and a wider spread of educational opportunities are bringing into the group of cultivated speakers a larger proportion of those who naturally had the postvocalic constriction; and with economic and cultural security, they feel less need to emulate any other model.' I am not wholly convinced that this account can be squared with the Hillsboro findings; but it is evident that, whatever the explanation, southern speech is tending to reverse the historical development of R Dropping and return to rhoticity.

This is all the more striking in the light of the fact that southern accents can appear more non-rhotic than any other accents of English anywhere. First, there is little or no /r/ sandhi (vol. 1, 3.2.3): not only no intrusive /r/ but also hardly any linking /r/. Second, lower-class or non-standard accents of the deep south delete /r/ variably in two environments where other non-rhotic accents do not, namely after /θ/ and intervocalically. Thus [r] is typically absent not only from *four apples* and *saw it* but also on occasion from *throw, throb, through,* and *hurry, very, Carolina* [kæˈlanə]; *Paris* may be homophonous with *pass* [pæɪs].

So southern accents may well require a synchronic, variable rule of R Dropping; and there is no evidence for rule inversion leading to the replacement of a deletion rule by an insertion rule, as in RP (vol. 1, 3.2.3). This raises the theoretical possibility, to put it no stronger, that all superficially non-rhotic southern speech is underlyingly rhotic, the synchronic R Dropping rule converting underlying /nɔrθ/ to phonetic [nɔθ], /lɛtər/ to [lɛtə], etc. Both Sledd (1966) and Bailey (1969b) adopt this view, Sledd announcing 'a belated conversion to the doctrine that the *r*-less dialects are *r*-ful'.

Two further arguments support this hypothesis: the parallelism in the behaviour of putative underlying /r/ and /l/ (6.5.9 below), and the pronunciation of words like *pattern*. In RP and similar accents, this is usually [ˈpætn̩ ~ ˈpæʔn̩], with the usual [n̩] output of underlying /ən/ after an alveolar plosive, just as in *Patton*. But in southern speech, so both McMillan (1946) and Bailey (1969b) insist, *pattern* is always [ˈpætən] ([-ɾ-, -d-]) and thus distinct from *Patton* [ˈpætn̩ ~ ˈpæʔn̩], a phonetic distinction which can be interpreted as proving that *pattern* contains /r/ between /ə/ and /n/, an /r/ which blocks the operation of Syllabic Consonant Formation before itself undergoing deletion by R Dropping.

Against the assumption of consistent underlying /r/ must be set the objections which apply in other apparently non-rhotic accents: that there is often no way in which the child exposed to a consistently non-rhotic accent could reasonably infer the presence of /r/ when there are no relevant alternations and when the output of posited /Vr/ is identical with the output of simple /V/. In southern accents this is often the case in the environment of a following voiced consonant: *card* and *cod* may be homophonous [kɑːd], and *lord* and *laud* as [lɔːd]. There is then no reason to suppose that they are not phonemically identical. (Given alternations such as *star* [stɑː] –*starry* [stɑːrɪ], *war* [wɔː]–*warring* [wɔːrɪŋ], a child might of course arguably infer underlying /r/ for all [ɑː, ɔː], and conclude that *cod* was /kɑrd/.) It also applies in the case of final [ə], where *manna* and *manner* can be homophonous, [ˈmænə].

If southern accents are all underlyingly rhotic, then the phonemic vowel system may be no greater than that set out in 6.5.2 above.

Various phonetic outputs occurring only as a reflex of historical /Vr/ can be accounted for as resulting from phonemic /Vr/ through the operation of synchronic rules of Pre-R Breaking and then R Dropping: e.g. [oə] in *door* /doʊr/, [ɜɪ] in *bird* /bʌrd/. Not only ['lɑrdʒɚ] but also ['lɑːdʒə, 'lɑədʒə, 'lɑɪdʒə] can be referred to phonemic /'lɑrdʒər/.

If, on the other hand, those varieties of southern speech which are pretty consistently non-rhotic in phonetic terms are analysed as underlyingly non-rhotic, too, then we must cater for a fair number of additional items in our vowel phoneme inventory – a largish part-system D.

6.5.8 Vowel plus /r/

In this section we consider the pronunciation of words belonging to the lexical sets not treated in 6.5.2 above: they contain a vowel followed by historical /r/, which remains as /r/ at least in accents which are categorically or variably rhotic.

The NURSE vowel is quite widely r-coloured in the south, [ɝ] etc. Any accent that keeps final or preconsonantal /r/ phonetically as such after other vowels always does so after the /ɜ/ (/ʌ/) of NURSE, usually coalescing them into a single r-coloured vowel; but the converse is not the case. Particularly in the tidewater speech of Virginia and North Carolina, r-coloured NURSE, [ɝː], may co-exist with the regular dropping of other nonprevocalic /r/s. In other non-rhotic southern accents, NURSE may be [ɜː] or, with lip rounding, [ɵː]; the precise quality and duration vary. In South Carolina, Georgia, and Alabama NURSE tends to have two very distinct allophones: in word-final position a monophthong or slight diphthong [ʌː ~ ɜː ~ ʌə], but in preconsonantal position a closing diphthong [ɜɪ ~ ʌɪ], thus *stir* [stɜː] but *dirt* [dɜɪt]. The word-final allophone is also used morpheme-finally before a suffix, as in *stir#ring*, *stir#red*, so that there are minimal pairs such as *bird* [bɜɪd] vs. *burred* [bɜːd]. There are also speakers who have [ɜɪ] before alveolars, [ɜ] before labials (*PEAS*: 108). The [ɜɪ] pronunciation, though stigmatized in the north as 'Brooklynese', is regarded in the south as rather elegant (particularly vis-à-vis the traditionally poor-white [ɝ]).

Turning to the lexical sets NEAR, SQUARE, CURE, FORCE, NORTH, note first a problem about syllabicity: words with these vowels followed by final /r/ or its reflex are 'varisyllabic'. Thus *near*, for example, may either be monosyllabic, with a diphthong [ɪˈə ~ ɛˈə ~ ɪˈɚ], or disyllabic, with the [ə ~ ɚ] element constituting a separate syllabic nucleus. Words of all the lexical sets mentioned may be subject to this varisyllabicity. Conversely, words such as *we're*, *player*, *higher*, *flower*, *who're*, *boa*, normally disyllabic, may readily be pronounced monosyllabically, with a phonetic diphthong. It is often difficult to distinguish between a centring diphthong and a disyllabic sequence of vowel plus [ə ~ ɚ].

There is also the problem of distinguishing centring diphthongs reflecting historical /Vr/ from those resulting from Breaking of lax vowels (6.5.3 above); this difficulty applies, of course, only in non-rhotic accents. Generally, it seems, non-rhotic *beard* is potentially distinct from accented *bid* [bɪəd]: *beard* has a diphthong of greater duration, [bɪˈɚd]. (There is a problem in transcribing these long diphthongs: neither [ɪːə] nor [ɪəː] seems wholly satisfactory.) In polysyllables and accentually non-salient monosyllables, where the lax vowels are not subject to Breaking, the contrast is a straightforward one of monophthong vs. diphthong, thus *bearded* ['bɪədɪd] vs. *bidder* ['bɪdə]. Hence the opposition between /ɪ/ (KIT) and /ɪə ~ ɪr/ (NEAR) is realized phonetically (i) as a difference in duration, [ɪə] vs. [ɪˈɚ], in a stressed final syllable; but (ii) as the presence vs. the absence of an in-glide, [ɪ ~ ɪ] vs. [ɪə], elsewhere. (In some cases there may also be other, qualitative, differences, as detailed below.) On occasion the duration difference may be neutralized, making *beard* potentially homophonous with *bid* and *bared* with *bad*.

Where the /r/ is prevocalic (with no intervening #), southern accents normally have a tense (< historically long) vowel. Thus *weary* has /i/, and *serious* begins differently from *Syria*; *Mary* has [eː ~ eɪ] /eɪ/, and is firmly distinct from *merry* and *marry*, while *various* begins differently from *very*; *story* has [oː ~ oʊ] /oʊ/, not the /ɔ/ of THOUGHT; and *curious* begins like *cue*, /kɪu ~ kju/. This means that both phonetically and phonemically the vowels in this type of word are different from those in words where the /r/ is or was preconsonantal/final: *serious* has /i/, *beer* /ɪr ~ ɪə/ (etc.); *dairy* has /eɪ/, *dare* /ær ~ æə/ (etc.). In the case of FORCE–CURE words (the sets are usually merged except /__rV/), while it is the case that *story* has the same /oʊ/ as *stow*, there is also the possibility of pronouncing *store*, too, as /stoʊ/, rather than with [oɚ ~ oə], though this pronunciation is stigmatized (and gives rise to the stereotype eye-dialect of *po'* for *poor*, etc.).

Where there is an intervening #, as in the case of verb stems in /-r/ with suffixed *-ing*, Bailey (1969b) reports an interesting pos-sibility, namely that of distinguishing phonetically between nouns and adjectives on the one hand, and verbal forms on the other, as set out in (245), e.g. *the b[ɛ]ring wasn't b[æ̈ə]ring the load properly.*

(245)

	Noun or adj.	Verb
steering	'stɪrɪŋ	'stɪərɪŋ ~ stjɛərɪŋ
daring, bearing	'dɛɪrɪŋ, 'bɛrɪŋ	'dæ̈ərɪŋ, 'bæ̈ərɪŋ
boring	'boʊrɪŋ	'boərɪŋ
mooring	'mʉurɪŋ	'mʊərɪŋ ~ moərɪŋ
barring	'bɑ(ə)ːrɪŋ	'bɑrɪŋ
firing	'farɪŋ	'faərɪŋ

(/-ɪn/ is always an alternative to /-ɪŋ/.)

It is not clear how widespread this kind of distinction is in the south: it is certainly not universal. Perhaps more widespread is a distinction between, say, *Mary* and *hair#y*, ['meːrɪ ~ 'mɛɪrɪ] vs. ['hæərɪ] etc. (compare also *Harry* ['hærɪ]).

We return now to the question of vowels in environments other than /—rV/. In southern mountain speech NEAR words sometimes have [jɚ], through syllabicity shift ([nɪɚ] → [njɚ]). This pronunci-ation is also found in Maryland, Virginia, and North Carolina, though in a lexically inconsistent way, e.g. much more frequently in *beard* than in *queer*. Otherwise, NEAR may be [ɪˑɚ] or [iˑɚ]. Further south, though, in South Carolina and Georgia, NEAR words tend to have [eˑɚ ~ ɛˑɚ] (or corresponding diphthongs with [-ɚ]). Usually this remains distinct from the /æə ~ ær/ of SQUARE, which has an opener starting-point; but in tidewater South Carolina the distinc-tion is often lost, so that *fear* = *fair*, *fare* [fɛˑɚ] (NEAR–SQUARE thus being merged as in the West Indies and some other places).

Conversely, there are southern accents with three distinct centr-ing diphthongs in NEAR–SQUARE words, e.g. *beer* [bɪə] vs. *here* [hɛ̈ə] vs. *hair* [hæ̈ə ~ hæɪə]. And the varisyllabicity discussed above may give rise to additional diphthongs in, for example, *via* [viə], *player* [pleə], *fire* [faə], thus producing a remarkable variety of similar but contrasting diphthongs. (At this point I abandon the transcrip-tional indication of the extra length in these diphthongs.)

So far we have implied that SQUARE words have /ær/ or its derivative. For those who have contrastive tense /æɪ/, however, it is often this rather than lax /æ/ which occurs in SQUARE, if we are to judge by the [æɪə] sometimes to be heard in *pair* (as in *pass*). An analyst who rejects the underlying-/r/ hypothesis is spared the necessity of choosing between /æ/ and /æɪ/, since he will merely identify a phoneme /æə/ in SQUARE, thus *pair* /pæə/, and any [ɪ] glide is merely allophonic.

The START vowel is of the type [ɑr ~ ɑː]. Non-rhotic START may differ from LOT in duration only, or in quality too; but the quality difference may be in either direction. In tidewater Virginia and the surrounding area, START is back and sometimes rounded, [ɑː ~ ɑɒ ~ ɒː]; it contrasts with the central [ɑ+] of LOT but is usually merged with NORTH. In parts of South Carolina and Georgia, on the other hand, START is central, [ɑ+ː], while LOT is back, [ɑ ~ ɒ]. In yet other parts of the south the qualities of START and LOT are identical, and the only difference is one of length (characteristically neutralized in many environments). Thus non-rhotic *cart* and *cot* may be distinct as [kɒːt] vs. [kɑ+t] (Va.), or as [kɑ+ːt] vs. [kɒt] (SC, Ga.), or simply as [kɑːt] vs. [kɑt]. In the latter type *card* and *cod* are potentially homophonous, [kɑːd].

There may be a similar relationship between NORTH and THOUGHT, with a contrast between non-rhotic *tort* [tɔːt] and *taut* [tɒt], but not between *lord* and *laud* [lɔːd ~ lɒʊd]. Non-rhotic *corn* rhymes with *lawn*.

In the western part of the south, too – west of a line approximately following the Mississippi – START and NORTH may be merged in popular speech. This makes *card* and *cord* identical, as [kɒːd ~ kɒrd] etc. According to some reports, there may even appear to be a switching of the two lexical types, so that *born in a barn* sounds like *barn in a born*. This is stigmatized wherever it occurs – in places such as Missouri, Texas, and Utah.

Where historical /r/ occurs between a back vowel and a palato-alveolar consonant, a palatal glide has developed in some kinds of southern accent, as for example in *large* [lɑːɪdʒ], *scorch* [skɔːɪtʃ], *porch* [pɔːɪtʃ] (otherwise [lɑːdʒ ~ lɑədʒ ~ lɑrdʒ] etc.). The fact that the [ɑːɪ] of *larger* is distinct both from the [aɛ] of *Elijah* and from the [æɪ] of *pass* in his own 'old-fashioned variety of Atlanta speech' was adduced by Sledd (1955) as important evidence in his brilliant refutation of Trager & Smith's purported overall pattern analysis of

English phonemics. If it is the case that the [ɪ] glide appears in *larger* but not in *rajah*, in *porch* but not in *coach*, Sledd's 1966 thesis that it is traceable to synchronic underlying /r/ does seem rather plausible. Most southerners, however, do not have these [ɪ] glides.

The PRICE vowel plus historical /r/, as in *fire*, is reflected as [ɑ+ɪə], triphthongal or disyllabic, in tidewater Virginia, but further south and west usually as a simple diphthong, [aə ~ aɚ]. This represents the monophthongal allophone of /aɪ/, [a], plus /ə/ with syllabicity loss (compare also [saəns] /'saɪəns/ *science*). In some kinds of rhotic southern speech, however, the vowel is backer, so that *fire* sounds like *far* [fɑr]. This variant, familiar in all kinds of midland speech, is nevertheless often considered substandard or incorrect. (It provided one of the variables investigated by Stolz & Bills (1968) in central Texas.) Monophthongs in MOUTH words (*flower, power*) are less usual, with the exception of the pronominal *our* /ɑː ~ ɑr/.

Southern accents characteristically keep FORCE distinct from NORTH (*hoarse* ≠ *horse*), while merging FORCE and CURE (*door* and *poor* rhyme). The merged vowel is a centring diphthong [oˑə] (rhotic [oɚ]), thus [doə ~ dor] *door*, [poək ~ pork] *pork*. The stigmatized use of [oʊ] for [oə ~ or] was mentioned above ([ʃoʊ] *sure* = *show*, [poʊ] *poor*, '*po'* ').

Some southerners, however, retain the FORCE vs. CURE distinction, with [ʊə ~ ʊɚ] in the latter set (or the corresponding unrounded quality). This applies, *PEAS* notes (p. 119), mostly to the speech of the cultured only, and presumably represents an innovation.

What, then, is the membership of part-system D of the typical southern vowel system? In a rhotic accent, nil, given that /ɑ/ has been included in part-system A, /ɔ/ in C, and that [ɝ] can be taken as /ʌr/. The same applies to a variably or categorically non-rhotic accent for the descriptivist who accepts the underlying-/r/ hypothesis. Those who reject it must recognize a part-system D such as (246).

(246) ɪə   ʊə
       ɛə   ɜː   oə
       æə   ɑː   ɔː

–or a subset thereof. In the table of incidence (247) (supplementary to (243)), the lefthand column relates to the prevocalic environment where there is no intervening # (e.g. *dairy*, *Mary*, but not *hair* # *y*); the centre and righthand columns relate to the environment __C and __ # . The centre column is applicable to rhotic accents, and to non-rhotic accents given the underlying-/r/ hypothesis; the righthand column relates to non-rhotic accents if the underlying-/r/ hypothesis is rejected.

(247)	NURSE	ʌr	ʌr = [ɝ, ɜɪ, ɜː]	ɜː = [ɜː, ɜɪ]
	NEAR	ir	ɪr, ɛr, ær	ɪə, ɛə
	SQUARE	eɪr	ær, æɪr, ɛr	æə, ɛə
	START	ɑr, ɔr	ɑr, ɔr	ɑː, ɑ
	NORTH	ɔr	ɔr	ɔː, ɔ
	FORCE	oʊr	oʊr, oʊ	oə, oʊ
	CURE	oʊr, ur	oʊr, ur, ʊr, oʊ	oə, ʊə, oʊ
	*lett*ER	ər	ər = [ɝ, ə]	ə
	*comm*A		ə, ər = [ɝ]	ə

6.5.9 Vowel plus /l/

The /l/ of southern accents follows rather the same patterns of realization as /r/. Lax vowels are subject to Shading and Breaking when it follows; and /l/ itself may under certain circumstances be deleted or, if not entirely lost, then articulated without any contact between tongue tip and alveolar ridge.

The vowel in southern *built* /bɪlt/ [bɪəɫt] exhibits Shading (ɪ → ɪ) and Breaking (→ ɪə), as does *belt* /bɛlt/ [bëəɫt]. In *talcum* /'tælkəm/ ['tæɫkəm] there is Shading, but (because it is not monosyllabic) no Breaking. In *doll*, *gull*, and *tool* the /ɑ/, /ʌ/, and /u/ respectively are often backer (because of Shading) than in *dot*, *gut*, *toot*.

The phoneme /l/ itself exhibits greater allophonic differences in the south than in other parts of North America, being notably clear between vowels (*silly*, *jelly*, *calling*): compare southern ['sɪlɪ] with midwestern ['sɪɫɪ]. It also tends to be clear after /aɪ/, /ɔɪ/ (*vile*, *oil*), as well as before /j/ (*million*). Retraction due to Shading, and Breaking, happen only before dark /l/. Hence *fill* and *filling* have three points of difference in their respective realizations of /fɪl/: *fill* is [fɪəɫ], while *filling* is ['fɪlɪŋ ~ 'fɪlɪn].

Dark /l/ is sometimes deleted in the environment of a following labial or velar, as in *help*, *bulb*, *golf*, *shelve*. This makes *help* [hëəp], homophonous with *hep* and a rhyme for *step* (the Shading and Breaking can be attributed to the /p/, independently of any intervening underlying /l/). This L Dropping is quite strongly stigmatized (it has been characterized to me by informants as 'hick' and 'low-class').

Where dark /l/ is not dropped it is potentially subject to a realization involving an unusual form of articulation. This is a kind of velar lateral, which may be symbolized [ʟ]: a lip-rounded vocoid with close back tongue position and unilateral velar closure.

> The back of the tongue is raised, no contact is made by the tip of the tongue, the sides of the tongue may or may not touch the upper teeth, and the back of the throat is constricted. . . . The speakers . . . believe that they form an *l*; and apparently the sound is heard as an *l*, even by those people who regularly have the normal lingual lateral in all positions in their speech. (Caffee 1940)

This [ʟ] coalesces with a preceding /ə/ to form a syllabic velar lateral in words such as *middle* ['mɪdʟ]. It also coalesces with a preceding /ʊ/ in words such as *full* /fʊl/ [fʟː], *bull*, *wolf*. In a peculiarity of lexical incidence, southern *bulge*, *bulk*, too, usually have /ʊl/ [ʟː] rather than the /ʌl/ of other accents.

Bailey (1969b: 206) draws attention to the fact that southern accents distinguish /l/ from /əl/ after back vowels, thus *school* vs. *dual*, *mule* vs. *renewal*, *stole* vs. *bestowal*, *drawl* vs. *withdrawal*. In each pair the first has tongue-tip articulation for the /l/, but the second has velar [ʟ].

6.5.10 Weak vowels

Southern accents, particularly if non-rhotic, characteristically retain an opposition between /ɪ/ and /ə/ as weak vowels, thereby making distinctions which are lost in most other American speech. Thus *rabb*[ɪ]*t* does not rhyme with *abb*[ə]*t*; *splend*[ɪ]*d* and *mended* do not rhyme with *tendered* [-dəd]; *get 'im* and *get 'em* are distinct, and so are *roses* and *Rosa's*, *sell it once* and *sell at once*; *palate* and *ballot* differ phonetically not only in the initial consonant and the weak vowel, but also (because of Umlaut) in the strong vowel, ['pælɪt] vs. ['bǽlət]; similarly *sheriff* vs. *seraph*. The incidence of /ɪ/ and /ə/ respectively corresponds in general to that of RP, although American southerners do have /ɪ/ in *-ad* and *-as* (where RP has /ə/) as well as in *-ate* (where RP traditionally has /ɪ/): thus *valid* and *salad* rhyme as /'vælɪd, 'sælɪd/ (RP /'vælɪd, 'sæləd/; GenAm both with [-ɪd]). *Texas* is locally often /'tɛksɪz/.

In *happ*Y the southern vowel is usually [ɪ] (though rhotic southerners may have [i]). Additional minimal pairs for weak /ɪ/ vs. /ə/ are therefore *Sophy* vs. *sofa*, *city* vs. *sitter*, *Commie* vs. *comma*, etc. Where the spelling is *-i*, there is fluctuation between /ɪ/ and /ə/, as in *Cincinnati*, *Missouri*, *Mississippi*, *ravioli*; a particularly southern pronunciation of *Miami* is supposedly [maˈæmə]. Actually, though, /-ə/ in *Missouri* and *Cincinnati* is by no means confined to the south. (Historically, /ə/ may have originated as a weakening of /aɪ/: Pace 1960.) Where the spelling is *-y*, /ə/ does not occur: *Kentucky* /kɪnˈtʌkɪ/ (not * /-kə/).

There is also fluctuation between /ɪ/ and /ə/ in *comm*A, although here /ɪ/ is definitely regarded as non-standard and is avoided by educated people. *PEAS* (pp. 168–9) reports [ɪ ∼ ɪ] in *sofa* and *china* particularly in West Virginia and the upper south (Va, NC). Where *sofa* is /ˈsoʊfɪ/, it of course becomes homophonous with *Sophy*. *Appalachia*, in standard speech /æpəˈlætʃə/, has a non-standard alternative pronunciation /æpəˈlætʃɪ/.

It is unusual to hear unstressed final-syllable /u ∼ ɪu/ in southern speech, except in the form of a schwa [ə] or its rounded equivalent [ɵ]. Thus *volume* is [ˈvɑ(l)jəm], *continue* [kənˈtɪnjɵ]. Before a vowel, [w] is inserted, thus *continuing* [kənˈtɪnjɵwɪŋ]. Final /oʊ/ can also be weakened in this way, as in *follow* [ˈfɑlɵ ∼ ˈfɑlə], *following* [ˈfɑlɵwɪŋ]; but in southern mountain speech there is also the (stigmatized) possibility of [ɚ], thus [ˈfɑlɚ, ˈfɑlɚɪn].

6.5.11 Consonants

In old-fashioned tidewater speech, /k, g/ are fronted to the palatal position, [c, ɟ], syllable-initially before a front vowel, and also notably before the [ɒː] (etc.) of START, as *garden* [ˈɟɒːdn̩] (perhaps to be phonemicized as /ˈgj-/).

An optional rule of NT Simplification deletes /t/ from the cluster /nt/ in the environment 'V__V, thus for example making *winter* a possible homophone of *winner* [wɪnə ∼ ˈwɪnɚ]; *Atlanta* [ətˈlænə]. This takes precedence over the Nasal Coalescence rule (244) (not *[ətˈlænə]). However, where the /nt/ is followed by a syllabic [n̩], the /t/ does not undergo deletion and Nasal Coalescence may occur: *sentence* [ˈsɛ̃tn̩s].

In many parts of the south, Cluster Reduction of final /st, ld, nd/ occurs very readily even where there is no consonant-initial word immediately following; this tends to be blocked by an intervening #, so that *banned* /bæn#d/ stays [bænd] (etc.) where *band* /bænd/ simplifies to [bæn]. This Cluster Reduction is widely, but not universally, regarded as 'substandard'.

Southern mountain speech tends to have [ʔ] for /t/ not only between nasals, or before a nasal within a word (as commonly in GenAm) but also before a nasal across a word boundary, as [ˈhɪtsə maˑʔ ˈnɔʊɪzɪ] *it's a mite noisy*, or before other sonorants, as [ˈkẽɪ̃ʔjə] *can't you?*, [hɪʔwəz ˈtɑm əz ˈstɒɚɹɪd ɔʊl ðə ˈʃiyʔn̩] *it was Tom as (who) started all the shooting*, [ˈsëʔlɚ] *settler*.

Some Texans use varieties of /s/ and /z/ made with the tongue tip up, almost retroflex [ʂ, ʐ]. (I do not believe this was merely a personal idiosyncrasy of the late President Johnson.)

Before /r/, /s/ rather than /ʃ/ seems to be widespread in the south, as in *shrink* [srɪŋk, ʂrɪŋk].

In *isn't*, *wasn't*, etc., pronunciations with [d] rather than [z] are usual, thus [ɪdn̩t]. Such forms are by no means confined to lower-class or non-standard speech.

The same cannot be said of TH Fronting ([f, v] for [θ, ð] in word-final position). This occurs only in lower-class, and particularly in black, speech: e.g. [boʊf] *both*, [brɪv] *breathe*. Its appearance in the southern United States is presumably quite independent of its use in popular urban accents of England.

Pronunciation of the pronoun *it* as /hɪt/ is a well-known charac-teristic of old-fashioned rural southern mountain accents, par-ticularly in the Ozarks. This represents a historical survival rather than an innovation. It has a weak form /ɪt/ (this weak form, generalized, is the presumed origin of the standard /h/-less pronunciation).

6.6 Black English

6.6.1 Introduction

The study of Black English, the dialect of black people in the United States, has after long neglect recently become rather fa-shionable. This is due in part to the problems which have arisen in so-called ghetto schools – schools in the inner city of those northern conurbations to which black people have moved from the south over the last few decades.

To what extent is Black English different from white English? More precisely, to what extent is popular Black English (Black English Vernacular, non-standard Negro English) something distinct from the non-standard popular English of white southerners? Views differ. Most Americans reckon that it is easy to identify a black person as such by his voice; yet it is reported that 'a test administered to middle-class white Chicagoans discloses that they consistently interpret the speech of urban-reared white Southern college professors as that of rural uneducated Negroes: the educated Southerner has all the superficial characteristics that Chicagoans associate with Southern Negro speech' (McDavid 1967a). On the basis of Linguistic Atlas records for the Bluegrass region of central Kentucky, Davis (1970) concludes that 'there simply were no systematic differences between the speech of the Negro and that of the Whites.... There is no real evidence that people can tell Whites from Blacks by linguistic cues alone.... All the informants in this study can more easily be characterized as South Midland than as either Black or White.'

This view has been succinctly expressed by McDavid as follows (1967a): 'it is safest to assume that in general the range of variants is the same in Negro and in white speech, though the statistical distribution of variants has been skewed by the American caste system.'

However, in a careful experiment involving 24 voices and 150 'judges', Tucker & Lambert (1969) showed that 'white judges can, in certain instances at least, distinguish white from Negro speakers'. For example, their northern white judges had an 87 per cent success rate in recognizing educated white southerners as white by their voices, 84 per cent in recognizing Mississippi-born black university students as black (but only 49 per cent success in recognizing as black southern-born university-educated blacks who had been living in New York City for several years). For southern white judges, the success rates were 96 per cent, 70 per cent, and 54 per cent.

If Black English is something distinct, do its special characteristics derive from the popular local dialects of England or from an African-language substratum? There was a time when scholars were disposed to deny all African influence. Nowadays, though, few would want to dissent from McDavid's pioneering insistence (McDavid & McDavid 1951) that just as there are recognizably Scandinavian linguistic survivals in Minnesota and the Dakotas, German linguistic survivals in Wisconsin and Pennsylvania, Dutch linguistic survivals in the Hudson Valley, so there are African linguistic survivals, culturally transmitted rather than racial, among American blacks. And it is now generally agreed that **Gullah**, spoken by blacks living along the coast of South Carolina and especially in the Sea Islands lying just offshore, is an English-based creole comparable to those of the West Indies (7.1.2 below). Gullah, however, is spoken only by a small minority of black Americans. The question is whether the speech of other black Americans, particularly of those who have not made it into the middle class, is just a dialect of English on a par with other regional varieties, or whether it too has its origins in creole.

Among those who argue strongly for the creole hypothesis is Stewart, who writes (1968):

evidence ... exists ... which practically forces the conclusion that the linguistic assimilation of the Afro-American population to the speech patterns of English-speaking American whites was neither as rapid nor as complete as some scholars have supposed. Of the Negro slaves who constituted the field labor force on North American plantations up to the mid-nineteenth century, even many who were born in the New World spoke a variety of English which was in fact a true creole language. . . . Indeed, the non-standard speech of present-day American Negroes still seems to exhibit structural traces of a creole predecessor, and this is probably a reason why it is in some ways more deviant from Standard English than is the non-standard speech of even the most uneducated American whites.

It is in syntax that the most convincing evidence for the creole hypothesis has been found. Work by Stewart (1967, 1968), Labov (1969a, 1972d; Labov *et al.* 1968), Dillard (1972), and others has identified important syntactic differences between Black English and Standard English; most of them are clearly attributable to creole influence and have their parallels in the West Indies and elsewhere.

Even in syntax, though, the argument over the separateness of Black English continues. While Feagin, having carried out a sociolinguistic study among white Alabamans, is firm that 'Black English has certain features which do not occur in Southern White, British dialects, or older stages of English and which are undoubtedly grammatical remnants of Creole' (1979: 263), Williamson (1970) claims to have observed in the informal speech of southern whites at least some of the features Feagin was to identify as exclusively black.

If it is true that Black English has a creole, African-derived substratum, it is also likely that there has been reciprocal influence between black and white southern speech, and that certain vocabulary items, at the very least, have percolated into general English from Black English. Convincing African etymons have been found for *goober* 'peanut', *okra, yam, juke(-box), jive, dig* 'understand', and many more, including *okay* (Dalby 1972). There are also the grunts sometimes spelt *uh-huh* and *uh-uh* respectively. The first, 'yes', is phonetically ['ə̃hə̃, 'ʌ̃hʌ̃, 'm̩m̩], hence nasal or nasalized; it usually has a rising tone pattern, [‿] (though other tones are possible). The second, 'no', is ['ʔəʔ'ʔə, 'ʔʌʔ'ʔʌ, 'ʔmʔ'm], sometimes with a lengthened final segment, an initial [h], and/or a final extra glottal stop; it is not necessarily nasal, and has an accented final syllable, with an obligatorily falling tone pattern, [ˋ] or [ˎ]. These are both constantly used by Americans of all races and regions. (In Britain, on the other hand, *uh-uh* 'no' is known only as a recent importation from the States or from West Indian English; some British people are confused by Americans' use of it. *Uh-huh* 'yes' is quite at home in Britain.) It thus seems likely that at least *uh-uh* 'no' was brought into English by black people.

6.6.2 Phonetic characteristics

There follows a listing of what to American northerners are the most striking characteristics of Black English phonetics and phonology. It must be remembered that some of these apply only to urban ghetto-dwellers of low socio-economic status: one must guard against supposing that all black Americans talk 'like the most ignorant teen-aged delinquents' (Sledd 1973).

It will be noticed that almost all of the following points were mentioned above in 6.5, The south. It may well be that any that were not should have been.

In the vowel system, there is the merger of CURE and FORCE, so that *poor* rhymes with *door* – either as [poə, doə], or else with the same vowel as GOAT, so that *poor* = *Poe* [poʊ] and *door* = *dough* [doʊ]. On the other hand, FORCE is distinguished from NORTH, *hoarse* ≠ *horse*. In some cases, NEAR may be merged with SQUARE, so that *fear* = *fair* [feə].

There may be subsystemic mergers of /ɪ/ and /æ/ in the environ- ment /__ŋ/, so that *drink* = *drank*, *ring* = *rang*, and of /ɪ/ and /ɛ/ in the environment of a following nasal, so that *pin* = *pen* and perhaps *Jim* = *gem*.

The PRICE vowel is monophthongal, [a], particularly in the environment of a following voiced consonant or #. Before a voiced consonant there may be a subsystemic merger with LOT, so that *ride* = *rod* [rad], *find* = *fond*; or the vowels may remain in contrast, [rad] vs. [rɑd] etc., but be distinguished in a way which northerners find difficult to perceive. It may also happen that there is monophthong- ing of MOUTH as well as of PRICE, which may lead to homophony of *pride* and *proud* [prad], *dine* and *down*, *find* and *found*. Again, this is mainly restricted to the environment of a following voiced conso- nant. Some speakers reportedly have a three-way neutralization, so that *pride* = *proud* = *prod*, *find* = *found* = *fond*.

Apart from this monophthonging, particularly in PRICE words, the vowel realizations which receive most comment are the [ɜ:] and [ɜɪ] realizations in NURSE (which are also of course traditional white New York City pronunciations), the lack of rounding in /ʊ/ (FOOT), and the rather open quality of /ɛ/ (DRESS).

Among the consonants, non-rhoticity means the potential for homophony of pairs such as *guard* and *god*, *farther* and *father*, *lord* and *laud* (as in various other accents); but also, more strikingly, of *sure–shore* and *show* [ʃoʊ], *their–there* and *they*, *you're–your* and *you* (the last with interesting syntactic repercussions), and of *Paris* and *pass*, *terrace* and *Tess*. There may also be an absence of /r/ after initial /θ/, as [θoʊ] *throw*, [θu] *threw–through*. The vocalization or deletion of final /l/ can lead to homophony of *tool* and *too*, *goal* and *go*, and perhaps three-way homophony in *pole* = *pour–poor* = *Poe*; deletion of /l/ before a consonant can make *help* homophonous with *hep* [hëəp]. Alternatively, /l/ in these words may be retained, but realized as [ʟ] or [ʊ].

The dental fricatives, /θ/ and /ð/, may be subject to TH Fronting in medial and final position, and occasionally to other processes. Thus *mouth* may be pronounced [mauf], *tooth* [tuf], and *nothing* ['nəfɪn], and similarly *smooth* as [smuv], *brother* as [b(r)əvə]. In the words *with* and *nothing* other possibilities are /t/ and zero corresponding to standard /θ/, thus [wɪt̬əm] *with 'em*, [wɪ 'mi] *with me*, [nət̬ʔn̩ ~ nəʔn̩ ~ nəɪn] *nothing* (Wolfram 1969: 83). TH Stopping is also reported for some other non-initial /θ/s, apparently particularly when preceded by a nasal and followed by a plosive, as *keep your mou*[t] *closed* (Wolfram 1969: 90). Note that in initial position [θ] occurs in Black English just as in standard accents: *thought* is [θɔ(ʊ)t], without either the Fronting of Cockney or the Stopping of West Indian accents. (Wolfram 1969: 130, does however mention the use of 'a lenis [t]' as a rare variant.) Stopping of initial /ð/, however, is frequent, just as in many other popular accents (*then* [dɛn]).

Final Cluster Reduction operates in Black English rather as in West Indian English (7.1.4 below). There may be no final [t] in words such as *list, missed, left, act*, no final [p, k] in *wasp, desk*, no final [d] in *find, cold, loved, named*. Words such as *list, desk* sometimes receive a syllabic plural ending (['lɪsɪz, 'dɛsɪz]), which suggests that at least for some speakers these words end underlyingly in /s/ rather than in /st/.

Single final /b, d, g/, as in *rob, bed, big*, are sometimes realized as a glottal plosive [ʔ] or as unreleased voiceless plosives [p̚, t̚, k̚] (perhaps with simultaneous [ʔ]). This does not usually lead to loss of contrast with /p, t, k/, however, because of allophonic effects on preceding vowels, thus for example *bet* /bɛt/ [bɛt] vs. *bed* /bɛd/ [bɛəʔt̚] (Wolfram 1969: 102). Final voiced plosives, and sometimes other final consonants, can also be straightforwardly elided (given zero realization). 'Some individuals appear to have generalized the process to the point where most of their syllables are of the CV type' (Labov 1973: 248). As a result there can be homophones such as *road* = *row, bid* = *big* (= *bit*), *poke* = *pope* = *poor, seed* = *see* (= *seat*). A morpheme-final consonant can also be lost before a suffix, thus [kɪːz] *kids*.

The initial consonant cluster in *street* may be [skr-] rather than [str-], so that *stream* and *scream* are homophones, [skrim ~ skrĩ]. Corresponding to standard /ʃr/, as in *shrink*, clusters such as [sw, sr, sɸ] may be found.

Oddities of lexical incidence include /'bɪdnɪs/ *business* (through the same process as gave ['ɪdn̩t] *isn't*), /æks/ *ask*, and initial stress in words like *police, defense, Detroit.*

Not only may *gonna* (*going to*) be [gõ] and *I'm gonna* [amo], but also *I don't know* can be simply ['aono].

7

The West Indies

7.1 General characteristics of Caribbean English

7.1.1 Introduction

The West Indies is a linguistic patchwork. In the West Indies proper – the Greater and Lesser Antilles and the Bahamas – and in the associated mainland coastal areas of Central and South America, we find speakers not only of Spanish, English, French, and Dutch, but also of creoles based on these: thus Papiamentu in Aruba and Curaçao, Sranan (Taki-Taki) in Surinam, Haitian Creole in Haiti, and Negro Dutch in St Thomas. On the mainland there are a variety of autochthonous Amerindian languages; no such languages now remain in the islands, although it is known that Arawak was once spoken in Trinidad, Carib (Karina) in Tobago and Grenada, and Island-Carib (which in spite of its name is an Arawakan language) in most of the Lesser Antilles The various European and European-derived languages of the area reflect the varying fortunes of the European powers which once battled for mastery of the Caribbean, along with the patterns of colonization which they succeeded in establishing. The Caribbean area also includes some 'imported' languages which are not European, such as Javanese in Surinam and Hindi in Trinidad and Guyana.

The most populous of the West Indian English-speaking territories is Jamaica in the Greater Antilles, with a population in excess of 2 million. Next comes Trinidad and Tobago, off the coast of Venezuela at the other end of the archipelago crescent, with rather over a million. Guyana, on the mainland of South America, has a population approaching three-quarters of a million. Then comes Barbados in the Windward Islands, with just over a quarter of a million. The population of the Bahamas is about 200,000. Each of these is treated individually in 7.2 below. Belize, in Central

America, stands rather apart in that many of its 150,000 population speak Spanish or an Amerindian language rather than English, although English is its official language. The remaining English-speaking territories each have populations of around or below 100,000. These include the Windward Islands of Grenada and St Vincent and the Leeward Islands of Antigua, Montserrat, St Kitts, Nevis, Anguilla, and the Virgin Islands. There are also the tiny Turks and Caicos Islands and the Caymans; and there are groups of English-speakers at various points along the Caribbean coast of Central America, including a sizeable group on the Miskito Coast of Nicaragua, where however the official language is Spanish. Lastly there is Bermuda out in the Atlantic, well to the north of the Caribbean but belonging linguistically with the English-speaking West Indies.

In this list we have omitted St Lucia and Dominica among the Windward Islands. Although these islands use English as their language of administration, education and officialdom, their inhabitants mostly speak a French-based creole. English is nevertheless beginning to displace creole French ('patois'), particularly in St Lucia, as it already has done in Grenada, which was also once French-speaking.

The demography of the West Indies is as complicated as its linguistic history. One fact, though, is obvious: that this area of the native-English-speaking world is the only one which is overwhelmingly black in its ethnic affiliation. There are black minorities in the United States, in England, and elsewhere; but it is only in the Caribbean territories that black people constitute the great majority of speakers of English as a first language. (We here exclude from consideration the speakers of English or English-based creoles in West Africa.)

With the possible exception of the Virgin Islands (of which St Thomas and St John once spoke a Danish-based creole, were never British, and are now American), West Indian English is British-oriented in its phonology. We find the BATH words, for example, typically pronounced with the broad vowel as in RP: *laugh* /lɑːf/, *pass* /pɑːs/ etc. *Mary*, *merry*, and *marry* are consistently distinguished from one another, as in all British but few American accents. TRAP words have the typical quality [a], thus *rat* [ɹat], which is common enough in Britain but virtually unknown in North America. But before considering the phonology of West Indian

English in detail, we look briefly at the nature of West Indian creoles.

7.1.2 Creole

The popular dialects in Jamaica and other English-speaking parts of the West Indies are referred to by linguists as **creoles**; the general public more often use the terms **dialect** or **patois**. What is implied by the term 'creole'? To what extent is the 'dialect' spoken in Jamaica or Guyana comparable to what I have called the traditional-dialect of the north of England?

Linguistically speaking, a creole is a language or dialect descended historically from a **pidgin**. A pidgin is a makeshift form of communication developed between groups of speakers of different languages who, having no language in common, employ a highly simplified version of the language of one group, with considerable influence from the language(s) of the other group(s). In this sense a pidgin has no native speakers (first-language speakers). It is typically characterized by a very reduced morphology, as compared with the language(s) on which it is 'based'. The ancestor of the present-day creoles spoken along the coast and on the islands off the coast on both sides of the Atlantic – in Africa and in the Americas – is believed to be a pidgin developed along the coast of West Africa in the fifteenth or sixteenth century by European traders (particularly slave-traders) and local African tribes. In one widely-held view, it was a Portuguese-based pidgin, subsequently relexified (given new vocabulary within essentially the same grammatical framework) in the case of those creoles which are now characterized by an essentially English or French (etc.) vocabulary.

Creolization is the process whereby a pidgin becomes established as the first language of a speech community, and very possibly as its only language. This happens when children are brought up by parents who use a pidgin as their common language within the family, or under other circumstances where the pidgin is the only common language of the adults with whom the child comes into contact. Once a pidgin acquires native speakers (first-language speakers) in this way, it is said to have become creolized, and is known as a creole. A creole characteristically is a much more complete language than a pidgin, since it is used by its speakers for all the various purposes for which speakers use their native language, not just for dealings with speakers from other groups.

Drawing the line between a pidgin and a creole is not always very easy. For example, both the West African Pidgin of Nigeria and Cameroon and the Neo-Melanesian Pidgin of the Solomon Islands and Papua-New Guinea are steadily acquiring first-language speakers and thus turning into creoles. As yet, though, it appears to be the case that the majority of their speakers have some other language as mother tongue. In the West Indies, on the other hand, the process of creolization lies essentially three centuries or more back in history. By the end of the seventeenth century English-based creoles were already well established in the slave societies of Barbados, the Leeward Islands, Jamaica, and Guyana/ Surinam.

In Surinam (ceded to the Dutch in 1667), English-based creoles have undergone three centuries of further evolution independent of any influence from standard English, or indeed of English of any other non-creole kind. As a consequence, they are now not in any way mutually intelligible with English. Sranan (also called Negerengels or Taki-Taki) is the language of the coastal region and the lingua franca of the whole country; there are also two other English-based creoles, not mutually intelligible with each other or with Sranan, namely Saramaccan and Djuka, spoken in the interior. All three must now be considered languages in their own right, their relation to English being only historical.

Elsewhere in the Caribbean, though, the fate of the English-based creoles has been rather different, in consequence of the fact that they have remained in contact with non-creole English. This is attributable mainly to the fact that they are spoken in what were or became British colonies, administered partly by expatriate British officials, economically organized principally as sugar plantations run by English owners. Officialdom and the upper strata of local society thus spoke English (whereas in Surinam they spoke Dutch). As education gradually became established and in due course extended to the mixed-race and black inhabitants, it was an education based exclusively upon the use of English as the language of instruction.

This means that for the last three centuries the English-based creoles of those West Indian territories which are or were formerly British colonies have been subject to the persistent and ever-increasing influence of standard English. They have been headed off from developing into quite distinct languages, as Sranan did; rather, they have in all probability become steadily more recognizable as varieties of English, acquiring more and more vocabulary from standard English and to some extent modifying their syntax in the same direction. So also in phonology: even the lowest-class Barbadian will know the pronunciation [θɪŋ] as an elegant variation of [tɪŋ] *thing* (whereas the speaker of Sranan, unless he has also learnt English, will not).

More importantly, the speech of the English-speaking West Indies now everywhere constitutes a continuum extending from broadest creole to standard English (perhaps with a local flavour). The situation is thus in many ways comparable to the traditional-dialect set-up in parts of the British Isles (discussed in volume 1, 1.1.3). In the terminology introduced by Stewart with reference to Black English in the United States, the continuum extends from the **basilect** (the variety most distinct from Standard English) through various degrees of **mesolect** to the **acrolect** (in this case educated West Indian English, which differs only trivially from other varieties of standard English). Individual speakers control a range of varieties (lects) along this continuum, and vary their speech in accordance with social context. Speech patterns in the community can be correlated with socio-economic class: the speech of an uneducated rural agricultural worker will typically be located towards the basilectal (broad creole) end of the spectrum, the speech of an educated urban white-collar towards the acrolectal (standard) end, the speech of others somewhere within the mesolect.

Basilectal and lower-mesolectal West Indian creole has many syntactic and morphological features differing sharply from anything found in traditional-dialects of Britain. In phonology, though, there are parallels between the two. Pronunciation involves social shibboleths in the West Indies in a way not dissimilar to the situation in England. A dropped /h/ is evaluated similarly in England and in Jamaica. A missing final /t/ in *next*, or [di] for *the*, may have a social meaning in the West Indies comparable to that of a glottalled /t/ or a vocalized /l/ in England.

If, then, we exclude the special case of Surinam, West Indian English as a whole is not just a creole. More precisely, it is describable as a **post-creole continuum** (DeCamp 1971). As the years pass, with increasing opportunities for contact with speakers of English from elsewhere, and under the influence of British or American cinema, radio, and television, the standard English end of the continuum gains steadily in dominance, and the process of gradual decreolization continues.

7.1.3 TH Stopping

One of the most striking phonetic characteristics of West Indian English is the neutralization, in popular speech, of the oppositions /θ/ vs. /t/ and /ð/ vs. /d/. Alveolar stops, [t, d], are used for both dental fricatives and alveolar plosives of standard accents. Thus the popular pronunciation of *thing* is [tɪŋ], that of *father* ['faːda]. Pairs such as *thin–tin, faith–fate, though–dough, breathe–breed* are homophonous.

Although this TH Stopping is found in popular speech throughout the English-speaking Caribbean, it is always subject to social and stylistic variability: the high-prestige and careful fricatives [θ, ð] vary with the lower-prestige and informal plosives [t, d]. In general, only the most educated speakers are consistent in their use of the fricatives in just the places where standard accents have /θ, ð/. Most speakers are inconsistent, sometimes using fricatives and sometimes plosives. There may also be some degree of hypercorrection, involving pronunciations such as [θʌŋ] *tongue*, [fʊθ] *foot*, [bɛð] *bed*. To the extent that this does happen, it demonstrates that the relevant lexical categories are not distinct in popular speech: if *faith* and *fate* are popularly homophonous as [feːt], they can also be homophonous in a would-be high-prestige form [feːθ].

The neutralization appears to operate particularly readily in the environment of a following /r/: thus *three–tree* [triː], *through–true* [truː]. In Jamaica, and possibly elsewhere, the resultant /tr/ may also be subject to (variable) merger with /tʃ/ (and similarly /dr/ with /dʒ/), so that *train* may be pronounced homophonously with *chain*, or *thrill* with *chill*. Usually, however, /tr, dr/ (corresponding to standard /θr, tr; ðr, dr/ remain distinct from the palato-alveolar affricates.

Standard-oriented speakers who are good spellers can consult their knowledge of the spelling in order to know whether [θ] or [t] is appropriate as a careful pronunciation for creole /t/. With the exception of a few special cases such as *Thomas* and *thyme*, *th* corresponds to standard /θ/ (or /ð/), while *t* corresponds to standard /t/. On the other hand a West Indian who is a poor speller may not be able to consult his pronunciation (as speakers of most accents of English can) in order to arrive at the correct spelling of a word with creole /t/. This is one respect in which most West Indians are placed at a disadvantage in comparison with speakers of most other local forms of English by the relationship between the standard orthography and the local accent.

7.1.4 Cluster reduction

As compared with standard accents, West Indian English tends towards a rather reduced range of possible consonant clusters. But the phonotactics of consonant clustering is sociolinguistically sensitive, with the most educated or careful accents having a range of consonant clusters just as wide as that of RP or GenAm. At the creole end of the continuum, there are no final clusters involving an obstruent plus /t/, nor any clusters involving /d/ as the second item. There is also some tendency to reduce initial clusters involving /s/.

Clusters involving an obstruent plus /t/ in standard accents include /ft, st, kt/, as in *left, nest, act*. In creole these lack their final consonant, and are (underlyingly as well as in surface phonetics) /lɛf, nɛs, ak/. Other standard word-final clusters following the same pattern are /θt, ʃt, pt, tʃt/, as in *earthed, pushed, stopped, touched*. All of these include the past tense ending -*ed*, which is not used in creole; so these clusters tend to be missing from popular West Indian English on morphosyntactic as well as on phonotactic grounds. Clusters of nasal plus voiceless consonant, however, are found in West Indian just as in other accents, thus [lamp] *lamp*, [tɛnt] *tent, tenth*, [baŋk] *bank*. So are those involving a liquid plus a voiceless consonant, at least as far as rhoticity allows: [(h)ɛlp] *help*, [(h)ɛlt] *health*, [mɪlk] *milk*, [ʃɛlf] *shelf*, and in some West Indian accents [paːrt] *part*.

Final clusters involving /d/ as the second item in standard accents include in particular /nd/ and /ld/, as *send, build*. In creole these too lose the /d/, thus /sɛn, bɪl/. The consonant-plus-/d/ clusters of standard *rubbed, bagged, loved, breathed* are again inapplicable in creole because of morphosyntactic considerations. In intermediate varieties, however, they can of course occur; though *breathed* can obviously only have a final cluster if its stem is pronounced with final [ð]. In rhotic varieties of West Indian English, /rd/ is regular in words such as *hard*.

Certain other final consonant clusters occur freely in West Indian English just as elsewhere: for example /ks/ in *six, box*, /ps/ in *lapse, Pops*. The clusters /sk/ and /sp/, however, do not: in popular West Indian speech *ask* is /a(:)ks/, while *mask* is /ma:s/. Historically considered, some /sk/ and /sp/ words have been subjected to metathesis, whereas others have undergone cluster simplification by loss of the plosive.

It was claimed above that creole *nest* is underlyingly /nɛs/ (and similarly with other words). The phonetic form [nɛs] is frequent in all forms of English, of course, as an optional preconsonantal variant (thus, *knocked the ne*[s] *down*). Why do we consider it to be underlying in creole, rather than derived from an underlying /nɛst/ by Elision? There are several reasons. The form [nɛs] occurs freely before vowels and in absolute final position. (So also [fa:sa] *faster*, [tɛsɪn] *testing*.) When pluralized with the standard English -(e)s suffix it tends to be ['nɛsɛz, 'nɛsɪz], so following the pattern of words like *horse/horses, bus/buses* rather than that of words ending in /t/ (*cat/cats, tent/tents*). And in intermediate varieties between broad creole and standard hypercorrections of the type [fe:st] *face*, [gɛstɪn] *guessing* are quite frequent.

Reduction of initial clusters involving /s/ is restricted to the broadest creole. There it shows up in forms such as [ta:t] *start*, [kratʃ] *scratch*. In intermediate varieties of speech it is responsible for occasional hypercorrections such as [stʌk] for *tuck*, [straɪv] for *thrive*.

7.1.5 Other consonants

At the creole end of the continuum there are three consonants which tend to be absent, though phonemically distinctive further up the sociolinguistic scale: /v/, /ʒ/, and /h/. The details vary considerably from territory to territory.

In place of standard /v/ West Indian creole may have /b/ or /w/. Thus *vex* may be pronounced [bɛks], *river* ['rɪba], and *love* [lʌb]. These pronunciations are however stigmatized, and are avoided by speakers with any education. Other words, more recently added to the everyday vocabulary, regularly have [v] for all speakers: thus [voːt] *vote*, for instance, seems never to be made homophonous with *boat*. So V–B Confusion, as we may call it, is nowadays perhaps always lexically restricted.

The alternative possibility is V–W Confusion. Bahamians, Bermudans, and Vincentians are among those for whom the use of [w] for standard [v], or a bilabial fricative [β] for both, has been reported. Thus *village* may be pronounced ['wɪlɪdʒ], and so on. In Montserrat this phenomenon is restricted to the speech of the older uneducated population, and even for them lexically restricted (since *vote* has [v], not [w]); the facts in all these territories await proper investigation. It is not clear whether this phenomenon is connected with the V–W Confusion of eighteenth- and nineteenth-century London Cockney, or whether it arose independently in the West Indies through the influence of an African substratum lacking /v/.

The African substratum is presumably responsible for the creole tendency to replace standard /ʒ/ with either /dʒ/ or /ʃ/, each of which differ by just one distinctive feature from /ʒ/. The commonest replacement is the affricate, giving rise to such pronunciations as ['plɛdʒa] *pleasure*, ['vɪdʒʌn] *vision*. These pronunciations, too, are stigmatized and restricted to the creole end of the continuum. Of course, there are not very many everyday English words which contain /ʒ/, and none which involve its occurrence in any environment other than 'V_V. Most words containing /ʒ/ belong to the relatively learned part of the English vocabulary, so that they would be used only by the more educated speakers, who control [ʒ].

H Dropping in much of Jamaica is virtually identical with the same phenomenon in England. In popular speech /h/ does not really exist as a phoneme, although [h] as a speech sound is quite common. Pairs such as *hair* and *air* are homophonous, both being sometimes [ɪɛr] and sometimes, particularly if stressed, [hɪɛr]. Alongside the frequent H Dropping of [aːf] *half*, [uɔl] *hole–whole*, etc., there is the frequent use of [h] in words such as *egg*, *off*, *end*. This can be seen either as hypercorrection (a speaker attempts to upgrade his speech by attaching [h] to words beginning with a vowel, but does not succeed in identifying the lexical items for which this is appropriate as against those for which it is inappropriate), or merely as an emphatic device used whenever a word beginning phonologically with a vowel is emphasized.

As in England, H Dropping is overtly stigmatized and regarded as incorrect. As in England, the educated and middle class do not on the whole drop /h/, while those slightly lower on the social scale use it variably. Jamaica is also similar to England in that there are rural pockets (particularly in the west) where H Dropping is unknown and everyone, from top to bottom of the social scale, uses phonemic /h/. (Its lexical incidence may differ, though, with *it* being /hɪt/, for example, and *him* /ɪm/.)

The situation in the other parts of the West Indies is not altogether clear. In many islands there is a phonemic /h/, just as in the standard accents, and instances of H Dropping are quoted to the visitor as an example of the bad speech Jamaicans (but not the inhabitants of the island in question) use. But there is also H Dropping in some of the Bahamas, and perhaps elsewhere.

In popular Jamaican speech /j/ and /w/ tend to appear in certain environments where they do not occur in standard accents. The palatal glide is to be heard between a velar consonant and a following open vowel, thus *cat* /kjat/, *gas* /gjas/, *car* /kjaːr/, *garden* /gjaːdn̩/. This does not apply, however, if the vowel corresponds lexically to LOT or to THOUGHT, NORTH: hence *cot* /kat ~ kɒt/, *corn* /kaːn ~ kɔːn/ have no /j/. Where /kj, gj/ are used, they may be realized as a single, palatal articulation, [c, ɟ]. Palatal allophones of /k, g/ are also often used before close front vowels, including [iɛ], thus *gate* [ɟiɛt]. I surmise, however, that the palatals are becoming obsolete in Jamaican speech: *garden* seems to be /gaːdn̩/ much more commonly than the traditional /gjaːdn̩/. The labial-velar glide, /w/, is found between a labial and a following /aɪ/, but only if the vowel corresponds lexically to CHOICE rather than PRICE: thus *point* /pwaɪnt/, *boy* /bwaɪ/ (but *pint* /paɪnt/, *buy* /baɪ/). This /w/ is not to be found in middle-class speech, although the /j/ after /k, g/ sometimes is. I am not sure to what extent these Jamaican pronunciations extend to other parts of the West Indies.

The foregoing consonantal characteristics are all socially and stylistically variable in the West Indies. There are certain others which apply much more generally to Caribbean accents of English. These include the particular phonetic qualities of /l/ and /w/.

West Indian /l/ is typically clear (lightly palatalized) in all environments, without the dark (velarized) allophones of many other accents. A word such as *milk* is [mɪl̡k], as in Ireland, rather than [mɪɫk], the GenAm and RP form.

West Indian /w/ is notable for the allophone [ɥ] (labial-palatal approximant), used in the environment of a following mid or close front vowel, thus [ɥiːk] *week*, [ɥɛt] *wet*. This [ɥ] is to be explained as an accommodatory (coarticulated) allophone, since it, like the front vowels it occurs before, is made with the front of the tongue raised towards the hard palate. The ordinary [w] allophone, used in all other environments, is of course made with the back of the tongue raised towards the soft palate.

As in England, Glide Cluster Reduction is usual in West Indian speech; thus *whine* is homophonous with *wine* [waɪn]. This point and the two preceding points are all illustrated in the word *wheel*, with a typical West Indian pronunciation [ɥiːl̡].

7.1.6 Vowels and /r/

The degrees of rhoticity to be found in the West Indies are as varied as those of England. Barbados speech is distinguished by its fully rhotic nature. The accents of Trinidad and the other Windward and Leeward Islands, and of the Bahamas, are non-rhotic. Jamaica and Guyana occupy intermediate positions, with variable semi-rhoticity. The vowel systems in the non-rhotic islands, as one would expect, include at least two additional phonemes as compared with the vowel system of Barbadian: one of the type /ea/ (phonetically [ea ~ eɐ ~ ɛː]) in the NEAR and SQUARE words, and one of the type /oa/ (phonetically [uɔ ~ ʊɐ ~ oa]) in the FORCE and CURE words. It is very usual in West Indian speech of all social classes for the paired lexical sets to be merged, both in non-rhotic and in rhotic accents: thus *beer* is typically homophonous with *bare–bear*, and *pour* with *poor*.

In West Indian vowels the most striking characteristic is the tendency to avoid central, [ə]-like qualities in favour of peripheral (unreduced) vowels. In popular Jamaican speech, for example, words such as *letter* and *comma* are usually pronounced with final [a

~ ɐ], which there is no reason not to assign to the same phoneme /a/ as in *flat*. The two syllables of *matter* rhyme: /'mata/. Words such as *and* or *at* have the same or similar vowel quality (/an(d), at/) whether stressed or not. As one progresses up the social scale, [ə]-like qualities become more common; it is very hard to find a satisfactory criterion for determining whether or not a phonemic opposition really exists between /a/ and a putative /ə/, but the existence of such a phoneme is something of a hallmark of educated speech. Even educated and middle-class West Indians, though, frequently use peripheral (unreduced) vowels in words and contexts where speakers of other accents would be likely to use /ə/ or some other reduction vowel. This is exemplified in words such as *governm*[ɛ]*nt*, *happin*[ɛ]*ss*, *purp*[ʌ]*se*, *wom*[a]*n*, *want*[ɛ]*d*, [a]*go*.

Where West Indian speech does have what seems like a reduction vowel, in environments where other accents vary between /ɪ/ and /ə/, it has a clear preference for /ɪ/: thus *or*[ɪ]*nge*, *runn*[ɪ]*ng* (/ɪn ~ ɪŋ/), [ə'bɪlɪtɪ] *ability*, etc.; similarly, /ɪ/ is regular in words such as *towel* and *channel* ['tʃanɪl], pronunciations which are very rare anywhere else.

Returning to the stressed vowels, we find in the West Indies a variety of different vowel systems. There are, however, certain points which they tend to have in common. The prestige norms for FACE and GOAT are /eː/ and /oː/, phonetically monophthongs, unaffected by the Long Mid Diphthonging (vol. 1, 3.1.12) of RP and GenAm. Diphthongs are used in some islands in words of these lexical sets, but they are opening diphthongs of the type [iɛ ~ iɐ], [uɔ ~ ʊʌ], which function as social/stylistic or allophonic variants of the monophthongs [eː], [oː]. (In the phonemic transcription employed by the *Dictionary of Jamaican English* (Cassidy & Le Page 1980), the vowels of FACE and GOAT are written /ie/ and /uo/ respectively.)

The other long vowels of West Indian English tend to be firmly monophthongal, without the diphthongal allophones commonly found in the accents of the United States or England: thus *see* and *two* are [siː], [tʰuː], often with almost cardinal-type vowels.

Of the diphthongs, the MOUTH vowel tends to be back and rounded throughout, [ɒʊ ~ ɔʊ]; the PRICE vowel is usually front, [aɪ ~ aɛ], though with considerable geographical variation. Among the short vowels, the /a/ of TRAP is open, front or central, [a ~ ɑ+], while the /ʌ/ of STRUT is typically rounded and back or centralized back, [ɔ ~ ɔ̈]. (It will be convenient, however, still to write it /ʌ/.)

There is an unusual development in words such as *down, round, count* – words in which other accents of English have the MOUTH diphthong plus /n/. In the Caribbean these are often pronounced instead with the STRUT vowel plus /ŋ/, making *down* homophonous with *dung* /dʌŋ/, and *round* (/d/-less) with *rung* /rʌŋ/. (An alternative possibility is a nasalized vowel, qualitatively like /ʌ/, with no nasal consonant: *down* [dɔ̃].) In Jamaica this pronunciation seems to be obsolescent, lexically restricted and avoided by educated speakers; but further south, in Trinidad and Guyana, it is much more generally to be heard, middle-class educated speech included: typical examples in more learned words are /ˈbʌŋdari/ *boundary*, /aˈkʌŋtansi/ *accountancy*. The origin of this development is obscure: it does not on the face of it appear to be due to the substratum influence of an African language, although it does occur in West African Pidgin English (9.2.1).

7.1.7 Prosodic features

The tendency towards non-reduction of vowels in unstressed syllables has an obvious effect on the rhythm of West Indian speech: to a European or American ear it sounds more evenly stressed, with less of a contrast between stressed and unstressed syllables than in other varieties of English. West Indian English is not, however, syllable-timed to the extent that the English of native speakers of African languages usually is.

In word stress there are many words belonging to the relatively educated vocabulary which receive final stress in West Indian English, although they have initial stress in RP and GenAm: thus *reaˈlize* (RP *ˈrealize*), *celeˈbrate* (RP *ˈcelebrate*). Compare also items such as *agriˈculture* (RP *ˈagriculture*). One might even say that West Indian English lacks the Alternating Stress Rule (Chomsky & Halle 1968: 77–9).

There are certain problems which arise in the analysis of West Indian word stress, problems that have not yet been satisfactorily resolved. It is quite common to find disyllabic words which appear to have the stress on the syllable which is unstressed in all other varieties of English: e.g. [kɪˈtʃɪn] *kitchen*, [krɪˈpl̩] *cripple(d)*. It is by no means clear whether this is the correct description of the stress pattern (even though that is what it sounds like to the outsider's ear). And it is not clear how far this prosodic effect, whatever it is, can be used for lexical distinctions.

Working with Jamaican informants, speakers of broad creole in the rural west of the island, I came to the conclusion (Wells 1973: 22) that there was an intonation or emphasis phenomenon which had the effect of shifting the surface stress rightwards by one syllable. Thus if a speaker says the creole sentence *A ena go ina di kichin*, or its standard equivalent *I was going into the kitchen*, with ordinary stress and intonation, then *kitchen* is front-stressed, /ˈkɪtʃɪn/. But with special, emphatic, intonation, the syllable /kɪ/ has medium or low pitch, and /tʃɪn/ a high fall, giving the auditory effect to an English ear of /kɪˈtʃɪn/. I concluded that it was best regarded as a special type of nuclear tone still located phonologically on the usual syllable, and wrote it /ˈkɪtʃɪn/. This view is supported by the fact that the surface-stressed syllable may even contain a syllabic consonant rather than any true vowel, as in the example [krɪˈpl̩] /ˈkrɪpl̩/ quoted above.

But from Barbados and Guyana there have been reports claiming lexical exploitation of stress (or tone?) in words of this kind. Holder (1972) lists words such as *bottle, table, wallet* as having final stress in Guyanese English, in contrast to the initial stress of *battle, wrestle, mallet*. He also reports minimal pairs such as 'father (parent) vs. fa'ther (clergyman). Pairs of this kind seem in fact first to have been pointed out for Barbadian English, by Collymore (1970; first edition 1955), who offers minimal pairs such as 'brother vs. ˈbrother (member of religious sect), 'copy (noun) vs. ˈcopy (verb). In fact there are a large number of such minimal pairs in which one item is a common noun, while the other is a personal name, thus 'tailor vs. Tay'lor (or ˈTaylor, depending on the analysis we adopt); similarly *Mason, Farmer*, etc. (Allsopp 1972).

It is clear that West Indian English differs from other varieties not only in stress but also in intonation. Although the non-weakening of vowels in unstressed syllables tends to reduce the perceptual difference between stressed and unstressed syllables, the use of a typically rather wide pitch range compensates for this by increasing the perceptual difference between those stressed syllables which are intonationally highlighted (accented) and those which are not.

It is reasonable to seek for traces of an African substratum not only in segmental phenomena in West Indian English but also, indeed particularly, in the prosodic features. An attempt to analyse the intonation of Guyanese English from this point of view was made by Berry (1976), who is himself an Africanist. He rejects the view that Guyanese English is a tone language (as some had surmised on the basis of the minimal pairs discussed above), and concludes that

the salient prosodic features of Guyanese English are, first, a pitch accent and second, a sentence intonation conspicuously different from the intonation of standard American or British English. Though high pitch in Guyanese English and heavy stress in Standard English often coincide.... The basic sentence intonation in Guyanese English is reminiscent of the terrace-tone languages of West Africa in which the pitch changes by discrete steps from syllable to syllable in an overall pattern of downdrift. (Berry 1976: 269–70)

Berry is, I think, right, in pointing out the importance of the tendency of pitch in a West Indian sentence to change by discrete steps from syllable to syllable, as opposed to the tendency in other accents for falls in the head, or rises anywhere, to be spread evenly over complete stress groups or longer stretches. His pointing out of patterns of downdrift and downstep in Guyanese intonation are not so striking, since downdrift and downstep are by no means phenomena restricted to African languages; indeed, they approach the status of linguistic universals. (The 'stepping head' of RP is a classical example of the downstep phenomenon; there are varieties of Scottish intonation which display downdrift of a kind which might be considered typically African, with successive high syllables separated by lower-pitched syllables, each high (and stressed) syllable being relatively lower than the preceding one. So downstep and downdrift are no guarantee of the existence of an African-language substratum.) (See further below, 7.2.3, 7.2.4.)

7.2 Individual territories

7.2.1 Jamaica

Jamaica is the largest of the English-speaking West Indian islands, and easily the most populous English-speaking territory in the

Caribbean area. It is not surprising, then, that Jamaican English (including its basilectal form, Jamaican Creole) is the best-known variety of West Indian English. This is the case not only among the general public, who tend (in England, at any rate) to equate 'West Indian' with 'Jamaican', but also among linguists, by whom Jamaican syntax (Bailey 1966), vocabulary (Cassidy & Le Page 1980), and linguistic history (Le Page & DeCamp 1960; Cassidy 1961) have been thoroughly explored. (It is perhaps only in the case of Guyanese syntax (Bickerton 1975) that some other variety of West Indian English has been covered in greater depth.) It was also the speech of Jamaicans living in London that I investigated in my study of accent-changing (Wells 1973).

Nearly 250 kilometres long and up to 80 kilometres wide, Jamaica is big enough to exhibit not only wide social variability in speech, but also some degree of geographical variability. For example, it used to be thought that popular (basilectal) Jamaican Creole has no phoneme /h/, but just the variable emphatic [h] described in 7.1.5 above. Although this is so for the capital, Kingston, and for many other parts of the island, it is now clear that it is not the case for certain westerly parishes, where a contrastive /h/ is consistently used at all social levels (Wells 1973: 12, 93). In the word *castle*, the usual Jamaican form is /kjasl/ (which goes against the general broad-BATH characteristic of Jamaican pronunciation); but speakers in the easternmost parishes say /kja:sl/ (Wells 1973: 93–4). A number of cases of geographical variation in vocabulary have been investigated and mapped by DeCamp (1961).

At the upper (acrolectal) end of the social and linguistic scale, Jamaican consonants are phonetically much as in the standard accents, apart from the use of clear /l/ in all environments and of the [ɥ] allophone of /w/ before /i:, ɪ, e:, ɛ/. Further down the scale, in the mesolect and basilect, the characteristics discussed in 7.1 emerge: TH Stopping, Cluster Reduction, avoidance of [ʒ] and some [v], H Dropping, semivowels in words such as /kjat/ *cat*, /bwaɪ/ *boy*. The distribution of /r/ is discussed below.

The vowel system is as set out in (248).

(248)

ɪ	ʊ	i:				u:
ɛ	ʌ	e:		(3:)		o:
a	(ɒ)	aɪ	(ɔɪ)	a:	(ɔ:)	ɔʊ

Phonetically, /ʌ/ is back and rounded, between [ɔ] and [ə]. Mid long /eː/ and /oː/ are monophthongs in middle-class speech, but in popular speech usually falling diphthongs, [ɪë ~ iɛ], [ʊö ~ uɔ], thus *face* acrolectally [feːs] and basilectally [fiɛs], *goat* [goːt] and [guɔt]. Contrastive /ɒ/, /ɔː/, and /ɔɪ/ are restricted to the higher part of the continuum, being replaced in popular speech by /a/, /aː/ and /aɪ/ respectively, so that *block* is acrolectally [blɒk] (or sometimes with an unrounded back vowel, [blɑk]) but basilectally homophonous with *black* [blak]; similarly *voice* may or may not be distinct from *vice* [vaɪs] or *form* from *farm* [faːm].

In NURSE words the Jamaican Creole (basilectal) pronunciation involves /ʌ/, with a following /r/ in morpheme-final position only; thus *bird* is homophonous with *bud* [böd] /bʌd/, while *fur* is [föɹ] /fʌr/. In the mesolect the /ʌr/ pronunciation is extended to all NURSE words, so that *bird* [böɹd] is distinguished from *bud* [böd] by its containing /r/, as /bʌrd/ vs. /bʌd/. In the acrolect the vocalic nucleus in NURSE words is a single long r-coloured mid central vowel, [ɝː] – very much as in GenAm, though possibly with some lip rounding. The usual problems of phonemicization therefore arise: it is possible to argue that it is still the realization of underlying /ʌr/, or that it represents an additional vowel in part-system D, either an /ɜː/ which is always followed by /r/, or else a consolidated /ɝː/.

In the phonemic notation used by the *Dictionary of Jamaican English* and many other scholarly works, /i e o u/ are used for my /ɪ ɛ ʌ ʊ/, and /ii ie ai ou uo uu aa/ for my /iː eː aɪ ɔʊ oː uː aː/. This is a very convenient notation for books dealing only with Jamaican English, but is awkward for comparative purposes, which is why I have not applied it here.

The lexical incidence of the vowels is shown in (249).

(249)

KIT	ɪ	FLEECE	iː	NEAR	eːr [iɛɹ *x* eːɹ]
DRESS	ɛ	FACE	eː [iɛ *x* eː]	SQUARE	eːr [iɛɹ *x* eːɹ]
TRAP	a	PALM	aː	START	aː(r)
LOT	a *x* ɒ	THOUGHT	aː *x* ɔː	NORTH	aː(r) *x* ɔː(r)
STRUT	ʌ	GOAT	oː [uɔ *x* oː]	FORCE	oːr
FOOT	ʊ	GOOSE	uː	CURE	oːr
BATH	aː	PRICE	aɪ	*happ*Y	[ɪ], occas. [i]
CLOTH	aː *x* ɔː	CHOICE	aɪ *x* ɔɪ	*lett*ER	a [ɐ] *x* ʌr *x* ə
NURSE	ʌ *x* ʌr *x* ɜːr	MOUTH	ɔʊ	*comm*A	a [ɐ] *x* ʌr *x* ə

The third column above demands fuller discussion, since the rhoticity situation in Jamaica is rather complicated. In the basilect, historical morpheme-final /r/ remains except in weak syllables: thus there is a phonetically realized /r/ in *near, square, star, war, four, fourth* and *poor,* but not in *letter, father* (the latter being basilectally ['faːdɐ] /'faːda/). Before a consonant within the same morpheme, historical /r/ is lost, so that basilectal *beard* is a homophone of *bathe* [biɛd] and *court* of *coat* [kuɔt], while *farm* and *form,* both /faːm/, rhyme with *psalm* /saːm/. In the lower mesolect, final /r/ is quite common in careful pronunciations of *lett*ER words, e.g. *father* ['faːdöɹ ~ 'faːðöɹ]. Nevertheless, the usual unmonitored pronunciation for all social classes in Jamaica is non-rhotic in respect of *lett*ER words, the height of the central vowel used evidently correlating with social class and style, from broad ['faːdɐ] to standard ['faːðə]. Mesolectally, rhoticity is extended by some speakers to all NEAR, SQUARE, FORCE and CURE words (as well as, as we have seen already, to NURSE words). This has the appropriate effect of distinguishing *beard* firmly from *bathe* (as /beːrd/ vs. /beːd ~ beːð/) and *court* from *coat* (as /koːrt/ vs. /koːt/). On the other hand hypercorrections are sometimes to be observed, as /beːrd/ *bathe* (as reported in Wells 1973: 98). In START and NORTH words, sporadic preconsonantal rhoticity is characteristic of many mesolectal and some acrolectal speakers: thus *short,* basilectally /ʃaːt/, may be pronounced either /ʃɔːrt/ or, more commonly, /ʃɔːt/, and similarly *start* /staːrt/ or /staːt/. In my survey of Jamaicans in London I found that phonetic /r/ was used by 55 per cent of respondents in *horse* but by only 8 per cent in *north,* with other comparable words spread between these extremes. As a last complication, some speakers may lose final /r/, particularly after /eː/ and /oː/, so that non-rhotic pronunciations of words such as *beer* and *four* (and, less commonly, of words such as *star* and *fur*) are sometimes encountered. It seems, though, that Jamaicans never make pairs such as *beer* and *bay, four* and *foe* homophonous; which argues that what is involved here is no more than a low-level rule deleting an underlying /r/ which has already had some allophonic effect on the preceding vowel.

7.2.2 Trinidad

Trinidad lies just off the coast of Venezuela. It has been English-speaking for only a rather short period (less than two centuries), having been a Spanish possession until 1797, when it was seized by the British. Between 1777 and 1821 there was a considerable influx of French-speaking planters and their slaves (speakers of French Creole), so that in the early nineteenth century Spanish gave way to French as the predominant language of Trinidad. Nevertheless, French and patois yielded in their turn in the course of the nineteenth century, as English gradually took over as the main language of the island. In the nineteenth century there was also considerable immigration to Trinidad from other parts of the West Indies, from the Indian subcontinent, from southern China, and from Portugal. All these groups of immigrants, or their descendants, in time became English-speaking. The Indians were the slowest to assimilate linguistically, and Hindi is still widely known and used in Trinidad (about 36 per cent of the population is East Indian), though English is by now the mother tongue of virtually all Trinidadians born since, say, 1940.

The Trinidadian accent is non-rhotic. For example, *star* is [sta ~ stɑ], *beer–bear–bare* (homophones) [bia ~ beə], and *four* [fɔ(:)]. This characteristic immediately distinguishes Trinidad speech from that of Jamaica, Guyana, and Barbados, all of which retain historical final /r/ in such words. It is tempting to link the non-rhoticity of Trinidadian pronunciation with the fact that metropolitan speech in England was generally non-rhotic by the time Trinidad became English-speaking. Against this, though, it must be said that this explanation is not available for the equally non-rhotic, but much longer established, English pronunciation of the Leeward Islands.

A striking characteristic of Trinidadian popular pronunciation, though not of the local standard accent, is the merger of certain vowels – such that *ham* and *harm* may be homophonous, as also may *cut* and *cot*. The latter merger may even be extended so that *caught* and *curt*, too, may be homophonous with *cut–cot*.

Where *ham* and *harm* are not distinguished, an open [a–], between front and central, is used in both words: we may write it /a/. It is used in all of the lexical sets TRAP, BATH, PALM, START. Where *ham* is distinguished from *harm*, as /a/ vs. /ɑ/, the distinction may depend on quality or duration or a combination of the two, the shorter/fronter /a/ being used in TRAP words and the longer/backer /ɑ/ otherwise. But there are certain anomalies in this lexical distribution; Warner (1967) notes *guardian* with /a/ and *magazine* with /ɑ/. She comments further that in cases of doubt the 'socially hyperconscious' appear to lean towards /ɑ/.

Acrolectal speakers have a four-way distinction between *cut, cot, caught* and *curt*, with /ʌ/, /ɒ/, /ɔ/ and /3/ respectively. The STRUT vowel, /ʌ/, is then usually realized as a central vowel, a variety of [ə], and so distinguished from the /ɒ/ of LOT which is back and rounded, usually of the [ɔ̈] type. (This means that an educated Trinidadian pronunciation of *sock* may well sound like the *suck* of Jamaicans or Barbadians.) The /ɔ/ of THOUGHT–NORTH–FORCE differs from this /ɒ/ mainly in duration, though it may also be backer, [ɔ̈: ~ ɔ:]. The merger of the lexical sets NORTH and FORCE is taken for granted by Warner (1967), even though most other West Indian accents retain the historical distinction here; I have encountered Trinidadian informants who claimed to make a distinction between the vowels of *short* and *sport*, but I suspect that this was achieved only at the expense of making *short* and *shot* homophonous, i.e. by using /ɒ/ in *short* as against /ɔ/ in *sport*. The fourth vowel under discussion here, the /3/ of NURSE, tends in acrolectal Trinidadian pronunciation to be rather close, ranging from [3] to [ɨ].

In popular pronunciation, as noted above, all four vowels /ʌ, ɒ, ɔ, 3/ may be merged in a single back open rounded vowel /ɒ/ (phonetically [ɔ̈] or thereabouts). Speakers using this merged /ɒ/ will have *bud, bod(y), board–bored* and *bird* as homophones. The name of the capital of the island, *Port-of-Spain*, thus varies between basilectal /'pɒtə'spen/ (with the first syllable being [pɔ̈t], just like that of *putty* or *pot*) and acrolectal /'pɔtə'spen/ (first syllable phonetically [pɔːt]).

Winford (1978) reports a slightly different pattern of possible mergers, including that of NURSE and GOAT (and hence hypercorrect *foam* as [f3m]); but he does not mention the merger of TRAP and START. (My account follows Warner, whose description agrees with my own observations.) The acrolectal vowel system, then, is (250).

(250)

ɪ ʊ	i	eə		u
ɛ ʌ	e	3		o
a ɒ	aɪ ɔɪ	ɑ	ɔ	ɔʊ

The basilectal system, set out in (251), has four fewer phonemes.

(251)

ɪ ʊ	i	eə	u
ɛ	e		o
	aɪ ɔɪ	a ɒ	ɔʊ

In popular speech, the /eə/ of NEAR and SQUARE is commonly a wide opening diphthong, approaching [ia], and could be correspondingly written.

The lexical incidence of the vowels is shown in (252).

(252)					
KIT	ɪ	FLEECE	i	NEAR	eə
DRESS	ɛ	FACE	e	SQUARE	eə
TRAP	a	PALM	a x ɑ	START	a x ɑ
LOT	ɒ	THOUGHT	ɒ x ɔ	NORTH	ɒ x ɔ
STRUT	ɒ x ʌ	GOAT	o	FORCE	ɒ x ɔ
FOOT	ʊ	GOOSE	u	CURE	ɒ x ɔ
BATH	a x ɑ	PRICE	aɪ	*happ*Y	i
CLOTH	ɔ x ɒ	CHOICE	ɔɪ	*lett*ER	a x ə
NURSE	ɒ x ɜ	MOUTH	ɔʊ	*comm*A	a x ə

Warner also notes the possibility of further mergers in the vowel system for speakers with patois (French Creole), Spanish, or Indian influence; it involves the failure to distinguish /i/ and /ɪ/ (*beat* vs. *bit*) and similarly /u/ and /ʊ/ (*pool* vs. *pull*). This is perceived as giving an old-fashioned rural effect. She further described some whose native language is Hindi as not distinguishing /aɪ/ and /ɔɪ/ (*tie* vs. *toy*), though apparently all speakers for whom English is the first language do make this distinction (unlike many non-Trinidadian West Indians).

Among the consonants, in addition to the matters discussed in 7.1.3–4, there is also a widespread tendency in Trinidadian speech to simplify certain initial consonant clusters. Thus the /r/ tends to be lost from initial /pr-/ and /fr-/ (*probably, pretend, from, Frederick*), while the /t/ is sometimes lost from initial /st-/ (*still, steady*).

Prosodically, Warner (1967) claims that the use of a final rising intonation contour is more frequent in Trinidadian than in RP.

It is noticeable that Trinidadians, together with people from the Windward Isles, have in their speech a process of Voicing Assimilation. This leads to the voicing of certain underlyingly voiceless obstruents in the environment of a following voiced obstruent, as [mɒz bi] *must be* (but in isolation [mɒs(t)] *must*). I have not investigated the extent of this process or the constraints operating upon it; as far as I know, no one else has ever reported its existence.

7.2.3 Guyana

Two particular points distinguish Guyana from the rest of the English-speaking Caribbean. One is geographical, in that Guyana is part of the South American mainland, rather than a West Indian island; and the other is ethnographical, in that immigration from the Indian subcontinent has played a very important rôle in the formation of its population.

From 1803 to 1970 Guyana was a British colony under the name British Guiana. An English settlement in the Guianas was first established in the seventeenth century, and by the time what are now Guyana and Surinam were ceded to the Dutch in 1667 the English-based creole Sranan had become established there as the language of black slaves. Sranan remains the main language of Surinam, but in Guyana has given way, through a century and a half of British influence, to a creole-to-standard-English continuum of the kind described in 7.1.2 above.

The labour shortage on the sugar plantations after emancipation in 1833 led to the recruitment of large numbers of indentured labourers from Europe, China, West Africa, and other parts of the Caribbean, but above all from India. By now Indo-Guyanese form just over half of the population, speaking little Hindi, being overwhelmingly English-speaking (speakers, that is, of Guyanese Creole or some variety along the continuum leading to Standard English). There is a clear tendency for Indo-Guyanese to live in the rural areas, speaking a more extreme ('basilectal') creole, while the Afro-Guyanese live in the towns and speak an intermediate ('mesolectal') variety.

It is estimated that over 95 per cent of Guyana's population lives on less than 2 per cent of the country's land area – namely, along a 250-kilometre coastal strip 8–16 kilometres wide, and along various rivers. Over a quarter of the population lives in the capital, Georgetown, or its suburbs.

Guyanese English is strikingly similar to Jamaican. This similarity is even more marked in the phonetics than it is in syntax and morphology; lexically, there are quite extensive differences. The Guyanese phoneme system, both extreme creole and prestige-norm, is isomorphic with the Jamaican. The main difference at the phonetic level is that the Guyanese FACE and GOAT vowels, /e:/ and

/oː/, are monophthongs lacking the opening-diphthong variants typical of Jamaican. Another point is that Guyanese English has [i] in *happ*Y, as against Jamaican [ɪ].
The vowel system, then, is as set out in (253).

(253)

ɪ ʊ	iː			uː
ε ʌ	eː			oː
a (ɑ)	aɪ (ɔɪ)	aː (ɔː)	ɔʊ	

/ʌ/ is phonetically back and rounded, [ɔ]. /ɑ, ɔɪ, ɔː/ are restricted to the educated/middle-class end of the continuum, being replaced in popular speech by /a, aɪ, aː/ respectively, so that *block = black* /blak/, *voice = vice* /vaɪs/, *form = farm* /faːm/. (Allsopp (1962) describes a *vice* vs. *voice* contrast depending on length, [vaɪs] vs. [vaˑɪs] etc. For speakers who do this, [aˑɪ] can be regarded as the realization of /ɔɪ/, a realization less prestigious than [ɒɪ].)
The incidence of these vowels is as shown in (254).

(254)

KIT	ɪ	FLEECE	iː	NEAR	eː(r)
DRESS	ε	FACE	eː	SQUARE	eː(r)
TRAP	a[1]	PALM	aː	START	aː(r)
LOT	a *x* ɑ	THOUGHT	aː *x* ɑː	NORTH	aː(r) *x* ɔː(r)
STRUT	ʌ	GOAT	oː	FORCE	oː(r)
FOOT	ʊ	GOOSE	uː	CURE	oː(r)
BATH	aː	PRICE	aɪ	*happ*Y	[i]
CLOTH	aː *x* ɔː	CHOICE	aɪ *x* ɔɪ	*lett*ER	a *x* ə
NURSE	ʌ *x* ʌr	MOUTH	ɔʊ	*comm*A	a *x* ə

[1] Certain TRAP words have /aː/ rather than the expected /a/, thus *bad* /baːd/, *land* /laːn(d)/ (in popular speech a potential homophone of *lawn*).

In 7.1.7 I mentioned the claim of final stress in the Guyanese pronunciation of the words *bottle, table, wallet*, as against initial stress in *battle, wrestle, mallet*. Holder (1972: 898) adduces only two actual minimal pairs (disyllables distinguished by stress in Guyanese English but homophonous in RP): in his notation, *fáther* (progenitor) vs. *fathér* (clergyman), and *Come óver* vs. *School ovér* (= school is over). It is not clear whether this is genuinely a matter of simple placement of stress, as assumed by Holder, or whether it is rather a question of two types of tonal stress (so ʼ*father* vs. ˎ*father* etc., as described for Barbados). Other words mentioned by Holder as having final stress are *orange, greenish, Patrick, voodoo, cotton,*

Billie, Mary, fairy, jelly, alley, water, paper, finger, picture, as against initial-stressed *porridge, selfish, basic, coward, dozen, husband, rhythm, silly, valley, better, butter, hammer, later, pepper, doctor, feature.* He also notes *windów* and *pillów* as against *yéllow* and *swállow.* A few trisyllabic words are affected too: as well as *yellowish* and *Bailiewick* Holder notes penultimate-stressed *manáger, bicýcle, baníster, caléndar, carpénter, miníster, passénger.*

Berry (1976) offers a useful account of Guyanese English intonation, to which the interested reader is referred. He finds a typical pattern of high stressed (pitch-accented) syllables and low unaccented ones, as in his example, (255).

(255)

'*Give the   old-* '*man a   * '*packet.*

He identifies three general types of 'falling' intonation, which are distinguished by ending in a fall, a low rise, and a mid-level after a preceding low respectively (in my terms, these would surely be different possible nuclear tones following a 'falling' variety of head). There is also a rising pattern (rising head). Yes–no questions and question tags have a higher rise nucleus, or a mid-low-high fall-rise. Emphasis can be added (i) by overriding the general downdrift tendency in the head; (ii) by expanding the pitch range; (iii) by the use of emphatic tones, e.g. a mid-to-high or low-to-high rise instead of a high level; (iv) pitch levelling; or (v) tone-shift (on vocatives, cf. discussion of examples *kitchen* and *cripple* in 7.1.7 above). And words of 'special semantic importance' are often 'drawled'.

7.2.4 Barbados

The most easterly of the Caribbean islands, Barbados was a British colony without interruption from 1627 until independence in 1966. It has thus been English-speaking almost twice as long as, say, Trinidad. The distance between broadest dialect and standard English is smaller in Barbados than elsewhere in the West Indies: the basilect (often referred to as ['beːdʒən] *Badian, Bajan, Bajun*) is more decreolized than elsewhere. Barbadians are in demand as schoolteachers in other islands, inasmuch as they enjoy a reputation for speaking good English.

The most striking characteristics of Barbadian pronunciation, when compared with that of other parts of the West Indies, are full rhoticity, the use of a glottal allophone of /t/, and the quality of the PRICE vowel. To an English ear Barbadian pronunciation is very reminiscent of the west of England; in particular, it puts one in mind of the speech of pirates, as popularly portrayed. Why treasure islands and the Spanish Main should implicitly have come to be associated in popular stereotype accent with Barbados, rather than with any other island, is not clear.

Barbadian is the only West Indian accent which is fully rhotic at all levels of society: /beːr/ *beer–bear*, /beːrd/ *beard*, /staːr/ *star*, /staːrt/ *start*, /wɒːr/ *war*, /ˈfɒːrtiː/ ˈfoːr/ *forty-four*, /koːrt/ *court*, /pjoːr/ *pure*, /bɜːrd/ [bɝːd] *bird*, /ˈbɛtər/ [ˈbɛtɚ] *better*.

Word-final /t/ frequently – in popular speech at least – has the glottal allophone [ʔ]. Thus *bit* may be heard as [bɪʔ], and similarly [ˈkwʌɪʔ ə ˈlɑʔ] *quite a lot*, [ˈpeːmɛnʔ] *payment*; also syllable-finally before a consonant, as [dɪˈpaːɹʔmənʔs] *departments*. Although T Glottalling is characteristic of many British accents, in the West Indies it is distinctively Barbadian, and may be a local innovation. Sometimes it extends to /p/ and /k/, as [baʔ] *back*.

The phonetic range of the first element of the PRICE diphthong is [ʌ ~ ɔ̈ ~ ə]: [nʌis] *nice*, [tʃʌil(d)] *child*, [ˈspʌiʔstöŋ, -tʌʊn] *Speightstown*. This quality is again unique in the West Indies, and is reminiscent of the speech of parts of the west of England or Ireland. The MOUTH diphthong, too, has a starting-point in this area: [hɔ̈ʊs] *house*. The same range, [ʌ ~ ɔ̈ ~ ə], characterizes the monophthong /ʌ/ (the vowel of STRUT). Unstressed [ə] seems rather commoner in Bajan than in the popular speech of other Caribbean territories, and probably belongs to the /ʌ/ phoneme: *elephant* [ˈɛlɪfənʔ], presumably /-fʌnt/. As in other rhotic accents, schwa coalesces with /r/ to give [ɚ], as [ˈɥɛdɚ ~ ˈɥɛðɚ] *weather*. Similarly, NURSE words have [ɝː], which we phonemicize as /ɜːr/, thus *shirt* [ʃɝːʔ] /ʃɜːrt/.

The vowels of FACE and GOAT, /eː/ and /oː/ respectively, may have monophthongal qualities rather noticeably opener than half-close: [ne̞ːm] *name*, [ɹo̞ːd] *road*. Alternatively, they may be centring diphthongs with closer starting-points: [ke̞ək] *cake*, [ˈɹeənˈkoəʔ] *raincoat*. (One informant, a university student, had the [eə, oə] allophones before voiceless consonants, with monophthongs elsewhere; but from others I have noted examples such as [te̞əˈbl̩] *table*, [ˈjɛloə] *yellow*.)

The short vowels /ɪ/ (KIT), /ɛ/ (DRESS) and /ʊ/ (FOOT) are relatively open in quality, as compared with RP or GenAm: [bɪʔ] *bit*, [bɛ̞ʔ] *bet* (often somewhat more open than cardinal 3), [pʊ̞ʔ] *put*.

Long and short /ɒː/ (THOUGHT), /ɒ/ (LOT) seem to be sometimes rounded, sometimes not (i.e. [ɑ(ː)]). The quality of /uː/ and of the second element of /ʌʊ/ is rather central.

The whole vowel system may be set out as shown in (256).

(256)

ɪ	ʊ	iː					uː
ɛ	ʌ	eː	ʌi	(ɔɪ)	[ɜː]		ʌʊ	oː
a	ɒ				aː	ɒː		

The lexical incidence of the vowels is as shown in (257).

(257)

KIT	ɪ	FLEECE	iː	NEAR	eːr
DRESS	ɛ	FACE	eː	SQUARE	eːr
TRAP	a	PALM	aː	START	aːr
LOT	ɒ	THOUGHT	ɒː	NORTH	ɒːr
STRUT	ʌ	GOAT	oː	FORCE	oːr
FOOT	ʊ	GOOSE	uː	CURE	oːr
BATH	aː	PRICE	ʌi	*happ*Y	iː
CLOTH	ɒː	CHOICE	ʌi *x* ɔɪ	*lett*ER	/ər/ [ɚ]
NURSE	[ɜː]	MOUTH	ʌʊ	*comm*A	ə

In 7.1.7 I mentioned the claimed Barbadian minimal pairs 'brother* (sibling) vs. ˆbrother* (member of religious sect), 'copy* (noun) vs. ˆcopy* (verb). In describing this phenomenon, Collymore (1970: 83–4) is insistent that the /ˆ/ pattern is the usual one for disyllables in Barbadian, and implicitly contrasts it with the 'Standard English' /'/ pattern. Other minimal pairs which he quotes include the following: 'Scotland* (in the UK) vs. ˆScotland* (in Barbados); 'sister* (family) vs. ˆsister* (sectary); 'worker* vs. ˆworker* (milliner); 'body* vs. ˆbody* (person); 'tailor* vs. ˆTaylor*.

7.2.5 The Leewards

The following relates to the speech of **Montserrat**, one of the smaller Leeward Islands, but the one with which I myself am familiar; it appears that the English pronunciation of the populous St Kitts and Antigua is generally similar.

The Leewards were the first parts of the West Indies to be

colonized and settled by the British. This took place in the first half
of the seventeenth century, well before the colonization of Jamaica
or the Windwards. There was a short break in their Britishness,
however, when they were briefly seized by the French in 1666–7.
Montserrat itself was probably first settled in 1633, by a group of
disaffected Irish Catholics from the nearby St Kitts.

It is popularly claimed that Montserratians speak with an Irish
accent (as reported, for example, by Fergus 1975: 10). While there
is no doubt about the Irishness of many Montserrat place-names
and surnames, or about the Irish rôle in the island's settlement
history, there is no justification for this claim. Characteristics of
Montserratian pronunciation include the use of /u/ as a reduction
vowel, a distinctive treatment of historical final /r/, and the shortening of final long vowels. The last point, at least, seems to be shared
not only by the other Leewards but also by St Vincent and Grenada.

The shortening of historically long vowels gives short vowels in
words such as *tea* [ti], *play* [ple], *Ma* [ma], *straw* ([stra] basilectally
but [strɒ] in the acrolect), *show* [ʃo], *two* [tu]. The shortening also
applies before a suffix comprising a separate syllable, as *agreement*
[a'griment], *payment* ['pement]; but not, apparently, before the
non-creole non-syllabic suffixes in *frees* [fri:z] (homophonous with
freeze). In checked syllables, however, and non-finally in general,
the opposition between long and short vowels applies as in other
accents: *beat* is distinct from *bit*, *bait* from *bet*, *bath* [ba:t ∼ ba:θ]
from *bat*, *boat* from *but*, *pool* from *pull*. Between the [a:] of *bath* and
the [a] of *bat* there is no difference of quality; and there seems often
to be little or no difference of quality between the long vowel of *beat*
and the short one of *bit* or between that of *boot* and that of *put*
(phonetically [bi:t], [bit], [bu:t], [put], where, as in all transcriptions
in this section, [i e u], long or short, stand for vocoids rather opener
than cardinal). With the mid vowels, *bait* and *boat* have long monophthongs in careful or educated speech, thus [be:t] (qualitatively
very similar to *bet* [bet]) and *boat* [bo:t] (qualitatively closer than *but*
[bɔt]); basilectally, however, they have opening diphthongs, thus
[biet], [buɔt]. (This opening diphthong is never used in *bay* and
show, which are monophthongal [be], [ʃo] in all styles of speech.)

The shortening of historical long vowels does not mean that there
are no final long vowels in Montserratian English. This is because
R Vocalization has left long vocoids where historical /r/ has dis-

appeared: not only in *start* [staːt], but also in *star* [staː], and not only
in *north* [naːt ~ nɒːθ] but also in *war* [waː ~ wɒː]. There are no final
long [iː, eː, oː, uː]; *near, steer–stare* etc. have opening diphthongs [iä],
while *four, sure–shore* etc. have [uo ~ ɔʌ].

As in Jamaica and Guyana, the front and back open vowels are
merged basilectally, but distinguished in careful or educated
speech. Thus *block* [blak ~ blɒk] may or may not be distinct from
black [blak], and *form* [faːm ~ fɒːm] may or may not be distinct from
farm [faːm]. This means that *jaw* vs. *jar* is a minimal pair for final [a]
vs. [aː] in popular speech, but not acrolectally, where they are [dʒɒ]
and [dʒaː] respectively.

Pairs such as *jaw* vs. *jar*, *stay* vs. *steer*, *snow* vs. *snore* are distinct
in both Jamaican and Montserratian English. But whereas Montserratian *face*, *goat*, *bath* sound like their Jamaican forms,
Montserratian *jar*, *steer*, *snore* sound like Jamaican *jaw*, *stay*, *snow*
(and vice versa): [dʒaː], [stiä], [snuɔ].

As in Jamaica, NURSE words exhibit some sociolinguistic variation. The basilectal form is with the STRUT vowel, thus *first* [fɔs]
(homophonous with *fuss*). Otherwise, speakers use a qualitatively
similar but long vowel, sometimes with r-colouring, thus [fɔːs(t) ~
fɔ˞ːs(t)]. It occurs finally in words such as *stir* [stɔ(ˈ)ː]. This constitutes a last trace of rhoticity in what is otherwise a non-rhotic
accent: /or/ is disappearing in favour of a new /ɜː/.

These developments mean that a taxonomic phonemicization of
the data yields an unusual vowel system, in which the [i] of *tea* is
identified phonemically with the /i/ of *bit* rather than with the /iː/ of
beat. Similarly, *two* has the /u/ of *put* rather than the /uː/ of *boot*.
Both *play* and *bet* have /e/. There is a quality difference between [o]
in *show* and [ɔ] in *cut*, but these vowels could still be regarded as
allophones of a single phoneme /o/. *Ma* has the /a/ of *bat*, not the /aː/
of *bath*; *straw* has the /ɒ/ (basilectal /a/) of *lot*, not the /ɒː/ (basilectal
/aː/) of *thought*. The basilectal opening diphthongs, [ie] in *bait* and
[iä] in *near*, are in complementary distribution; we can write them
both as /ie/. Similarly with [uɔ] /uo/ of basilectal *boat* and *four*; here
there is no quality difference. (Basilectally, *beard* is a homophone of
bathe, and *court* of *coat*.)

In careful or educated speech, the monophthong [oː] of *coat* and
road is distinct from the diphthong [oɔ] of *court* and *board*, and so
probably is the [eː] of *bait, face* from the [iɐ] of *near, stare* (thus

587

pace ≠ *pierce*). So non-basilectally we must recognize /oː/ distinct from /uo/, and /eː/ distinct from /ie/.

The vowel system can no longer be usefully subdivided on the checked vs. free criterion, but only as short vs. long. It is as shown in (258).

(258)

i	u	iː					uː
e	o	ie					uo
		(eː)		(3ː)			(oː)
a	(ɒ)	ai	(ɒi)	aː	(ɒː)	ou	

The incidence of these vowels has mostly been discussed above. On the whole, BATH words have /aː/, thus /laːf/ *laugh* etc.; but BATH Broadening has not applied in the environments involving a following nasal, thus /dans/ *dance*. CLOTH words have long /ɒː/, basilectal /aː/. The *happ*Y vowel is, of course, short but close, [i].

The use of /u/ as a reduction vowel, although common, is stigmatized; there are always competing pronunciations with /a/, acrolectally [ə]. Examples include /'brokfus/ *breakfast*, /'aiun/ *iron*, /'haːbu/ *harbour*, /mu'ʃiːn/ *machine*, /'slipuz/ *slippers*.

Montserrat English phonology includes a rule simplifying sequences of two identical plosives; thus /'plietaːt/ *plate-tart*. It also applies to affricates: /'wɪ'tʃortʃ/ *which church*.

7.2.6 Bahamas

The Bahama Islands are scattered over quite an extensive area to the north of Cuba. From Grand Bahama and Great Abaco in the north to Great Inagua in the south is over 800 kilometres, with the dozen or so principal islands strung out between them, mostly well separated from one another; so it is only to be expected that there should be considerable geographical variation in Bahamian English.

It is estimated that about 85 per cent of the 210,000 population are black; and of the white minority many are expatriates from Britain, the United States, or Canada. It has been suggested (Shilling 1975) that the speech of the 20,000 or so native-born white population does not, as elsewhere in the English-speaking Caribbean, constitute an upper extreme (acrolect) in a creole continuum, but can be sharply distinguished from black Bahamian speech. I am not in a position to judge whether this is in fact so. In phonology, Shilling claims that TH Stopping is entirely absent from white speech, even in the most casual style, whereas it is only those blacks whose grammar is almost completely standard who achieve consistent use of [θ] and [ð] as against [t] and [d]. However certain other non-standard consonantal characteristics – H Dropping, Final Cluster Reduction, and V–W Confusion – are found in both white and black speech.

H Dropping appears to be both geographically and socially variable in the Bahamas. Some islands have a standard-type opposition between /h/ and zero (*harm* consistently distinguished from *arm*), whilst in others H Dropping occurs freely (and is noticed and stigmatized). Not only is [h] absent where it would be present in standard accents (thus [a:m] for *harm*, making it homophonous with *arm*), but also hypercorrect insertion is frequent (thus sometimes [ha:m] for *arm*, as well as sometimes for *harm*) – as in eastern Jamaica. Shilling's description implies that H Dropping (and hypercorrect insertion of [h]) is much commoner with white speakers than with black.

As well as the usual Final Cluster Reduction (/bɛs/ *best* etc.), Shilling reports some use of [ʔ] for syllable-final /t/ by white speakers (and 'infrequently' by blacks).

As far as concerns V–W Confusion, claims have been made that '/w/ and /v/ seemed to be interchangeable for many [white] speakers' (Holm 1979) and that while 'there may well be some [black] speakers who do not have an underlying v ~ w distinction, all white speakers ... used [β] variably with "correct" v and w' (Shilling 1975). Questioning a white Bahamian informant leads me to suspect that the essence of the admittedly frequent V–W Confusion is not the regular replacement of standard /v/ by [w], nor the replacement of standard /w/ by [v], nor the use of [β] indifferently for both /v/ and /w/, but the phonemic merger of standard /v/ and /w/ into a single phoneme with the allophones [w] and [v] in complementary distribution. The [w] allophone occurs in initial position, thus *vine* = *wine* [wʌɪn], *very* ['wɛrɪ], *voice* = *worse* = *verse* [wəis], but the [v] allophone elsewhere, thus *love* [lʌv], *river* ['rɪvə].

It seems that popular speech may lack the voiced fricatives /z/ and

/ʒ/, the voiceless counterparts being used in their place – thus ['iːsɪ] *easy*, ['wɪsɪt] *visit*, ['plɛʃə] *pleasure*, ['wɪʃən] *vision*. This is a characteristic of some Celtic accents (vol. 2, chapter 5), but has presumably developed independently in the Bahamas.

Bahamian speech, both black and white, is non-rhotic. The vowel system seems to be as shown in (259). (This system, and everything in this section, is tentative.)

(259)

ɪ	ʊ	iː			uː			
ɛ	ʌ	eː	əi		oː	ea	(ɜː)	oa
a	ɒ		ʌɪ	ɑʊ		aː		ɑː

Qualitatively, /a/ is central rather than front, [a̠-]. Both /ɑ(ː)/ and /ʌ/ are extremely back. I suspect that the phonetic distance between /a/ and /ɑ/, and between /aː/ and /ɑː/, increases the higher one goes up the social scale; the vowel I have written /ɑː/ is rounded and half-open, [ɔː], in middle-class speech, thus [sɔːf(t)] *soft*, [θɔːt] *thought* (popularly [sɑːf], [tɑːt]). It is possible that the oppositions /a/ vs. /ɑ/ (*rat* vs. *rot*) and /aː/ vs. /ɑː/ (*last* vs. *lost*) disappear in lower-class speech, as in Jamaica. Shilling (1975) claims further that in black speech the vowels of PRICE and MOUTH are monophthongs and that they fall together (she transcribes them both [a]). If this is so, one wonders about their distinctiveness vis-à-vis BATH–START and THOUGHT–CLOTH. She further states that in white speech, where these vowels are distinct and diphthongal, the first element of MOUTH is [æ], while that of PRICE is [a]. My informant uses qualities of the kind implied by my transcriptions, [ɑʊ] and [ʌɪ].

The vowel /ɜː/ is restricted to the upper end of the social scale. In popular speech, NURSE words instead have the same /əi/ as CHOICE, phonetically [əi] or perhaps with a rounded first element, [ɵi]. Thus *bird* varies socially between [bɜːd] and [bəid]; the second form, the usual one for black speakers, makes it homophonous with *Boyd*. My informant insists that this applies even in free syllables, so that *stir* [stəi] can be a perfect rhyme for *toy* [təi]. Unusually for the West Indies, however, the lexical sets CHOICE and PRICE are not merged; but the lexical sets NORTH and FORCE – again unusually for the West Indies – are, with *horse* and *hoarse* homophonously /hoas/.

Lexical incidence of the vowels is shown, again tentatively, in (260).

(260)

KIT	ɪ	FLEECE	iː	NEAR	ea
DRESS	ɛ	FACE	eː	SQUARE	ea
TRAP	a	PALM	aː, ɑː	START	aː
LOT	ɑ	THOUGHT	ɑː	NORTH	oa
STRUT	ʌ	GOAT	oː	FORCE	oa
FOOT	ʊ	GOOSE	uː	CURE	oa
BATH	aː	PRICE	ʌɪ	happY	[ɪ]
CLOTH	ɒː	CHOICE	əi	lettER	ə
NURSE	əi	MOUTH	ɑʊ	commA	ə

8

The southern hemisphere

The Australian and New Zealand accents of English are very similar to one another. South African, although differing in a number of important respects, also has a general similarity to Australian. These facts are not surprising when we consider that all three territories were settled from Britain at about the same time, the English language becoming established in each around the beginning of the nineteenth century. All reflect, therefore, the developments which had taken place in the south of England up to that time: they are non-rhotic and have BATH Broadening. The intervening 150–200 years have been quite long enough for them to have developed their own characteristic local accents. Notable are the loss of the weak-syllable contrast /ɪ/ vs. /ə/, and the raising of the short front vowels of TRAP and DRESS. From the fact that these accents have little or no T Glottalling (vol. 1, 3.4.5), we can infer that at the time their accents were essentially formed this development had not yet taken place in Britain. It is appropriate to group these three regional forms under the common heading of southern-hemisphere English.

Another, very small, native-English-speaking community in the southern hemisphere is the 2000-strong population of the Falkland Isles. Interestingly enough, the brief samples of Falklands pronunciation I have heard were rather reminiscent of an Australian accent. The vowels are not of the Scottish type the settlement history would lead one to expect.

8.1 Australia

8.1.1 Introduction

English is the language of virtually all native-born Australians other than Aboriginals; the latter, who to some extent still speak one or more of the many Australian languages, constitute only about 1 per cent of the total population of Australia (estimated in 1978 as somewhat over 14 million).

In view of the fact that Australia was first colonized by the English less than two centuries ago – considerably later, then, than North America – it is not surprising that an Australian accent is very much more similar to the accents of present-day England than are those of the United States. Nevertheless, enough time has passed for Australia to have developed a distinctive accent of its own, easily recognized as different from any accent of England.

Australian English is quite remarkably homogeneous, particularly if one considers the enormous size of the territory over which it is spoken. From Perth to Sydney is over 3000 kilometres, yet their accents are practically indistinguishable. Such geographical variation in pronunciation as there is tends to be a matter of urban versus rural, the rural accent being somewhat slower and broader than the urban; apart from this, accent variability in Australia is social and stylistic rather than geographical. This uniformity of spoken English in Australia is attributed by Bernard (1969) to two principal factors: first, that the early white Australians entered through a very small number of seaports, and remained in contact by sea through these ports; and second, that they built up a social solidarity (whether as convicts or as free migrants) against their Britain-based officials and administrators. This 'Mixing Bowl' theory clearly contains a large part of the answer. But it is perhaps also true that the pronunciation of all southern-hemisphere English, and particularly Australian English, carries forward trends already present in the popular accents of the south-east of England in the early nineteenth century, but enabled to develop more rapidly and thoroughly as a consequence of their being freed from the omnipresent restraining influence of RP. In a village or small town of, say, Bedfordshire in 1800, a man would be in regular contact with RP speakers (squire, rector, doctor), and the social pressures to admire and imitate qualities associated with this culturally dominant social class were strong; there was no doubt considerable sociolinguistic stratification such as persists in England today, with innovative trends in popular speech encountering resistance, overt and covert, from RP-type models. But someone transported to an antipodean penal settlement, or migrating inde-

pendently to seek a new life in a far country, thereby cut himself
free both from the hierarchical pressures of English social stratification and from regular contact with RP speakers. This, combined
with the 'Mixing Bowl' effect, had the consequence of sharply
reducing the social variability of speech in the new colonies as
compared with the mother country.

Gold rushes and other economic booms and failures ensured that
the early Australian population remained a mobile one, with little
chance to develop regional differences. It appears that a distinctive
Australian accent had arisen by the 1830s or 1840s, although the
proportion of native-born Australians did not exceed that of
immigrants until the 1860s.

In describing present-day Australian pronunciation it is usual,
following Mitchell & Delbridge (1965), to distinguish three main
types: **Broad**, **General**, and **Cultivated**, identified principally
by differences in the quality of certain vowels. In Cultivated
Australian, the FLEECE, GOOSE, FACE, GOAT, PRICE and MOUTH
vowels have realizations similar to those of RP, whereas in General
Australian they have undergone Diphthong Shifting similar to that
found in the south-east of England. Broad Australian is similar to
General, but has extra duration in the first element of the
diphthongs.

At first hearing, General Australian and Cockney may give the
impression of being very similar. They do share such striking
characteristics as Diphthong Shift and (variable) H Dropping.
However they can readily be distinguished by the fact, inter alia,
that Australian lacks the T Glottalling and L Vocalization so typical
of contemporary London speech. And from this we can infer that
these latter Cockney characteristics have become established in
south-east England only in the last century and a half, since the
formation of Australian English.

The phonetic differences between General and Cultivated
Australian, and between informal and formal styles of speech, are
the basis for the 'Strine' series of booklets, whose humour has
enjoyed considerable success both in Australia and in Britain. The
first of these, entitled *Let Stalk Strine* (i.e. 'Let's Talk Australian'),
claimed as its author one Afferbeck Lauder, 'Professor of Strine
Studies, University of Sinny'. It contains a glossary of 'Strine'
words and phrases – spellings, each of which, when interpreted in

accordance with Cultivated pronunciation (or RP), sounds more or less precisely like the General (or Broad) Australian pronunciation of some quite different word or phrase. Thus *flesh in the pen* is glossed as 'momentary brilliance' and given an extensive spoof disquisition on its supposed derivation from the early Strine settlers' use of goose quills: it depends, of course, on the phonetic similarity between General Australian /æ/ (TRAP) and RP /e/ (DRESS), whereby an Australian's *flash* may sound to British ears like *flesh*, and his *pan* like *pen*. Another Strine expression, *Tan Cancel*, 'the elected local government authority', hangs on the fact that Broad or General /æʊ/ (MOUTH) is reminiscent of Cultivated or RP /æ/ (TRAP). *Calm bear klyter*, 'return in an hour or two', involves PALM–STRUT, SQUARE–TRAP, and PRICE–FACE.

Several Strine forms depend on an assumed equivalence between Strine fortis consonants and Cultivated/RP lenis ones, thus *garbler mince* (couple of minutes), *egg jelly* (actually). It is doubtful whether this reflects any real phonetic difference.

The author of the *Strine* books followed them up with the *Fraffly* ones, purporting to reveal the language actually spoken by those stuck-up Poms in London (Lauder 1968, 1969). In this case, of course, the joke depends on the interpretation of RP (perhaps U-RP) forms in terms of Australian phonetics. Thus 'Ready? Repeat after me' is travestied as *Reddeh? Ropee tofter me*, highlighting the RP–Australian difference in *happ*Y and BATH-START.

8.1.2 The vowel system

Phonologically, all Australian English is very close to RP; phonetically, it is not. That is to say, the Australian vowel system can be set in one-to-one correspondence with the RP system (which is also that of the south of England in general, if we ignore certain recent developments). Furthermore, the lexical incidence of these vowels in stressed syllables is virtually identical with that found in RP. The correspondence in unstressed syllables breaks down mainly because of the Australian avoidance of unstressed [ɪ] in favour of word-internal [ə] (8.1.6 below) and word-final /iː/.

Realizationally, the differences are minor when we compare RP with Cultivated Australian, but considerable when we compare it with General or Broad Australian. It is these differences, together

with certain characteristics of voice quality, rhythm, and intonation, which appear to play the principal rôle in making an
Australian accent sound Australian.

In the vowel system the parallelism with RP extends as far as the
same hesitation about the phonemic status of /ʊə/, /ɔə/, and long
/æ:/. It seems correct to include /ʊə/ as a phoneme in the vowel
system of Cultivated Australian, although as in England it is gradually, by a process of lexical diffusion, merging with /ɔ:/; otherwise,
though, Australians use /u:/ or /u:ə/ in CURE words (8.1.5 below).
Equally, [ɔə] can on the whole be taken as a positional allophone of
/ɔ:/, used by some speakers word-finally; and [æ:] must be accorded
distinctive phonemic status vis-à-vis /æ/ only if morphological
environments are ignored in the phonology (thus [hæ:mə] 'one who
hams', ham # mer vs. [hæmə] hammer, 'mallet-like instrument'.)

In view of the range of realizational variability to be found in
Australian English (particularly among the closing diphthongs), it
is not easy to select a phonemic notation which will serve satisfactorily for all accents. In the following tabulation, the symbolization
/i:/ for the FLEECE vowel could equally well be shown as /ɨi/ or /əɪ/ or
/ɪi/ or /ɪ:/, all with some phonetic justification; and GOOSE could be
written /ɪʊ/ or /əʊ/ or /ʊʉ/ or /ʉ:/ instead of /u:/.

The vowel system is as shown in (261).

(261)

ɪ	ʊ	i:	ɪə	(ʊə)	u:
e		ʌɪ ɔɪ	eə ɜ: ɔ:		ʌʊ
æ ʌ ɒ		ɑɪ	a:		æʊ

The lexical incidence of these vowels is as shown in (262).

(262)

KIT	ɪ	FLEECE	i:	NEAR	ɪə ~ i:ə ~ i:
DRESS	e	FACE	ʌɪ	SQUARE	eə
TRAP	æ	PALM	a:	START	a:
LOT	ɒ	THOUGHT	ɔ:	NORTH	ɔ:
STRUT	ʌ	GOAT	ʌʊ	FORCE	ɔ:
FOOT	ʊ	GOOSE	u:	CURE	ʊə x ɔ: ~ u:ə ~ u:
BATH	a:[1]	PRICE	ɑɪ	happY	i:
CLOTH	ɒ	CHOICE	ɔɪ	lettER	ə
NURSE	ɜ:	MOUTH	æʊ	commA	ə

[1] See discussion below, 8.1.4.

As far as concerns the details of lexical distribution, there is little difference between Australian and British speech. A few more noteworthy pronunciations are set out in (263).

(263) *aquatic* /əˈkwɒtɪk/, compare RP /əˈkwætɪk/
      auction /ˈɒkʃən/, compare RP /ˈɔːkʃən/
      chassis /ˈʃæziː/, compare RP /ˈʃæsɪ/
      immediate /əˈmiːdiːət/, compare RP /ɪˈmiːdʒət/
      Melbourne /ˈmelbən/, compare RP /ˈmelbɔːn/
      oral /ˈɒrəl/, compare RP /ˈɔːrəl/
      Queensland /ˈkwiːnzlænd/, compare RP /ˈkwiːnzlənd/.

The word *basic* has an Australian variant /ˈbæsɪk/, alongside the expected /ˈbʌɪsɪk/.

8.1.3 Closing diphthongs

It is /iː, ʌɪ, ɑɪ, uː, ʌʊ, æʊ/ – the vowels of FLEECE, FACE, PRICE, GOOSE, GOAT, and MOUTH – which, as mentioned above, constitute the principal phonetic criterion for distinguishing between the various accents of Australian English. In the Cultivated accent they have a quality similar to that found in RP, while in the General and Broad accents they reflect the development we have designated Diphthong Shift.

Tabulation (264), which is based partly on a combination of Mitchell & Delbridge (1965) and Cochrane (1959), details typical phonetic realizations in the three Australian accent types identified by Mitchell. The symbol [ʌ] is to be interpreted as implying the quality of Australian STRUT, i.e. between half-open and open, just fronter than central, unrounded: intermediate between [æ] and [ɒ].

			Cultivated	*General*	*Broad*
(264)	/iː/	FLEECE	[ɪi]	[ɪi]	[əːi]
	/ʌɪ/	FACE	[ɛɪ]	[ʌɪ]	[ʌːɪ, a–ːɪ]
	/ɑɪ/	PRICE	[a–ɪ̞]	[ɒɪ̞]	[ɒːɪ̞]
	/uː/	GOOSE	[ʊu]	[ɪʉ, ʊʉ]	[əːʉ]
	/ʌʊ/	GOAT	[ö̞ʊ]	[ʌʉ]	[ʌːʊ, a–ːʉ]
	/æʊ/	MOUTH	[a–ʊ]	[æo]	[ɛːo, ɛ̃ːɣ]

Thus Cultivated differs from the other two accent types by having unshifted diphthongs; Broad differs from General principally in respect of diphthong speed, the mainly rural Broad type having noticeably slow diphthongs. The Cultivated vowels /iː/ and /uː/ do have monophthongal variants, particularly in shortening environments such as — [voiceless C]V, thus *keeping* ['kipɪŋ], *loofah* ['lʉfə]. (The monophthongal variant of /uː/, and its endpoint when diphthongal, might well be transcribed with the symbol [ʉ̞] rather than [ʉ], since the lip rounding is open rather than close.)

Diphthong Shift means that FLEECE and GOOSE share virtually the same starting-point, [ɪ]; so likewise do FACE and GOAT, with [ʌ]. But PRICE–MOUTH Crossover means that these two diphthongs have very different starting-points, that of PRICE being back and perhaps rounded, [ɒ], but that of MOUTH being front, [æ ~ ɛ].

Vowels and diphthongs are somewhat retracted before /l/. This is particularly noticeable in the case of /ʌʊ/, which has an allophone of the type [ɔʊ] in this environment, as *solo* /'sʌʊlʌʊ/ ['sɔʊlʌʊ], *coal* [kɔʊɫ] (compare *coat* [kʌʊt]).

Mitchell & Delbridge (1965: 84) report a 'curiously variable' glide in their discussion of GOAT in that subtype of Cultivated Australian, perceived as 'affected', which they label 'Modified Australian'. In South Australia it was found to range from [ëʊ] to [ëÿ] and from [ɔʊ] to [ɒy]. They claim that a glide starting [ɒ] is very typical of this Modified accent.

8.1.4 Monophthongs

Compared with most other accents of English, Australian English (particularly in its broader varieties) is characterized by the raising of the front short vowels and the fronting of the GOOSE, START, and NURSE vowels.

To the English speaker from the northern hemisphere it is the DRESS vowel, /e/, which is most strikingly different from that heard in most other accents. Qualitatively it is hardly opener than cardinal 2, [e]. The other short front vowels, the /ɪ/ of KIT and the /æ/ of TRAP, also tend to be rather closer than the qualities usual in RP or GenAm. In Broad Australian /ɪ, e, æ/ may be even closer than in General or Cultivated, as well as possibly being pharyngealized and, in the case of /æ/, nasalized. Since the effect is one of squashing up the front short vowels towards the upper part of the vowel area, Collins (1975) has referred to this development as 'pancake vocalism'.

The fronting of the /ʌ/ of STRUT towards the cardinal 4 area, [a–], can be seen as a drag-chain consequence of the movement of /æ/ up and away from cardinal 4. This quality of STRUT, however, is also found in London Cockney.

The START vowel is central to front, [a–ː], noticeably fronter than in RP. Accordingly we transcribe it /aː/, as against the symbol /ɑː/ we use for the corresponding vowel in RP and South African; and it is the quality of this vowel which presents one very important difference within the southern-hemisphere accents as a group, the Australian–New Zealand front quality contrasting with the very back South African quality.

The same /aː/ is used not only in the START set, but also in PALM thus /ˈkaː ˌpaːk/ *car park*, /ˈfaːðəz ˈkaːm/ *father's calm*. In general, BATH words, too, have /aː/ in Australian English, thus /laːf/ *laugh*, /paːs/ *pass*, /laːst/ *last*, etc. But in certain words of this set some Australians use /æ/, the vowel of TRAP. These words are mainly those where the vowel is followed by a nasal plus another consonant, e.g. *advantage, chance, demand, example, plant* (cf. vol. 1, 2.2.7). In this subset many Australians from the eastern states consider /aː/ high-class, even indicative of affectation, pedantry, or snobbishness, as against the popular pronunciation with /æ/. But in South Australia /aː/ is usual, thus *dance* /daːns/ (compare Sydney /dæns/).

The fronting of /uː/ and /aː/ means that the /ɔː/ of NORTH–FORCE–THOUGHT is left as the only really back long vowel in Australian English. The general trend towards fronting also affects NURSE, since Australian /ɜː/ is often rather front of central. More striking, though, in comparison with RP, is its closeness: it is typically half-close (level with cardinal [e]) or even closer. Qualitatively it is thus a kind of lowered [iː]; the auditory distance between /uː/ and /ɜː/ (*shoot* vs. *shirt*) does not seem to be very great.

8.1.5 Centring diphthongs

The centring diphthongs are /ɪə/, /eə/, and /ʊə/, although the last-mentioned is absent from the Broad Australian system. The phonetic realization of the centring diphthongs tends towards the monophthongal, particularly before /r/.

The monophthonging of /ɪə/ and /eə/ yields long monophthongal realizations qualitatively similar to the /ɪ/ and /e/ of KIT and DRESS,

599

but longer, thus *weary* /'wɪəriː/ ['wɪːɹəi], *vary* /'veəriː/ ['veːɹəi], etc. The starting-point of /eə/ is thus noticeably closer than in RP (often being around cardinal 2). For some Australians the distinction between *shed* and *shared* is one of duration only, [ʃed] vs. [ʃeːd].

Although words such as *beard* have /ɪə/ in all kinds of Australian English, the broader varieties restrict this diphthong to preconsonantal environments, using rather the sequence /iː/ plus /ə/ in final position. Thus Broad Australian *beer* is [bəɪə], which we write phonemically as /biːə/; the Cultivated variant is [bɪə] /bɪə/. The monophthonging in the environment ＿rV mentioned above means that there is an uncertainty of phonemicization in words such as *hero*, where [ɪː] represents the neutralization of the opposition between /iː/ and /ɪə/.

Partly comparable considerations apply to the CURE set. Cultivated pronunciation typically has [ʊə] in *poor* /pʊə/ and *pure* /pjʊə/, [ʊə] or [ʊː] in *boorish* and *security*. But in words such as *poor* and *pure* broader accents have /ɔː/, and the use of /ɔː/ for traditional /ʊə/ is spreading, as in England, to educated accents as well. In the environment ＿rV, as *security*, Broad Australian typically has a quality to be identified as /uː/, thus [səˈkjɪʊɹətəi].

Words such as *beard* and *pierce* establish the status of /ɪə/ for all varieties of Australian English. But since there are no words in general use with (Cultivated) /...ʊəC.../, it follows that no parallel justification for recognizing a phoneme /ʊə/ in General or Broad Australian exists. Since this phoneme clearly does exist in Cultivated Australian, it constitutes a unique case of systemic variability in Australian English.

The tautosyllabic [ɔə] is restricted to the Cultivated accent (so Cochrane claims (1959) and I have no reason to doubt him). There it is no more than a free variant, with [ɔː], of the phoneme /ɔː/. A disyllabic sequence [ɔːə] occurs in rare items such as *drawer* 'one who draws' (compare *drawer* 'boxlike container', usually monosyllabic [drɔː ~ drɔə]).

Words such as *fire, power,* are disyllabic in Australian English, thus /ˈfɑɪə, ˈpæʊə/; RP-type Smoothing is not an Australian habit.

8.1.6 Weak vowels

Australian English has a phoneme /ə/, restricted in occurrence to weak syllables. It contrasts with all other vowels; Cochrane (1959: 82) adduces the pairs shown in (265) to demonstrate this.

(265) /ə/ vs. /ʌ/   pickaback [...kɪb...]   vs.   hiccuping [...kəp...]
                     endure [ən...]   vs.   undo [ʌn...]
       /ə/ vs. /ɪ/   bannock ['bænɪk]   vs.   panic ['pænik]
       /ə/ vs. /ɜː/ catarrh [kɪ'taː]   vs.   curtail [kə'teɪl].

This gives a slightly misleading picture, though: the opposition between /ə/ and /ɪ/ is really very tenuous, being restricted to the environment of a following velar. In this position /ɪ/ is very frequent in the suffixes -ing and -ic, while of course /ə/ is rather rare: to supplement bannock vs. panic above we must have recourse to pairs such as paddock vs. nomadic, cassock vs. classic, barrack vs. Garrick. Some speakers have no contrast here; they pronounce paddock as ['pædɪk] (hence the caricature spelling 'paddick'). For them [ɪ] and [ə] are in fully complementary distribution and therefore allophones of a single phoneme. In environments other than before a velar there is generally no opposition between /ɪ/ and /ə/, the latter occurring to the exclusion of the former. Thus there is no distinction in pairs such as those shown in (266) (usually distinct in RP):

(266)   boxes and boxers, both /'bɒksəz/;
        founded and foundered, both /'fæʊndəd/;
        valid and salad rhyme, both end /-əd/;
        rabbit and abbot rhyme, both end /-ət/;
        bucket and ducat rhyme, both end /-ət/;
        Alice and callous rhyme, both end /-əs/;
        Armidale, NSW, is homophonous with Armadale, Vic.

Australian English thus has a considerable number of homophones which in many other accents are distinct, either because of different weak vowels or because of the presence/absence of /r/. This applies to boxes–boxers and founded–foundered above, and to many others. Thus tended and tendered are usually distinct in RP as /'tendɪd/ vs. /'tendəd/, and in GenAm as /'tendɪd/ ~ 'tendəd/ vs. /'tendərd/. An Australian newsreader who worked on British television for a time gave rise to complaints not just for having an overseas accent but more specifically for seeming to report that the

Queen had *chattered* to factory workers (in fact she had *chatted*), and that an electricity breakdown had meant that a hospital had to continue with the use of *tortures* (actually *torches*).

The suffixes spelt -*ate*, -*ess*, -*est*, -*et*, -*id*, -*ist*, -*less*, -*let*, -*ness* accordingly all have /ə/ in Australian speech. So does -*age*, as *cabbage* /'kæbədʒ/, *village* /'vɪlədʒ/ (compare British /'kæbɪdʒ/, /'vɪlɪdʒ/). But one must perhaps not be too categorical about these suffixes where Cultivated Australian is concerned: there do seem to be some speakers who have /ɪ/ not only in -*age* but also in -*ive*, thus *massive* /'mæsɪv/ (usual Australian form: /'mæsəv/).

The words *it*, *is*, and *him*, as a result of this tendency, have distinct strong and weak forms in Australian English, e.g. stressed *it* /'ɪt/, unstressed /ət/. Thus *pack it* is still homophonous with *packet*, both /'pækət/. Hence weak *it* and *at* are phonetically identical, as are weak *is* and *as*.

The *happy* vowel is /iː/. Pairs such as *studied* and *studded* (homophonous in RP with /-ɪd/) are sharply distinguished by Australians, as /'stʌdiːd/ vs. /'stʌdəd/. The prefixes *be-*, *de-*, *e-*, *pre-*, and *re-* all fluctuate between /iː/ and /ə/; they do not, of course, have RP-style /ɪ/. Thus *pretend* can be /priː'tend/ or /prə'tend/. However *se-* is apparently always /sə-/, thus *select* /sə'lekt/.

The Australian trend towards merging of all unstressed vowels in /ə/ may lead also, for example, to identity between the initial syllables of *July* and *Geelong*, thus /dʒə'laɪ/, /dʒə'lɒŋ/.

The fact that the final vowel of *Latin* and *Martin* is phonemically /ə/, not /ɪ/, causes these and similar words to be subject to Syllabic Consonant Formation: ['lætn̩, 'maːtn̩] (compare the usual RP ['lætɪn, 'maːtɪn], where Syllabic Consonant Formation is blocked by the presence of /ɪ/ in the structural description).

The phonotactic constraints on Australian /ɪ/ also mean that the rival forms of -*ing* differ not only in the place of articulation of the nasal but also in the vowel: high-prestige /ɪŋ/, low-prestige /ən/. Hence the prevalence in Broad Australian of forms such as ['rɒɪdn̩] *riding*, ['ræbətn̩] *rabbiting* (a pronunciation regarded as 'normally unacceptable' by Mitchell & Delbridge 1965: 48).

Comment is perhaps called for on the pronunciation of the pronoun *you*. In broader types of Australian English the weak form /jə/ is very common; and this is rather frequently reduced by Elision to /j/ in the environment of a following vowel, as /jaːnt/ *you aren't*,

/'jæftə/ *you have to.* (Compare also /aːmiː lɑɪf tʌfnzʒʌp/ *army life toughens you up*, quoted by Mitchell & Delbridge 1965: 52.) While such reductions are not unknown elsewhere, they do seem particularly prevalent in Australia.

8.1.7 Consonants

The consonants of Australian English are fairly unremarkable. The non-rhotic distribution of /r/ and the variable dropping (except in Cultivated Australian) of /h/ contribute to the general impression of Englishness as against Americanness. To an English ear the most noticeable consonantal phenomena are perhaps T Voicing and the quality of /l/.

Intervocalic /t/ may undergo T Voicing (vol. 1, 3.3.4), though it is perhaps more accurately described as variably subject to leniting, i.e. to becoming [d̥], thus ['bʌd̥ə] *butter*. This phenomenon has been little studied in Australian speech, and it is not clear to me whether the /t–d/ opposition can be affected (as in GenAm), nor whether articulatory acceleration (Tapping) is usually involved. It is interesting in this connection to observe the treatment of English words borrowed into native Australian languages. Thus in Dyirbal, where the consonant system lacks any /p/ or /t/ but does include an alveolar plosive *d*, a 'semi-retroflex' continuant *ɾ*, and an alveolar tap or trill *r*, the word *peanut* appears as *binara* (Dixon 1972: 326). That is, the English final /t/, which is potentially intervocalic across a word boundary, has interpreted as the equivalent of the tap/trill rather than of the plosive (since it would also have been possible for the word to assume the form ** binada* or even ** binaɾa*). Similarly, *potato* appears in Dyirbal as *burira*.

Nor has the quality of Australian /l/, it seems to me, yet been adequately remarked upon. The impression I have is of a pharyngealized (rather than a velarized) quality, i.e. [lˤ], occurring in all environments. There may be variations in the extent of this colouring in initial and final positions, but no sharp clear vs. dark allophony as in RP. It is therefore particularly noticeable to English ears in prevocalic environments, as *blade, telephone, happily*.

It has been claimed that Australians use /s/, not /z/, for the possessive singular ending on agent nouns with the suffix *-er*, making *teacher's* /'tiːtʃəs/ distinct from the plural *teachers* /'tiːtʃəz/

(Pilch 1971: 273). My informants do not confirm this, although they do admit that *Surfer's Paradise*, NSW, can sound homophonous with *surface paradise*. Nor do they confirm Pilch's claim (1971: 272) that Australians all lack /w/ in words such as *quarter*, *quart* (making these homophonous with *caught her*, *caught*, respectively): as in England, it appears, some have /kwɔ:-/ and some have /kɔ:-/.

8.1.8 Prosodic characteristics

There is one Australian intonation pattern which calls for special mention. It is a tune consisting of a high head plus a rising nucleus, similar to that typically used in yes–no questions in RP and similar accents; what is characteristically Australian is its repeated use in simple statements. Mitchell & Delbridge (1965: 56) designate it 'the interview tune', and suggest that it is used when answering interview questions in a way which seems to express the meaning 'I've finished with that. What are you going to ask me next?' They also, with no evident justification, characterize it as 'abnormal', which suggests that it is stigmatized in Australia.

As long ago as 1844 a British visitor to Australia was complaining that local-born Australians had 'just the same nasal twang as many Americans have'. This was a Mrs Charles Meredith, in her *Notes and sketches of New South Wales* (quoted by Mitchell & Delbridge 1965: 62). As always, it is difficult to pin down exactly what observers mean when they refer to the 'nasality' or 'nasal twang' of some accent. But it is true that Australian speech is often perceived as having this quality. Mitchell & Delbridge, having surveyed the pronunciation of over seven thousand Australian schoolchildren, conclude that of their 2400 subjects whose accent was classified as Broad (34 per cent of the total sample) some 14 per cent had noticeable nasality, as against less than 5 per cent of General speakers and 1 per cent of Cultivated speakers. This covered both contextual nasality (adjacent to a nasal consonant) and 'pervasive' nasality; the latter was most marked with /æ/ (a special quality of this vowel confirmed by Mackiewicz-Krassowska 1976). Is an American-style TRAP Raising (æ → ẽə) beginning to affect Australian English too?

We have already seen that one of the defining characteristics of Broad as against General Australian is rhythmic: the use of slow diphthongs with a lengthened first element. Quite apart from this, a larger proportion of Broad speakers than of others were judged to speak unusually slowly (Mitchell & Delbridge 1965: 64).

8.2 New Zealand

8.2.1 Introduction

New Zealand English is very like Australian English. The most important differences seem actually to be lexical rather than phonological, the New Zealand vocabulary including inter alia several words of Maori origin. (The Maoris, whose own language is a Polynesian one, constitute about one in ten of the New Zealand population, a quarter of a million out of a total of nearly 3 million.)

As far as pronunciation is concerned, a New Zealand accent is so similar to an Australian one that it is difficult for outsiders to tell them apart. Nevertheless, New Zealand English does include a number of phonological characteristics which it does not share with Australian. As Hawkins puts it (n.d.):

Native speakers of NZ can distinguish an Australian pronunciation quite readily, though the converse is not always true: Australians tend to classify a NZ accent as coming from a distant and unfamiliar part of Australia, such as Tasmania. Native speakers of English from other parts of the world, on the other hand, can usually not distinguish an NZ from an Australian pronunciation.

British settlement in New Zealand began in the late eighteenth century, and the territory was annexed in 1839–41 (as part of New South Wales). New Zealand English was probably formed in its essentials by the 1840s, say perhaps ten years later than Australian English. In view of this history, the similarity between the two accents is not surprising.

The most important difference between the Australian and New Zealand accents concerns the KIT vowel, which in New Zealand has become a central vowel not distinct from /ə/. This is discussed in 8.2.2 below.

In New Zealand, as in Australia, there is a range of accents extending from Cultivated to Broad. Geographically, they are homogeneous, without regional characteristics that would enable one, for instance, to distinguish the speech of the North Island from that of the South Island. There is apparently one exception to this generalization: one area of New Zealand does have a specific regional accent. This is the 'Southland burr' of Otago and Southland, the southernmost provinces of the South Island. Its distinguishing characteristic is that it is rhotic. Regrettably, I have never heard this accent spoken, nor as far as I am aware does there exist a phonetic account of it. Turner says merely (1966: 105) that 'the /r/ is not trilled or different – except in its frequency of occurrence – from /r/ elsewhere in New Zealand'. It is believed to result from Scottish influence, Otago being a Scottish settlement. Does this Scottish influence extend to the absence of /ʊ/ vs. /uː/? Bennett (1943) is surely exaggerating when he labels Otago speech 'a modified form of Scots'.

8.2.2 Central KIT

The New Zealand vowel in words of the standard lexical set KIT is commonly a central vowel, rather than a front one: it may be narrowly transcribed [ɨ], being an unrounded central vowel between close and half-close, a lowered [i]. Thus *this thing* is pronounced ['ðɨs 'θɨŋ] (compare Australian ['ðɪs 'θɪŋ], South African ['ðɪs 'θɪŋ], both with [ɪ] denoting a vowel rather closer than in RP).

New Zealand [ɨ] does not contrast with [ə], and New Zealanders studying phonetics usually find it unrealistic to attempt to distinguish the phonemic symbols /ɪ/ and /ə/. Accordingly it seems sensible to symbolize the New Zealand KIT vowel as /ə/, as /'ðəs 'θəŋ/. When in final position, /ə/ has a rather opener realization (as in other accents), thus *dinner* /'dənə/ ['dɪnə]. Elsewhere, the quality is such that in RP terms it would be taken as /ə/ rather than as /ɪ/: *dismiss* [dɪs'mɪs] /dəs'məs/, *distinction* /dəs'təŋkʃən/, *phonetics* /fə'netəks/. (Whether we symbolize this phoneme as /ə/ or as /ɪ/ is arbitrary. If, like Hawkins (n.d.), we write it /ɪ/, we must be consistent: *alive* is then /ɪ'laɪv/, and *mother* /'mʌðɪ/ – or conceivably /'mʌðʌ/. My choice of /ə/ for KIT enables us to retain the more familiar appearance of /ə'laɪv/ and /'mʌðə/.)

Australians can identify New Zealanders at the quayside by the fact that they speak of /ʃəps/, unlike Australians who call them /ʃɪps/.

The centrality of New Zealand KIT means that there is no doubt at all about the *happy* vowel: it belongs with FLEECE, /iː/, and not with KIT. *City* is /'sətiː/; *invisibility* is /'ənvəzə'bələtiː/ (compare old-fashioned RP /'ɪnvɪzɪ'bɪlɪtɪ/, nowadays usually /'ɪnvɪzə'bɪlətɪ/).

8.2.3 The remainder of the vowel system

We have noted that TRAP and DRESS are typically rather closer in Australian than in RP (8.1.4 above). This applies also to New Zealand English – if anything, rather more so. New Zealand /æ/ of TRAP is no opener than half-open, [ɛ], while the /e/ of DRESS is half-close, a somewhat centralized cardinal [e], or even closer. In fact /e/ can range as close as [ɪ]; NZ *neck* can readily be heard as RP/GenAm *nick*. When we remember the centrality of KIT, this is not surprising: the vowel in *set* can become indefinitely closer without risking confusion with *sit* [sɪt]. New Zealand /e/ often has some degree of diphthonging, thus *bed* [bɪəd], *yes* [jɪəs] (sometimes almost [jiəs]).

Given that KIT is central and DRESS now the closest short front vowel, it is logical to take the New Zealand short vowel system (part-system· A) as set out in (267), with only two phonologically significant degrees of height, with two front vowels (DRESS, TRAP), two central vowels (KIT, STRUT), and two back vowels (FOOT, LOT):

(267) e   ə   ʊ

æ   ʌ   ɒ

Hawkins (1976) argues persuasively for this analysis, claiming further that this constitutes a more balanced, stable system than the awkward RP one, which cannot be satisfactorily specified in terms of solely binary features. But I am not convinced that RP is moving towards a New Zealand type of short vowel system, as he supposes.

New Zealand /uː/ (GOOSE) is usually a close central [ʉː], or a lip-diphthong [iʉ], thus *choose* /tʃuːz/ [tʃʉːz ~ tʃiʉz]. In broader accents, noticeable diphthonging may occur, but with rather less lowering of the first element than in Australian: *two boots* ['tiʉ 'biʉts]. The same comment applies to /iː/ (FLEECE), thus *three* /θriː/ [θɹɪi ~ θɹɪi].

The long monophthong /ɜː/ (NURSE) is rounded in New Zealand English; it is realized as a centralized front mid vowel, [œ̈ː]. In some broader accents it is as close as cardinal 2, thus [ö̈ː]. Hearing the New Zealand linguist Turner pronounce his own surname, I was very much reminded of German *Töne*. Prima facie, New Zealand English thus contradicts the supposed phonological universal that if a language has only one front rounded vowel that vowel must be close, /y/; because NZ NURSE (we could write it /ø:/ instead of /ɜ:/) is only half-close, if that. But the fronting of /u:/ (GOOSE) perhaps allows us to recognize two phonologically front rounded vowels in this accent, so that the long monophthongs are moving towards the pattern shown in (268).

(268) i: y: FLEECE GOOSE
       e: ø: o: SQUARE NURSE THOUGHT
       a: START

The centring diphthongs also call for some discussion. The quality of New Zealand /eə/ (SQUARE) is like that of RP /ɪə/ (NEAR), i.e. it has a half-close starting-point, [eə ~ ɪə], considerably closer than RP [æə ~ ɛə]. New Zealand *fair* sounds like *fear* to an Englishman. New Zealand NEAR, in its turn, involves a very close starting-point, [iə], and may not be distinct from /i:/ plus /ə/: thus *beer* [biə], *beard* [biəd]. Words like *serious* have /i:/, thus /'si:ri:əs/. Some speakers, however – particularly children, according to Hawkins – have merged the two front centring diphthongs, so that pairs such as *fair* and *fear*, *bear* and *beer*, *stare* and *steer* are homophonous, as [fɪə], [bɪə], [stɪə] respectively. (This NEAR–SQUARE Merger is also, as we have seen, a characteristic of West Indian and some East Anglian accents.) The situation is further complicated by the tendency towards a diphthongal /e/ (DRESS) in certain environments, notably before /d/, so that *shed* and *shared* fall together as [ʃɪəd]. This would seem to make a three-way homophony *shed–shared–sheered* a real possibility. Hawkins comments further [n.d.], 'the sounds in this area are undergoing significant changes at present, and the patterns that will eventually emerge are by no means certain'.

Making no firm conclusions on the subject of these speculations, we are left with the vowel system set out in (269) for New Zealand English.

(269)

e	ə	ʊ	i:		(iə)		(ʊə)		u:
æ	ʌ	ɒ	ʌɪ	ɔɪ	eə	3:	ɔ:		ʌʊ
				ɑɪ		a:		æʊ	

The lexical incidence of these vowels is shown in (270).

(270)					
KIT	ə	FLEECE	iː	NEAR	iə, iːə ~ iː, eə
DRESS	e	FACE	ʌɪ	SQUARE	eə
TRAP	æ	PALM	aː	START	aː
LOT	ɒ	THOUGHT	ɔː	NORTH	ɔː
STRUT	ʌ	GOAT	ʌʊ	FORCE	ɔː
FOOT	ʊ	GOOSE	uː	CURE	ʊə, uːə ~ uː, ɔː
BATH	aː	PRICE	ɑɪ	*happ*Y	iː
CLOTH	ɒ	CHOICE	ɔɪ	*lett*ER	ə
NURSE	ɜː	MOUTH	æʊ	*comm*A	ə

8.2.4 The lateral and its influence

New Zealanders whose speech I have listened to myself do not vocalize /l/, although, like Australians, they tend towards a rather dark /l/, possibly pharyngealized, in all environments. Hawkins, whose phonetic reliability I respect, nevertheless reports vocalization as the norm in New Zealand: 'In NZ English final and pre-consonantal /l/ has entirely lost the alveolar tongue-tip contact, so that it is in fact realized as a back vowel close to [o] ...' (Hawkins 1976: 62 fn.). The truth of the matter may well be that L Vocalization is a variable rule in current New Zealand speech.

Be that as it may, /l/ certainly exerts a noticeable influence on any preceding vowel. While /uː/ generally is central, thus *tomb* [tɵːm], preceding /l/ it is back, thus *tool* [tuːɫ] (or perhaps [tʊː]?). The diphthong /ʌʊ/ (GOAT) is also strongly affected, being realized as [ɒʊ] in the environment of a following /l/. For some speakers the opposition between /ʌʊ/ (GOAT) and /ɒ/ (LOT) is neutralized in this environment, making *dole* and *doll* homophonous. For others we may be justified in recognizing an extra phoneme /ɒʊ/, as in London.

More widespread in New Zealand English, it appears, are two other vowel neutralizations in this environment: that of the oppositions /ɒ/ vs. /ʌ/ (*doll–dull*) and /e/ vs. /æ/ (*fellow–fallow*). The first neutralization, according to Hawkins, is particularly common in the environment __lC, as in *pulse, result, ulcer*, which New Zealand students of phonetics often elect to transcribe with /ɒ/. (They commonly feel, though, that *dull* and *doll*, where the /l/ is word-final, are not identically pronounced, even granted that they are very similar.) They also, he reports, frequently transcribe *relevant*, etc., with /æ/, despite the pressure in favour of /e/ which we would expect orthographic *e* to exert.

There is also a variable neutralization of the opposition /ə/ vs. /ʊ/ (KIT vs. FOOT) in this environment, making homophones of pairs such as *bill–bull, fill–full, Wilf–wolf.*

8.2.5 Other consonants

Many New Zealanders retain the opposition between *whine* /hwɑɪn/ and *wine* /wɑɪn/ and similar pairs, with /hw/ realized as [hʍ]. Turner reports (1966: 105) that approximately half of a 1964 sample of first-year Christchurch students made the distinction.

Several Maori names contain orthographic *ng* in syllable-initial environment. This corresponds to phonetic [ŋ] in Maori, which in other environments gives no difficulty to speakers of English: *Wanganui* /ˈwɒŋəˈnuːiː/. But when Maori words with initial *ng* are borrowed into English they are pronounced with simple /n/: *ngaio* (a kind of tree) is /ˈnɑɪʌʊ/, and Sir Apirana *Ngata* is /ˈnaːtə/.

8.3 South Africa

8.3.1 Introduction

In the Republic of South Africa English, for all its dominant cultural position, is in terms of its number of mother-tongue speakers very much a minority language. About three-quarters of the country's 20 million population speak as their first language a Bantu language (Zulu, Xhosa, Tswana, Sotho, and others). Of the 4 million or thereabouts who are native speakers of a language of European origin, those who speak Afrikaans outnumber those who speak English by about three to one. The community generally referred to as 'the English-speaking South Africans' consists of about a million and a half whites of British extraction; it is their speech which is here described.

This leaves out of account the 700,000 Indians in South Africa, who have progressively abandoned Hindi, Gujarati and Tamil and taken up English as their first language. Through ignorance, I cannot offer any report on the phonetic characteristics of South

African Indian English, although it is reported that they include typical Indian features such as V–W Confusion and monophthongs in FACE and GOAT (Lanham 1978a).

Although English is thus the native language of relatively few South Africans, it is widely known and used as a second language. It is, of course, one of the country's two official languages (the other being Afrikaans); it is the principal language of commerce and industry. There are a fair number of coloureds and Afrikaners who are bilingual in Afrikaans and English. Many others, including many blacks, have some knowledge of English. All of these speakers tend to pronounce English with the interference patterns typical of a second language. South African blacks characteristically fail, for instance, to distinguish such pairs as *heat* vs. *hit*, *paper* vs. *pepper*, (see 9.2.3). These are distinct in all native varieties of English in the world, although the way in which they are distinguished does vary considerably from place to place.

The first English-speaking community in southern Africa arose from the British occupation of the Cape in 1806; it was consolidated by the arrival of 5000 settlers in 1820. This early Cape English seems to have been considerably influenced phonetically by Afrikaans (by then already established in South Africa for a century and a half). Later settlements of English speakers in Natal in the 1850s were less subject to Afrikaans influence. The more recently established English-speaking society of Johannesburg and the surrounding Witwatersrand, dating from the last part of the nineteenth century, combines characteristics of both the Cape and Natal. The twentieth century has seen the gradual displacement of RP as the prestige norm in favour of a new indigenous prestige norm (in which, for example, *valid* rhymes with *salad*, while the vowels in *kit* and *pit* are rather clearly different from one another). At the present day one can draw a distinction between a 'Conservative' South African accent differing only slightly from RP and a 'Respectable' South African accent differing from RP more extensively; both of these are distinct from a broad (or 'Extreme') South African accent which includes a number of stigmatized features (Lanham 1978b).

The accent of local-born native speakers of English in Zimbabwe (formerly Rhodesia) appears to be generally similar to South African. As far as I am aware, it has not been systematically studied.

8.3.2 The KIT Split

Historical /ɪ/, the KIT vowel, has undergone a phonemic split in South African English. The difference between the two resultant sound types is clearly heard if a word such as *sing* [sɪŋ ~ sɨŋ] is compared with one such as *limb* [lïm ~ ləm]. Description of this phenomenon is complicated by the fact that both the vowel qualities used and the conditioning environments are variable. It is possible to adopt various views on the phonemicization of the sound types in question: Lanham at one time (1967) argued for the recognition of three distinct phonemes, though he now (e.g. 1978b) considers that only one phoneme is involved. We shall here tentatively adopt the view that there are two.

A relatively close front vowel, [ɪ], is typically used in South African English for the KIT vowel when adjacent to a velar consonant, as *kiss, gift, lick, big, sing*. It is restricted to stressed syllables: compare *chicken* ['tʃɪkən] etc. It is also used after /h/, as *hit*, and word-initially, as *inn*. It is also very generally used before /ʃ/, as *fish*, and also, by many speakers, before other palato-alveolar consonants, as *ditch, bridge* (though here a broad South African accent is more likely to have [ə]).

A centralized or central vowel, [ï], is used in the complementary set of environments. Examples are *bit, lip, tin, slim*; [ï] occurs in both syllables of *minutes* and in all three syllables of *limited*.

In conservative accents [ï] may contrast with [ə] in weak syllables, as *haggis* [-gïs] vs. *bogus* [-gəs]. But most South Africans have no such contrast. For them, too, pairs such as *illusion* and *allusion*, *except* and *accept* are homophonous; and so are *scented–centred* ['sentəd], *sources–saucers*, *Lenin–Lennon* etc. This means that it is generally possible to regard [ï] and [ə] as allophones of the same phoneme, /ə/, in South African English. This approach is supported by the fact that in broad accents [ï] tends to be replaced by an opener [ə] quality even in stressed syllables, as ['dənə] *dinner*, ['ləmətəd] *limited*. (Lanham refers to what I write [ï], [ə] as 'high schwa' and 'low schwa' respectively.)

A broad South African accent is also characterized by a tendency to front and raise the /ɪ/ of *kiss*, etc., making it virtually cardinal, thus [big] *big*. In an accent of this type a pair such as *kit* [kit] and *bit* [bət] clearly do not rhyme, and it is this which makes one reluctant to regard their vowels as still belonging to the same phoneme. It seems more satisfactory to regard [ɪ ~ i] as /ɪ/ and [ï ~ ə] as /ə/, the latter having become one of the stressable vowels in South African English. If this line of reasoning is accepted, *kiss* [kɪs ~ kis] is to be taken phonologically as /kɪs/, and *dinner* ['dïnə ~ 'dənə] as /'dənə/; *chicken* is /'tʃɪkən/.

The final vowel in *happy* words may be short but close and front, ranging from [ɪ̞] to [i]. (In view of the possibility, mentioned above, of short [i] as a realization of /ɪ/, it seems reasonable to identify this as the taxonomic phoneme /ɪ/: which means that ['pïti] *pity* is /'pətɪ/.) But another possibility, apparently increasing, is a long [iː], particularly in pre-pause position. This is a consequence of a more general trend towards strengthening final unstressed syllables at the end of an intonation group in which the nuclear tone is rising. These final syllables acquire added duration and pitch prominence. *Pity* in this environment may thus be auditorily ['pï,ti]. (Another characteristically broad South African pronunciation very possibly linked to this phenomenon is the use of [ən, əl] rather than syllabic [n̩, l̩] in words such as *button, middle, listen* ['lə,sən].)

8.3.3 Other front vowels

The DRESS and TRAP vowels tend to be closer in South African English than in RP. The SQUARE vowel tends to be not only closer but also monophthongal.

The quality of the vowel in DRESS is typically around cardinal [e], thus [ɹed] *red*. The vowel is closest in a broad South African accent, less close (and within the RP range) in a conservative accent. The vowel of TRAP has undergone a similar development, ranging from a conservative [æ] to a broad-accent [ɛ], cardinal 3 or closer, thus [bɛd] *bad*. The stage stereotype of a South African yokel is one who keeps saying ['jẹs mɛn] *Yes, man*. An average South African pronunciation of *rack* is readily heard as *wreck* by English ears.

The vowel of SQUARE in South Africa ranges from a formal or conservative [ɛə] (as in RP) to a general or popular [eː], around half-close in height and monophthongal, thus [feː] *fair*. The distinction between *shared* and *shed*, *Cairn* and *Ken* may thus depend solely on duration, [ʃeːd] vs. [ʃed] etc.

8.3.4 Diphthongs

The FACE and GOAT vowels have in South Africa undergone a development similar to the Diphthong Shift of the south of England. So have PRICE and MOUTH, in broad accents; but PRICE is also noticeably subject to a quite different development, namely the weakening or loss of the second element of the diphthong, so that a monophthong or near-monophthong results. Weakening of the second part of the diphthong is also characteristic of FACE, GOAT, CHOICE, and MOUTH in some kinds of South African speech.

For the FACE vowel, most South Africans have a centralized or central starting-point, not a front one: the quality is [ëɪ] or [əɪ]. In a broad accent the starting-point is opener and backer, giving the quality [ʌɪ] or, with weakened glide, [ʌe]. The starting-point for GOAT covers more or less the same range. A conservative accent has [əʊ] much as in RP, while a popular accent has [ʌʊ] or, with monophthonging, [ʌː], thus *nose* [nʌːz], *telephone* ['telǝfʌːn]. Both FACE and GOAT are subject to stylistic and sociolinguistic variation, so that *say so* varies between careful-cultured ['sëɪ 'səʊ] and casual-popular ['sʌɪ 'sʌː]. Afrikaans-influenced English, however, typically retains a prominent off-glide, thus ['sʌɪ 'sʌu].

Diphthong Shift of PRICE and MOUTH gives the qualities [ɒɪ] and [æʊ] respectively, much as in Cockney or Australian. Conservative accents retain RP-type [a–], [a–ʊ]. In popular speech, the tendency towards weakening the second element gives the variants [ɒː], [æǝ]. However, PRICE–MOUTH Crossover has gained by no means so firm a hold in South Africa as in some other places. Presumably through a process of counter-correction, it is now very usual for South Africans to have the first element of PRICE a front vowel, around cardinal [a], well forward of the first element of MOUTH, which may be almost as back as cardinal [ɑ]. These variants seem to be becoming commoner, and to be implicitly accorded social approval (8.3.8 below). This is particularly true of the front-vowel realization of PRICE, as [baɪ] *buy*, [laɪǝn] *lion*. In certain environments, though, the Glide Weakening process comes into play with these vowels too, giving qualities such as [aː], [ɑɣ], thus [taːm] *time*, [dɑɣn] *down*. This gives the kind of pronunciation of a phrase such as *nice house* which strikes me, as an outsider, as the most typically South African variant: ['naːs 'hɑɣs]. But there are also South Africans who say ['na–ɪs 'ha–ʊs], ['nɒːs 'hæǝs], or ['naɪs 'haʊs].

With a speaker for whom PRICE has a back starting-point and is subject to Glide Weakening, the opposition between /aɪ/ and ɑː/ may disappear, leading to potential homophones such as *kite–cart, dine–darn, life–laugh*. This remains an optional neutralization: speakers do not confuse the two lexical sets in question, even if they may fail to distinguish them realizationally.

8.3.5 Long monophthongs

The long monophthongs of THOUGHT–NORTH–FORCE and NURSE follow the same trends as in other southern-hemisphere accents; but the South African development of START–BATH–PALM is strikingly different from that found in Australia and New Zealand, since this vowel tends to be very back and sometimes rounded. Again unlike Australia and New Zealand, South African FLEECE and GOOSE remain as monophthongs or very narrow diphthongs.

The /ɔː/ of THOUGHT, NORTH, and FORCE is becoming closer, as in England: it may now be as close as [oː]. Lanham comments that this trend is 'entirely below social consciousness', adding that there is 'no evidence of stylistic variation' between this and the older half-open type (1978b: 154).

The trend to make NURSE somewhat closer and fronter than in RP (as in Australia and New Zealand) appears to be on the increase in South Africa. The trend is towards a weakly rounded [ö:] quality, thus *first* [föːst], but in more conservative speech [fɜːst] or sometimes (presumably by counter-correction) [fɐːst].

South Africans can often be readily recognized as such by the very back quality of the /ɑː/ of START, BATH, and PALM. In broad speech it may also be weakly rounded, thus becoming qualitatively identical with the /ɒ/ of LOT. Thus *last part* ranges from conservative ['lɑːst 'pɑːt] to broad South African ['lɒst 'pɒːt]. This broad variant is, however, stigmatized and so subject to stylistic alternation with a less back [ɑ+ː].

The possible loss of contrast between PRICE and START (/aɪ/ and /ɑː/) was discussed in 8.3.4 above.

The quality of START finds an echo in the quality of the /ʌ/ of STRUT. Both are central to back in South African English (as against central to front in Australian English).

As mentioned above, the /uː/ of GOOSE remains on the whole

monophthongal in South African English. But it is often central, [ʉː], rather than back. As expected, this variant is particularly favoured by preceding /j/, as *new* [njʉː]. Lanham (1978b: 153) calls [ʉː] 'widespread', 'apparently below social consciousness', and 'maintained in formal style'. This agrees with developments in the south of England and Australia–New Zealand, except that South Africa lacks the competing trend towards diphthonging of /uː/ found in the other places mentioned.

The complete stressed vowel system can be set out as (271). Incidence is as (272).

(271)

ɪ	ʊ	iː			uː	ɪə	ʊə
e	ə	ʌ	əɪ	ɔɪ	əʊ	eə	3ː	ɔː
æ	ɒ		aɪ		aʊ			ɑː

(272)

KIT	ɪ ; ə	FLEECE	iː	NEAR	ɪə
DRESS	e	FACE	əɪ	SQUARE	eə
TRAP	æ	PALM	ɑː	START	ɑː
LOT	ɒ	THOUGHT	ɔː	NORTH	ɔː
STRUT	ʌ	GOAT	əʊ	FORCE	ɔː
FOOT	ʊ	GOOSE	uː	CURE	ʊə
BATH	ɑː	PRICE	aɪ	*happ*Y	[ɪ ~ i]
CLOTH		CHOICE	ɔɪ	*lett*ER	ə
NURSE	3ː	MOUTH	aʊ	*comm*A	ə

8.3.6 The liquids

South African /r/ is often an obstruent – a fricative, tap, or roll. The other liquid, /l/, is important not so much for its own phonetic characteristics (though it does tend to be neutral or clear in quality, without the dark allophones common elsewhere), as for the effects it may have on preceding vowels.

South African English is non-rhotic, with no /r/ in words such as *start* or (prepausal) *star*. Where historical /r/ is preserved, however – prevocalically, that is – South African speech tends to be characterized by a 'strengthened', i.e. obstruent, realization of /r/. This involves the use of a tap, [ɾ], or a post-alveolar fricative, [ɹ], rather than the approximant found in most other accents of English. The tap allophone is particularly associated with intervocalic position, as *very sorry* ['veɾi 'sɒɾi], and with the environment of a preceding velar plosive or /θ/, as *cream* [kɾiːm], *grey* [gɾʌɪ], *thrill* [θɾvl]. The fricative allophone, as well as occurring in the clusters /tr, dr/ as in many other accents, is also associated particularly with word-initial position, as *red* [ɹed]. In a broad South African accent, however, obstruent allophones are to be found in other environments too. They are commoner in Cape Province than elsewhere, being 'apparently stigmatized' in Natal and Johannesburg, though not necessarily subject to stylistic variation and correction (Lanham 1978b: 151).

A trill realization, [r], as opposed to a single tap, is a characteristic of the English pronunciation of those whose first language is Afrikaans. Afrikaans-influenced English is also usually rhotic (at least as far as stressed syllables are concerned). But in the relevant environments (i.e. non-prevocalically) the /r/ of rhotic Afrikaans English is realized as an approximant or weak fricative; the trill allophone is restricted to prevocalic position.

The people of Malmesbury, 60 kilometres to the north of Cape Town, are popularly reputed all to use a uvular /r/. I do not know to what extent this is true.

Although South African /l/ is not really dark in any environment, it nevertheless exerts a lowering and retracting effect on certain vowels. This tends to apply particularly to /e/, /ə/, and /əʊ/, in the environments __lC and __l# . Thus we may have *belt* and *bell* with [æ̈], *milk* and *still* with [ÿ], and *cold* and *roll* with [ɒː]. Only the second of these seems to be sociolinguistically sensitive: parents tell their children off for saying 'mulk' (i.e. [mÿlk]) instead of [mɪlk] *milk*. A broad-accent pronunciation of *pill* sounds like a conservative pronunciation of *pull*.

The influence of /l/ on a preceding /æ/ leads to the loss of opposition between /e/ and /æ/ in this environment, so that *elf* and *Alf*, *shell* and *shall*, become homophonous [ælf, ʃæl].

These effects of /l/ are associated with Natal rather than with the Cape.

8.3.7 Other consonants

The most important remaining variable involving consonants is the question of presence or absence of aspiration of voiceless plosives. In a broad South African accent /p, t, k/ are characteristically unaspirated. Thus corresponding to the [pʰɑːk] *park* of other accents (including conservative South African) there is the variant [p⁼ɑːk], which Lanham describes (1978b: 153) as 'regionally associated with Cape (all social classes) and with Extreme South African English as a sociolect elsewhere'. This non-aspiration presumably arose through phonetic interference from Afrikaans. It is now reported to be receding, though remaining unstigmatized. Many speakers show inconsistency in the presence or absence of aspiration.

Afrikaans influence is also probably responsible for another characteristic of much South African pronunciation, namely the audible release of plosives in plosive clusters, e.g. of the [k] in *doctor* /ˈdɒktə/ or the [p] in *captain* /ˈkæptən/ (compare RP /ˈdɒktə, ˈkæptn/ where the first plosive in each cluster is not audibly released, owing to the temporal overlapping of the articulatory gestures for the two plosives concerned).

T Voicing is quite common in South African English in the environment ˈV—V. This results in an alveolar tap, [ɾ], in free or stylistic variation with [t], thus *better* [ˈbeɾə ~ ˈbetə]. Since [ɾ] is also, as mentioned above, one of the possible realizations of /r/, it follows that there is occasional neutralization of the opposition between /t/ and /r/, with *Betty* and *berry* variably homophonous as [ˈbeɾi].

In Glide Cluster Reduction, Yod Dropping, and Yod Coalescence, South African speech is much the same as that of England. *When* and *whine* are almost universally pronounced with simple /w-/; the rare variant with /hw-/ is associated, as in England, with the careful formal style of the speech-conscious. Those who use it may do so hypercorrectly. *Suit* and *assume* generally have /suː-/; /sjuː-/ is less common and associated with conservative speech. *Tune* and *duke* are generally /tjuːn/ and /djuːk/, but with broad variants /tʃuːn/, /dʒuːk/.

Linking and intrusive /r/, too, follow the English model, though with perhaps a greater tendency to avoid the /r/ sandhi by using a glottal stop. One usage which I have noticed from one or two South Africans, which is definitely unknown in England, is intrusive /r/ in the phrase *they are* [ðeːɾ ɑː] (the pronunciation expected for *there are*). I have no explanation for this phenomenon, which is perhaps syntactic rather than phonological.

Certain consonantal phenomena are perhaps restricted to the speech of Afrikaans–English bilinguals. The most striking of these is the devoicing of final voiced obstruents, leading to neutralization of the voicing opposition in this environment: thus *bed* and *bet* may become homophonous as [bet], and likewise *dog* and *dock* [dɒk], *slide* and *slight* [slɑːt] (etc.). Another such feature is the use of a nasalized vowel before a fricative in place of a vowel plus nasal consonant, thus [dɑ̃ːs] *dance*, [bĩːs] *beans* (with final obstruent devoicing). There is also the use of a voiced /h/, namely [ɦ], i.e. a breathy-voiced vocoid onset to the following vowel, thus [ɦɑːd] *hard*. (This realization of /h/ is sometimes regarded as characteristic of South African English as a whole, e.g. by Carter & Kahari (1979: II, 3); but I am of the opinion that it is only used by Afrikaners or Afrikaans–English bilinguals.)

The voiceless uvular fricative, [χ], has acquired a marginal status in South Afrikan English through Afrikaans loan-words such as *gogga* ['χɒχə] 'insect, creepy-crawlie'. Zulu [ɬ], though, proves no more tractable in English than does the same sound in words of Welsh origin in Britain: *Hluhluwe*, Zulu [ɬuɬuːwɛ], usually becomes something like /ʃlʊˈʃluːwəɪ/.

The consonant systems of the Bantu languages of South Africa include certain consonants known as depressors. These have the characteristic of exerting a lowering effect on the pitch of a following vowel, giving a following high-tone vowel a low-pitched onset (Rycroft & Ngcobo 1979). Among the depressor consonants are, generally speaking, those corresponding to the voiced obstruents of English, i.e. /b, d, g, v, (ð), z, ʒ, dʒ/, and also the voiced [ɦ] used by some South Africans for English /h/. It has been suggested (Rycroft 1980) that the principle of depressor consonants has to some extent been borrowed into South African English, so that *Come here* might have a different pitch pattern from *Come out* in spite of identical phonological conditions of stress and intonation, as shown in (273).

(273)

ˈkʌm ˈɦɪə   ˈkʌm ˈaʊt

Rycroft calls this depression feature 'an optional component of stress' in South African English. I do not know if it ever extends to the voiced obstruents as well as to /h/ [ɦ]; this would give a phrase such as *Dry my goat*, for example, a different pitch pattern from *Try my coat* (again, both with high head plus high fall nucleus) as shown in (274).

(274)

| ˈdraɪ | maɪ | ˈgəʊt | | ˈtraɪ | maɪ | ˈkəʊt |

8.3.8 Regional and social variability

In a pioneering piece of sociolinguistic research, Hooper (1945) investigated certain aspects of the speech of South African school-children. He looked into the phonetic quality of the FACE, PALM, CHOICE and MOUTH vowels and also, to some extent, that of the more central vowel resulting from the KIT Split. He was able to demonstrate that 'non-standard' variants such as [əɪ], [ɒː], [oɪ], [æʊ], [ə], as against RP-like variants, were (i) commoner among pupils from a lower economic group than from a higher, (ii) commoner among boys than among girls, and (iii) commoner among younger pupils than among older ones. For the social-class comparisons he took pupils from two schools, school H, described as drawing its pupils 'for the most part from a higher economic group', and school L, drawing pupils 'from the relatively lower economic group', but being nevertheless 'situated in a good, upper middle-class district' and paying attention to the pupils' speech. His findings are summarized in (275).

(275) South African high-school pupils in 1944: percentages using non-standard pronunciations in certain words

| | Johannesburg | | Transvaal | |
	School H	School L	girls	boys
gate	9	36	38	100
can't	42	72	38	100
boy	33	77	85	100
out	0	33	15	75
swim	12	60	no data	no data

Mean for six schools

	Younger group	Older group
gate	75	42

A very much more extensive and sophisticated account of social and regional variability in South African pronunciation is now available through the work of Lanham and his colleagues. On the basis of a 1973 survey involving over 400 speakers, Lanham & Macdonald (1979) recognize three sets of phonological variables which they call CE (Cape English) variables, NE (Natal English) variables, and General SAE (South African English) variables.

The CE variables are the most salient ones for characterizing the stigmatized broad South African accent. They include the realizations of /r/, /ɑː/, and /aʊ/, where a high score (broad accent) would typically involve the variants [ɹ ~ ɾ], [ɒˑ], and [æʏ] respectively. It is believed that variants of this type arose or became established in the earliest organized British settlements in South Africa, the Eastern Cape colony dating from 1820. Now, though, although still quite widespread, these variants are believed to be receding: Lanham & Macdonald find them to be less common in their younger subjects than in their older ones.

The NE variables have a quite different social connotation. They represent prestige innovations. Among them are the realizations of /aɪ/, of vowels before /l/, and of /ɜː/. A high score, typically involving variants such as [aː] in *time*, [æ] in *shelf*, and [ɜ+ː] in *first*, while sounding characteristically South African (as against RP), receives general social approbation and represents the new local standard. The front PRICE vowel, often with little or no diphthongal glide, is regarded as the most important indicator of the trend, and appears to be increasing fast in popularity: Lanham & Macdonald found that among Witwatersrand women it was characteristic of 11 per cent of their respondents aged over sixty-five, but of 67 per cent of those aged between eighteen and twenty-four. It is hypothesized that this and other NE characteristics are traceable to the Natal settlement, established rather later than the Cape and with somewhat different social origins.

The General SAE variables recognized by Lanham & Macdonald comprise most of the remaining traits which we have noted as potentially distinguishing South African pronunciation from RP. They are as follows (after each variable is shown the most 'advanced' – broadest, most typically South African – variant). Realization of /əɪ/ in FACE, [ʌe]; realization of /əʊ/ in GOAT, [ʌˑ]; the vowel quality in KIT words where the environment is other than an adjacent velar or #, [ə]; realization of /e/ in DRESS, [e], /eə/ in SQUARE, [eː], and /æ/ in TRAP, [ɛ]; the vowel of *happ*Y, [iː] with 'raised stress'; the realization of /ɔː/ in THOUGHT–NORTH–FORCE, [oː].

The trend towards greater homogeneity in South African English pronunciation can be seen from the fact that Lanham & Macdonald's younger respondents tended to have high values for all three sets of variables (except to some extent in Natal, where the CE variables were not prominent), while their older respondents more usually had high values either for the CE variables (particularly the older males of the East Rand) or for the NE variables, but not both.

The social-class composition of English-speaking South Africa is quite different from that of other English-speaking societies in that it contains no real manual labouring class. Manual labour in present-day South Africa is performed virtually exclusively by non-whites, and non-whites mostly speak a language other than English as their first language. (Is this the reason why South African, uniquely I think among varieties of English, has no -*ing* variable, all speakers consistently using [ŋ] in -*ing*? And why South Africans, unlike English people and Australians, include no H droppers?)

A relatively lower social class can nevertheless be distinguished from a higher one within South African English-speaking society on grounds of restricted education and also by place of residence. Lanham & Macdonald selected five electoral districts of the East Rand as representative of their lower class, with predominantly blue-collar or low-status clerical occupations. It was among this group that the CE and General SAE variables were highest scored.

9

The imperial legacy

There are several parts of the world where English is spoken as a first language by very few of the local inhabitants, but where a historical background of British or American colonization or empire has meant that English plays an important national rôle as a second language. Some such places have, furthermore, developed characteristic local varieties of English.

It could be argued that Indian and African accents of English qualify for inclusion in a work about mother-tongue accents no more than do French or Russian accents of English. Like them, their phonetic characteristics are to be accounted for almost entirely in terms of interference from the patterns of the native language. The justification for admitting some brief discussion of these 'post-imperial' accents is that they are characteristic of English as a second language rather than as a foreign language. They are used in countries where English is an official language, or the official language, of the state. In the South Asian subcontinent, and in 'anglophone' black Africa, English is widely used in administration, for secondary and higher education (sometimes even for primary education), in political life, and in commerce. Indians use English for communicating with other Indians, Africans use English for communicating with other Africans. In France, on the contrary, the language used for all the purposes just mentioned is French, and Frenchmen use English only for communicating with foreigners; and so with Russia.

Furthermore, the characteristic Indian and African pronunciations of English represent independent cultural traditions. On the whole, Indians learn English from other Indians, Africans from other Africans; and it has been argued that the resultant locally-coloured varieties of English are just as valid, in the post-independence situation, as the local varieties of Australia, Ireland, or Canada. The same arguments apply to the English of Singapore and the Philippines.

9.1 India

9.1.1 Introduction

The expression 'Indian English' is commonly used, though inaccurately, to refer not only to the English spoken in India proper (Bharat) but also to that of Pakistan, Bangladesh, Sri Lanka (formerly Ceylon), and Nepal, as well as to that spoken by those originating in these areas but now living in such places as South Africa, East Africa, the Caribbean, and Britain. The discussion which follows applies principally to the English of India proper, although that of the other countries mentioned is generally similar.

There are Indians educated at British public schools whose accent is unquestionably RP. There are Indians with a fair knowledge of English whose accent is nevertheless so impenetrable that English people can understand them, if at all, only with the greatest difficulty. Between these extremes there are two types of accent of particular interest. One is the Anglo-Indian accent associated with the community of the same name, who speak English as their first language; formerly known as Eurasians, they are of mixed British and Indian ethnic origin. The other is the accent of educated Indians for whom English is a second language, the first language being Hindi or some other indigenous language of the subcontinent.

The Anglo-Indians number something over 100,000. They are greatly outnumbered by Indians with some command of English as a second language, who constitute between 1 and $2\frac{1}{2}$ per cent of the population of India (and thus number perhaps 10 million). (In Sri Lanka the proportion of those knowing English is higher, perhaps 6 per cent; I have no data on Pakistan, Bangladesh, or Nepal.)

9.1.2 Anglo-Indian

The characteristic Anglo-Indian accent, known derogatively as a **chee-chee** accent, stands phonetically between RP and educated Indian English. Systemically, it is identical with RP (except perhaps for the absence of a firm /ʌ/ vs. /ə/ opposition). It also agrees well with RP in phonotactic distribution and lexical incidence of vowels and consonants. The respects in which it differs noticeably from RP are in the realization of certain phonemes and in its prosodic characteristics.

The voiceless plosives are unaspirated in all positions, thus [p⁼ɪn, t⁼ɪn, k⁼ɪn], [p⁼ep⁼ə] *paper*. The dental fricatives, /θ/ and /ð/, although realized as fricatives in careful speech and before stressed vowels, are often pronounced as plosives, [t̪, d̪] (perhaps with affrication) in rapid speech. The lateral, /l/, is clear in all positions, thus [fi:l̥] *feel* (compare RP [fi:ɫ]). The phonemes /v/ and /w/ 'are distinguished, but the latter is not normally lip-rounded' (Spencer 1966: 65) – /w/ is realized as a kind of approximant [β]. There are no retroflex consonants: /t, d, n/ are alveolar.

In the vowel system, FACE and GOAT are monophthongs, [e:] and [o:] respectively. (This may reflect the pronunciation used by English people at the time English first became established in India: in volume 1, 3.1.12, we put the date of Long Mid Diphthonging at about 1800, and the Anglo-Indians, as a group, date from before that time.) This is perhaps the most striking difference from RP in vowel realization; others are the relatively closer quality of /ɒ/ (LOT) and /ɔ:/ (THOUGHT), the relatively opener quality of /æ/ (TRAP) and the less than open starting-points of the PRICE and MOUTH diphthongs (phonetically of the type [ʌɪ, ʌʊ]). The vowel in SQUARE is a monophthong, [ɛ:] (compare the centring diphthong [ɛə] usual in RP). The *happ*Y vowel is a close [i:] (caricatured in eye-dialect by spellings such as 'funnee').

It is in its prosodic characteristics that an Anglo-Indian accent differs most noticeably from RP. Its patterns of stress and intonation are strikingly reminiscent of a south Welsh accent of English, as has often been remarked; hence the use of expressions such as 'Bombay Welsh' to refer to this kind of pronunciation. The difference between stressed and unstressed syllables depends hardly at all on intensity, rather on pitch and duration characteristics. Such 'stressed' syllables (more properly, accented syllables) are characterized very frequently by a falling or low-rising pitch, usually with a rise on the following syllables; and the syllable-final consonant, if there is one, is usually lengthened, thus ['kɒp:i:] *copy* (for similar lengthening of consonants in Welsh English, see volume 2, 5.1.6). In Spencer's description (1966: 67), 'the typical prosodic pattern, therefore, is characterised by only small variations in stress, by marked dips in pitch on the emphatic syllables, the intervening syllables and any final unstressed syllables being on a varying higher pitch.'

9.1.3 Vowels

Turning to general Indian English, we find a vowel system quite like that of RP. Length distinctions, however, are not always consistently made; there is often no phonemically distinct NURSE vowel; and the status of the oppositions /ʌ/ vs. /ə/ and /ɒ/ vs. /ɔ/ is dubious or variable. In what from an RP point of view is a striking archaism, the historical distinction between the lexical sets FORCE and NORTH is maintained; while FACE and GOAT are usually monophthongal.

The vowel system is as set out in (276). When one considers it as a system in its own right, the fact that Indian English is generally rhotic inevitably casts doubt on the correctness of including the part-system D items in it. All Indian writers on the subject, though, assume without question that it is correct to do so.

(276)

ɪ	ʊ		i		u	ɪə		(ʊə)
ɛ	ə	(ʌ)	e		o	eə	(3)	(ɔ)
æ	ɒ		aɪ	ɔɪ	aʊ		a	

(If /ɔ/ is missing from the system, then /ɒ/ properly belongs in the D-system, since it can in this case occur in free syllables.)

The lexical incidence is basically as set out in (277). It must be remembered, though, that divergences/errors in lexical incidence are rather frequent, particularly in the speech of those whose command of English is relatively weak.

(277)

KIT	ɪ	FLEECE	i	NEAR	ɪə(r)	
DRESS	ɛ	FACE	e	SQUARE	eə(r)	
TRAP	æ	PALM	a	START	ɑ(r)	
LOT	ɒ	THOUGHT	ɔ[4]	NORTH	ɒ(r) ~ ɔ(r)	
STRUT	[ʌ ~ ə][1]	GOAT	o	FORCE	o(r)[5]	
FOOT	ʊ	GOOSE	u	CURE	ʊə(r)[5]	
BATH	a[2]	PRICE	aɪ	*happ*Y	ɪ, i	
CLOTH	ɒ, ɔ	CHOICE	ɔɪ	*lett*ER	ə(r)	
NURSE	ər ~ ʌr[3]	MOUTH	aʊ	*comm*A	a, ə	

[1] phonemic status not clear: may be allophone of /ə/ or independent phoneme /ʌ/.
[2] or sometimes /æ/.
[3] or, less commonly, /ɜ/.
[4] or /ɒ/ for those who lack /ɔ/.
[5] or [oə(r)]; occasionally [ɔə(r)].

It appears that speakers usually control a possible opposition /ɛ/ vs. /æ/ (DRESS vs. TRAP), even if their first language has no such phonemic distinction. But the use of /ɛ/ in TRAP words, or of /æ/ in DRESS words, is not infrequent. Sethi (1980) suggests that 'the two vowels are quite often kept apart where minimal pairs exist in the vocabulary of the speaker (e.g. *bed–bad*)', but not otherwise (e.g. *tax* /tɛks ~ tæks/). There is also some alternation between /a/ and /ɒ/ (PALM vs. LOT) and /a/ and /ɔ/ (PALM vs. THOUGHT), particularly in cases where LOT or THOUGHT words are spelt with *a* (thus /a/ in words such as *want, sausage, all, caught, saw*).

In NEAR and SQUARE words where the vowel is followed by /rV/, thus *period, area*, Indians usually have /i/ and /e/, respectively, rather than /ɪə/ and /eə/: ['pɪrɪəd], ['eːrɪa].

Indian English very commonly has strong vowels in what in other accents would be weak syllables. Thus *cottage* has [e ~ ɛ] in its second, unstressed, syllable (compare the [ɪ] of RP and the [ɪ] or [ə] of various other accents). Other typical examples (Bansal 1969: 123) include *arrive* [æˈraɪʊ], *consider* [kɒnˈsɪdər], *introduce* [ɪntroˈdjuːs], *cricket* [ˈkrɪkɛt], *bravest* [ˈbreːʊɛst], *different* [ˈdɪfrɛnt], *Oxford* [ˈɒksfoːrd]. Nor are weak forms of words which have them (at least in other accents) regularly used: thus *was* may be [ʊɒz] or [ʊas] in all environments (compare the [wəz] used in RP except when stressed or constituent-final); *to* is always [tʊ]; *from* is always [frɒm]; *the* is often [di ~ dɪ] even before an initial consonant; *a* is often always [e] or [je].

9.1.4 Consonants

As a system, the consonant system of Indian English is often identical with that of RP and other accents of English except in one respect, namely the absence of the opposition /v/ vs. /w/. However, some speakers also lack /ʒ/; some use /ʃ/ rarely if at all; and some do not distinguish between /dʒ/ and /z/.

Nevertheless, in spite of the fact that all or most oppositions found in other accents are present, the actual realization of consonants diverges quite strikingly in some cases from what is found elsewhere.

The voiceless plosives, /p, t, k/, are typically unaspirated in all positions: [p⁼eː] *pay*, [t⁼aɪ ~ ʈ⁼aɪ] *tie*, [k⁼ʌm ~ k⁼əm] *come*. Nearly all Indic and Dravidian languages exploit the presence vs.

absence of aspiration phonologically; but the English phonemes have come to be equated with the unaspirated rather than the aspirated phonemes of local languages. (Where aspirated plosives are used in Indian English, it is usually as the equivalent of what in other accents are fricatives, including particularly [ʈʰ] corresponding to RP etc. [θ]: see below.)

The articulation of /t/ and /d/ is often retroflex, [ʈ, ɖ]. Retroflexion being a gradient rather than an all-or-nothing matter, the degree of retroflexion in these consonants varies considerably, though generally speaking one can say that the further south one goes in the subcontinent the greater the retroflexion. In the north some Indians use alveolar [t, d] indistinguishable in place from those of RP and GenAm. Retroflexion of /t/ and /d/ nevertheless remains a sure way for an impressionist to suggest an Indian accent.

It is very usual for Indians to use /d/, rather than the /t/ of other accents, in the -ed inflection after voiceless consonants, thus [treːsd] *traced*, [ɛd'ʋhansd] *advanced*, ['dɛʋləpd] *developed* (RP /dɪ'veləpt/), [pækɖ] *packed* (these and other examples from Bansal 1969: ch. 13). This means, of course, that pairs such as *trust* and *trussed*, homophonous elsewhere, are distinguished in Indian pronunciation.

In words spelt *gh-*, spelling pronunciation leads northern Indian speakers of English to use /gh-/ [gɦ], thus [gɦost] *ghost*. No other accent of English, of course, admits this cluster (RP /gəʊst/).

The affricates /tʃ, dʒ/ are articulated with the tip down; sometimes they are palatals without a great deal of affrication, [c, ɟ]. There are some people who use blade-alveolar [ts, dz] instead. Where the affricates are doubled, as in *watch-chain, a large jug*, most people treat them like doubled plosives, lengthening only the hold stage, thus ['wɒttʃen] etc. (compare RP ['wɒtʃtʃeɪn]).

Some speakers, as noted above, do not distinguish between /dʒ/ and /z/, and use pronunciations such as ['brizɪz] *bridges*, [zɔːn] *John*, ['lʌgɪz] *luggage*.

Turning to the fricatives, we note first that some people pronounce [ɸ] or [pʰ] in place of standard [f]. The second of these leads to particular difficulties in comprehension for speakers of other kinds of English, since the Indian's [pʰɪt] is interpreted as *pit* instead of the intended *fit*, etc.

We have already mentioned the very common absence in Indian English of the opposition which other accents make between /v/

and /w/ (*vine* vs. *wine, vest* vs. *west*). The realization most frequently used by Indians for their /v ~ w/ is [ʋ], a labiodental approximant. Some people use [w], too, but in free or positional variation with [ʋ]. For example, some tend to use [w] post-vocalically (thus [bɪ'heːw] *behave*, ['praɪwet] *private*), but [ʋ] initially ([ʋɛl] *well*). Other possibilities for standard /v/ include [ʋɦ, b, β, bɦ]. The preposition *of*, which in standard accents has /v/ as its consonant, is usually pronounced with /f/ in Indian English – in origin this was no doubt a spelling pronunciation.

Dental fricatives are rarely used by Indians. Most people use dental plosives, [t̪ʰ] and [d̪] (or sometimes [d̪ɦ]) respectively, where standard accents have [θ] and [ð]. The phonemic oppositions are preserved: *thin* differs from *tin* as [t̪ʰɪn] vs. [tɪn ~ ʈɪn], *then* from *den* as [d̪ɛn] vs. [dɛn ~ ɖɛn] (compare RP etc. [θɪn] vs. [tʰɪn], [ðen] vs. [den]). A few speakers, however, use non-dental [t(ʰ), d] or [t(ʰ), ɖ] instead. As in other accents where plosives are used rather than dental fricatives (Irish, West Indian), the cluster /tθ/ is avoided: *eighth* has the Indian form [et̪ʰ] (rhyming with *faith*; compare RP [eɪt̪θ ~ eɪʔθ] vs. [feɪθ]).

Because of the vagaries of English spelling, many Indians use /z/ in words where standard accents have /s/, or vice versa. Thus on the one hand we may have [luːz] *loose*, ['pɜːpəz] *purpose*; and on the other hand ['hɛsteːt] *hesitate*, [haʊsd] *housed*. It is particularly common to use /s/ in inflectional -(*e*)*s*, thus [dɒːgs] *dogs*, [kiːs] *keys*, [fɑls] *falls*. (In standard accents, of course, the /s/ allomorph is used only after voiceless consonants.)

Speakers with certain first-language backgrounds replace standard [z] by [dʒ] or [dz], thus *is* [ɪdʒ ~ ɪdz], *zoo* [dʒuː] (= *Jew*). Others replace standard [ʃ] by [s] or [sj] and [ʒ] by [ʃ], [dʒ], or [z]. Examples include *she* [siː] (= *see*), ['mɛdʒər ~ 'mɛzər ~ 'mɛʃə] *measure*. The use of /ʃ/ for RP–GenAm /ʒ/ is regarded by Nihalani *et al.* (1979) as usual in the speech of educated Indians. Like the palato-alveolar affricates, the [ʃ, ʒ] of those who use them are typically made with the tongue tip down and are [ɕ, ʑ]-like.

Indian /l/ is clear in all positions. The other liquid, /r/, is phonetically either a post-alveolar fricative or approximant, [ɹ], or else an alveolar tap or trill, [ɾ ~ r]. Most speakers have a more or less fully rhotic pronunciation, pronouncing /r/ in all cases where there is *r* in the spelling. Unlike many rhotic accents, though, Indian English does not show the tendency towards coalescing /V/ plus /r/ into an r-coloured vowel: *burn* is [bərn ~ bʌrn], not *[bɚn].

Some speakers distinguish words spelt with *wh* from those spelt with plain *w* by pronuncing the former with [ʋfi] or [wfi], thus *which* [ʋfiɪtʃ ~ wfiɪtʃ] vs. *witch* [ʋɪtʃ ~ wɪtʃ]. This can only be a spelling pronunciation: the conservative British-American forms with /hw-/ seem to be unknown in India, and no accent of first-language English has /wh-/.

The semivowels /j/ and /w/ are regularly omitted by some speakers when the following vowel is a mid or close one agreeing in backness with the semivowel: thus *yet* [ɛt], *won't* [oːnt]. Conversely, other speakers add a semivowel before an initial vowel in just these conditions: *every* ['jɛʋri], *about* [je'baʊt], *old* [woːld], *own* [ʋon].

Certain English consonant clusters present difficulties for some Indians. There are two common ways of resolving such difficulties: initial clusters may be broken up by the addition of a prothetic or anaptyctic vowel, while final clusters may be reduced by omission of one or more consonants. Examples: *still* [ɪ'stɪl ~ ɛ'stɪl], *slow* [sə'lo]; *desk* [ɖɛs], *works* [ʋərs]. The clusters of phonetic consonants which arise in other accents through the rule of Syllabic Consonant Formation (which converts [ə] plus a sonorant into a syllabic sonorant in specified environments) are obviated through non-application of the rule: thus *metal* ['mɛʈəl], *button* ['bʌʈən] (compare RP ['metl̩], 'bʌtn̩]). Some speakers (Biharis in particular) tend to add a final vowel to any word ending in a consonant cluster or even in a single consonant: Bansal (1969: 142) cites the examples *subject* ['sʌbdʒɛktə], *burn* ['bʌrnə], *thought* ['ʈhɒːtə], *is* ['ɪdzɛ]. But this is not typical of most Indians' speech.

9.1.5 Prosodic characteristics

The questions of word stress, sentence accent, and intonation raise in acute form the problem whether certain typical pronunciation characteristics of Indian English should be regarded as belonging to an autonomous variety of English, with its own systems, structures, and rules, or as straightforward errors.

'A very common fault among Indian speakers', reports Bansal (1969: 143), 'is the incorrect stressing of English words, that is, differently from the usual RP pattern' (and, we might add, the pattern of other native-speaker varieties). I well remember how as a listener I experienced first incomprehension and then annoyance when listening to a highly qualified Indian university lecturer who kept referring to ['iːʋɛnts] (*events*, in all other accents stressed on the final syllable). Among the examples listed by Bansal are [nɛ'sɛsəri] *necessary*, [su'teːbl] *suitable*, ['ɛbaʊt] *about*, ['prɪpəreːʃənz] *preparations*, [pro'dʒɛkt] *project* n. (RP /'prɒdʒɪkt ~ 'prɒdʒekt/), [rɪ'kɒːrd] *record* n. (RP /'rekɔːd/), ['mɪstek] *mistake*, [mɪ'nɪstər] *minister*. Many of these pronunciations appear to be idiosyncratic to individual speakers, and thus may justifiably be regarded as errors (since not institutionalized). Bansal found that it was these, more than any other characteristics of Indian English, which tended to cause unintelligibility: for example, *defence*, pronounced ['dɪfɛns], was misinterpreted as *difference*, and *atmosphere*, pronounced [ɛt'mɒsfɪə], was heard as *must fear* (1969: 161–2).

On rhythm, sentence accent (sentence stress), and intonation, I cannot do better than quote Bansal yet again (1969: 144).

The sentence stress in Indian English is not always in accordance with the normal RP pattern, and the characteristic English rhythm is not maintained. The division of speech into sense groups and tone groups is sometimes faulty, and pauses are made at wrong places. The location of the intonation nucleus is not always at the place where it would be in normal English. The rising tone sometimes used as the end of statements must sound unusual to the RP-speaking listeners.

Among his examples are '*I* know ˈwhat you mean; ˌGet me a ˈcup of tea, please (with no contrastive meaning intended); and '*Don't take any 'notice of .them* (where English people, reading the same sentence under the same test conditions, pronounced either ... ˈnotice of them or else notice of ˈthem).

9.1.6 Interference and intelligibility

A large number of different languages are spoken in India. In order of the size of mother-tongue speech community, the most widely spoken are Hindi, Telugu, Bengali, Marathi, Tamil, Urdu, Gujarati, Kannada, Malayalam, Oriya, Punjabi, and Assamese. Although some of these languages belong to the Indo-European family and some to the Dravidian, they have many similarities in their phonetics; so that phonetic interference of the various languages in English tends to be of a similar kind. Nevertheless, it is not identical: 'within India there are a large number of regional varieties [of English pronunciation], each different from the others in certain ways and retaining to some extent the phonetic patterns of the Indian language spoken in that particular region' (Bansal 1969: 11).

In his study of the intelligibility of spoken Indian English, Bansal (1969) found that mutual intelligibility in English between Indians of different mother tongues was around 74 per cent (compared with 97 per cent between RP-speaking English people). British listeners understood Indian English almost as well (or badly) as Indian listeners (70–3 per cent); Nigerian listeners found it considerably more difficult to understand (53 per cent intelligibility), as did Germans (57 per cent).

What are the phonetic factors responsible for making Indian English relatively difficult to understand? In descending order of frequency, Bansal found the most important ones to be wrongly located stress; absence of stress; use of [ḍ] for /ð/; use of [ʋ] for /v/; use of [ʋ] for /w/; unfamiliar proper names; 'wrong usage'; use of short [e] for FACE; elision of syllables; and non-aspiration of /p, t, k/ in stressed initial positions.

9.2 Africa

9.2.1 Introduction

English has been inherited as a second language in almost all those parts of black Africa which once belonged to the British Empire, as well as in at least one country which did not. In West Africa English is the official state language of Nigeria, Ghana, Sierra Leone, and the Gambia; also of Cameroon (where it shares this rôle with French) and of Liberia (which was never British). In East Africa English is or has been official in Kenya, Uganda, and Tanzania, though in these countries it has a serious rival for the rôle of common language in Swahili. Further south, English is the official state language in Malaŵi, Zambia, and Zimbabwe, and is also official in Botswana, Swaziland, Lesotho, and Namibia, and also, of course, with Afrikaans, in the Republic of South Africa (for the speech of white South Africans, see 8.3 above).

English is spoken as a first language by white settlers and their descendants in Zimbabwe, Namibia, Kenya, and elsewhere. But there is only one country in Africa where English is spoken as a first language by black people. This is Liberia, where some 20,000 people descended from nineteenth-century black American settlers live. Among the remaining 99 per cent of the population of Liberia, English is known (if at all) only as a second language; but the influence of the Americo-Liberians has been decisive in causing educated and official Liberian English to follow American norms (as opposed to the British norms which prevail in English everywhere else in Africa). See further in 9.2.2 below.

There are also in West Africa two 'marginal' languages: creoles of English origin, spoken by some as their first language and by others as a second language. One is **Krio**, spoken in Sierra Leone, particularly in and around the capital, Freetown. Krio is estimated to have 120,000 mother-tongue speakers (Hancock 1971b), and is used as a lingua franca by many thousands more (total number of speakers put at half a million by Jones 1971). The other goes by various names: I shall refer to it as **West African Pidgin English** (WAP), although it is also known as Wes Kos, Bush English, Cameroon Creole, Broken English, etc. It is used as a second language by over a million people, particularly in Cameroon and Nigeria. Mafeni (1971) describes Nigerian Pidgin, the WAP of Nigeria, as

part of a larger group of English-based pidgin and creole languages, or dialects, spoken mostly in coastal areas, and especially in cities and towns, but also in the hinterland, from the Gambia to Cameroon. Naturally, these dialects are to be found mainly in English-using West Africa [...] but speakers of WAP are also to be found among coastal West African communities in what were formerly French – and before 1918 German – colonies, as well as in the Portuguese and Spanish West African territories.

The number of those speaking WAP as a mother tongue is relatively small; they are found particularly in towns and among the children of inter-tribal or international marriages.

Because Krio speakers have been employed in key posts throughout British West Africa, there has been considerable influence of

Krio on all WAP. It seems clear that Krio and WAP are converging, and both are gradually being anglicized, since only Standard English is admitted to the classroom and for official purposes. In Krio, for instance, the traditional forms /nɔba/ 'never', /nɛf/ 'knife', /sto/ 'store' are increasingly replaced by the anglicizing /nɛva/, /naif/, /stɔ/ (Berry 1961). Similarly in WAP /grɔŋ/ 'ground' and /vait/ 'divide' are giving way to /graun/ and /di'vait/ (Dwyer 1966).

The pronunciation of English in West Africa is variable, depending on the degree to which the phonetic imprint of the first language has been eradicated. There is thus as yet no stable, homogeneous pronunciation. Such general phonetic characteristics as have begun to emerge are mainly distinctive prosodic features relating to syllabification and rhythm. (Spencer 1979)

This comment perhaps demands to be amplified by some reference to the vowel systems of African English, which are characteristically monophthongal and smaller, for instance, than that of Indian English; but with this amplification Spencer's comment appears to apply to English as a second language in all parts of black Africa. And the range of first languages is very large indeed: in Africa as a whole it is estimated that close on a thousand distinct languages are spoken. Another factor which may need to be considered is the accent of expatriate teachers of English in the various countries concerned: although this has mostly been RP or something near to it, one hears reports (as yet anecdotal) of a distinctly Scottish accent in the speech of Africans in Malaŵi, where Scottish missionaries have played an important part in teaching English.

9.2.2 Liberia

Standard English in Liberia is pronounced in accordance with American models, with a generally southern flavour. 'Although no precise data are available, the standard appears to be an acquired dialect, familiarity with which is regarded as a mark of education and cultural achievement' (Hancock 1974). The following notes, based on Hancock's article, relate rather to **vernacular Liberian English** (VLE), the informal and domestic speech of those of settler stock, which shows clear links with the Black English of the United States (6.6 above). It is not to be confused with **Liberian Pidgin English** (a variety of WAP), which predates the establishment of Liberia as a country, or with the **Kru Pidgin English** (closely related to Krio) spoken by Kru fishermen.

Unlike most African English, VLE has firm qualitative distinctions between /i/ and /ɪ/, /u/ and /ʊ/ (thus /tu fʊ/ *two foot*). The vowel system includes [i, ɪ, e, ɛ, æ, a, ʌ, ə, ɑ, ɔ, o, ʊ, u], although it is not certain that all are contrastive; there are also a number of diphthongs, including [aɪ, aʊ, əɪ]. Vowels can be nasalized, though this appears to be merely as a result of a realization rule /VN/ → [Ṽ] (except prevocalically). Examples: [hɪ] *his*, [hĩ] *him*; [dʒẽ] *James, Jane*; [æs] *ass*, [æ̃s] *ant(s)*; [tɔ̃ː] *thorn*; [bə̃ɪ] *burn*; [sɪdãʊ̃] *sit down*.

The *happ*Y vowel is usually /ɛ/ (compare the [i] of other kinds of African English): thus /twɛnɛ/ *twenty*, /hɛvɛ/ *heavy* (compare [hɛvẽ] *heaven*), /grɪdɛ/ *greedy*, /bebɛ/ *baby*. But a closer quality can occur in weak final syllables under nasalization, thus [pleːĩ] *playing*, [soĩ] *sewing*, [kɛʃĩ] *catching*.

There is a strong preference for 'free' as opposed to 'checked' syllables. When words are said in isolation, there is usually no consonant corresponding to historical final /t/, /d/, or fricatives (cf. 6.6.2 above for a similar tendency in US Black English). Examples: [blʌ] *blood*, [swi] *sweet*, [tʃæ] *child*, [ræ] *rice*, [grahapa] *grasshopper*, [klo] *clothes*. This rule is not absolute: [tot] *tote* 'carry', [wes] *waste* 'spill', [tɔf] *tough*. (In another article, dealing with **Kepama**, the variety of VLE spoken in Cape Palmas, eastern Liberia, Hancock (1971a: appendix) shows that in this dialect certain final consonants are synchronically deleted or changed in accordance with a context-sensitive rule; thus *got* is [gatˀ] in isolation, [gad] prevocalically, and [ga] preconsonantally. Similarly, *clothes* is [klo ~ klos], although *blood* is invariable as [blʌ]. It seems likely that this sort of variation characterizes Monrovia VLE, too, which implies underlying forms such as /gat/ *got*, /klos/ *clothes*, in spite of the free-syllable phonetic forms quoted.)

In [kɛʃ] *catch* and [riʃ] *reach*, a historical affricate has lost its stop component. Historical /θ, ð/ usually appear as /t, d/ initially, but as /f, v/ finally: [təɪd] *third*, [dæ] *that*, [maʊf] *mouth* (Kepama [mɔ ~ mɔf]), [briv] *breathe*. Historical /v/, on the other hand, sometimes appears as [w]: [ˈoːwə] *over*.

Historical liquids are lost as such when final or preconsonantal, and sometimes when intervocalic. Thus VLE is to be counted among the non-rhotic varieties of English. Examples: [sɪsə] *sister*, [hɔ] *her*, ['bɪɛ] *beard* (Kepama), [kɛ:] *care, carry*, [fɔ ~ fɔkˈ] *fork*, [gɛ:] *girl*; [lɪto] *little*, [kɪʊ] *kill* (with prevocalic alternants [lɪtol], [kɪl], at least in Kepama).

Historical /h/ is preserved, and there is no Glide Cluster Reduction (vol. 1, 3.2.4): [hwæ] *why*, [hwɪʃ] *which*, [hwaɪ(t~d)] *white* (Kepama).

Between vowels, /t/ may be realized as [ɾ] (Tapping, vol. 1, 3.3.4), thus [wɔɾə] *water* – a clearly American feature. African influence is seen in the retention of double-articulated [kp, gb] in words of African origin, thus [gbojɛ] 'hard-boiled egg'.

9.2.3 Vowels

We turn now to the phonetics of English as a second language in Africa. The vowels have often been noted as one of the major areas of difficulty for Africans learning English. Most African languages have a relatively small vowel system (though the consonant systems are often elaborate). In many instances there are only five contrastive vowels: this is the case in Swahili, Shona, and most other Bantu languages, with just /i, e, a, o, u/. Other languages have slightly larger systems, but still considerably fewer vowels than in the RP system of twelve monophthongs and eight diphthongs. Krio has a seven-term system, /i, e, ɛ, a, ɔ, o, u/; there are also some Bantu languages with this system. WAP varies regionally, having either this seven-term system or else a six-term one lacking the /e/ vs. /ɛ/ opposition. The Sudanic languages in Uganda have larger systems, which 'may in part account for the fact that [their speakers] are often said to have a better pronunciation of English' than speakers of Bantu languages (Ladefoged *et al.* 1972: 37).

In some languages with a relatively large vowel system there may nevertheless be phonotactic constraints which interfere with some English oppositions. In Igbo, for example, there are eight contrastive vowels, /i, ɪ, e, a, ɔ, o, ʊ, u/, which suggests that the distinction between, say, *beat* and *bit* would offer no problems to Igbos speaking English. But Igbo has a vowel-harmony rule which precludes the co-occurrence of a vowel from the set /i, e, o, u/ in the same word as one from the set /ɪ, a, ɔ, ʊ/. This means that to pronounce the English word *beating* as [bitɪŋ] would violate Igbo vowel harmony, and hence people tend to pronounce it as [bitiŋ] instead.

In fact there are few Africans who can make the distinction

between FLEECE and KIT (RP /iː/ vs. /ɪ/) without special training. It is difficult for speakers of most African languages just as it is difficult for speakers of French, Italian, or Spanish. Absence of this distinction is one of the most characteristic features of African English, with homophones such as *leave–live, beat–bit, seen–sin, Don't sleep on the floor–Don't slip on the floor*. A word such as *ticket* is usually [tikit]. (In Krio, /il/ means both 'heel' and 'hill'; in WAP, /bik/ 'big' rhymes with /wik/ 'week'.) From a survey of twelve Nigerian languages and the problems faced by their speakers in learning English pronunciation (Dunstan 1969), it appears that nearly all have a problem with /iː/ vs. /ɪ/: most have no such contrast, and of the three which do Igbo has the vowel-harmony complication mentioned above, Hausa has /iː/ only in free (unchecked) syllables, and Fula has a distinction between /iː/ and /i/ which is one of length only, with no quality difference. The FLEECE vs. KIT opposition is mentioned as a difficult one for Ghanaians, too (Sey 1973), even though Twi, Ewe and Gã have a contrast of this type. It is also a problem for East Africans whose first language is a Bantu language (as in the case of the Ugandans mentioned above), and for Zambians (McGregor 1971: 135). In contrast, there are no mother-tongue varieties of English which lack the opposition: every accent and dialect, including those spoken by people of African ancestry in the Caribbean and North America, has a distinction between *beat* and *bit*, *leave* and *live* (v.), *sleep* and *slip*.

Rather similar considerations apply to several other potential vowel oppositions. The English pronunciation used by speakers of Yoruba in Nigeria has been analysed by several scholars (Shafer 1967; Afolayan 1968; Bamgboṣe 1969; Tiffen 1974): it typically involves only the seven vowels of Yoruba, [i, e, ɛ, a, ɔ, o, u]. The lexical incidence of these vowels in English is shown in (278).

(278)	KIT	i	FLEECE	i	NEAR	ia
	DRESS	ɛ	FACE	e	SQUARE	ia, ɛa
	TRAP	a	PALM	a	START	a
	LOT	ɔ	THOUGHT	ɔ	NORTH	ɔ
	STRUT	ɔ	GOAT	o	FORCE	ɔ
	FOOT	u	GOOSE	u	CURE	ua, ɔ
	BATH	a	PRICE	ai	*happ*Y	i
	CLOTH	ɔ	CHOICE	ɔi	*lett*ER	a[1]
	NURSE	ɔ, a	MOUTH	au	*comm*A	a

[1] or other vowels, depending often on the spelling.

A vowel followed by /n/ is typically nasalized, often with loss of the actual nasal consonant, thus *pen* [pɛ̃n, pɛ̃], *question* [kɛʃɔ̃]. This may extend to other sequences of vowel plus nasal, thus *working* [wɔkĩ].

It is obvious that the incidence pattern tabulated in (278) involves very considerable homophony. Not only the FLEECE vs. KIT opposition is missing (RP /iː/ vs. /ɪ/), but also many others:

(i) Yoruba [a] covers TRAP, BATH, PALM, and START, so that there is no distinction corresponding to RP /æ/ vs. /ɑː/. This means that *cat* and *cart* are homophonous, [kat], as also are *pack–park* [pak], *match –march* [matʃ], *batter–barter* [bata]. A lecture on *famine* [famĩ] could easily be mistaken for one on *farming*. Since [a] is often also used in NURSE words, and in the weak syllables of *lett*ER and *comm*A, there can also be homophony between, for example, *heard* and *had–hard* [had], *stir* and *star* [sta].

(ii) Yoruba [ɔ] covers LOT, STRUT, CLOTH, THOUGHT, NORTH and FORCE, so that there is no distinction corresponding to RP /ɒ/ vs. /ʌ/ vs. /ɔː/. (Africans with other language backgrounds may keep STRUT distinct from LOT, but still not make any distinction corresponding to RP /ɒ/ vs. /ɔː/.) This means that *cot, cut, caught,* and *court* are homophonous, [kɔt]; so are *stock, stuck, stalk,* and *stork,* [stɔk]. This vowel is also used in NURSE words when spelt with *o,* or *u,* so that *work* is a homophone of *walk* [wɔk], and *turn* a homophone of *torn* and *ton* [tɔn].

(iii) Yoruba [u] covers FOOT and GOOSE, so that (as in Scottish English) there is no distinction corresponding to RP /ʊ/ vs. /uː/. This means that *look* and *Luke* are homophonous, [luk]; but the functional load of FOOT vs. GOOSE is low in any case.

(iv) Since Yoruba has no diphthongs, the [ai, ɔi, au] of PRICE, CHOICE and MOUTH respectively are properly vowel sequences, and therefore bisyllabic. The same applies to the [ia] of NEAR, the [ia ∼ ɛa] of SQUARE, and the [ua] of CURE; when SQUARE has [ia], furthermore, there is no distinction corresponding to RP /ɪə/ vs. /ɛə/, so that pairs such as *fear–fair* are homophonous, [fia].

Of course the Yoruba speaking English is not forced to limit himself to the vowel sounds of his first language, any more than is the English person speaking French. But to do so will always be easier than learning to make new, unfamiliar vowel contrasts; and where the target language is used mainly as a second language (as

English is in Nigeria) rather than as a foreign language, the social pressures favour remaining within the local vowel system.

The precise details of phonological interference from the first language obviously vary from language to language. But many of the vowel mergers we have noted in Yoruba English apply equally to other kinds of African English. It is usual to have no FLEECE vs. KIT or GOOSE vs. FOOT oppositions; it is usual to have no separate NURSE vowel (RP /ɜː/), but to use instead vowels of the [ɛ], [a] or [ɔ] type in NURSE words; it is usual to have peripheral vowel qualities rather than [ə] in weak syllables. It is also usual to have monophthongs, of the types [e] and [o], in FACE and GOAT (RP /eɪ, əʊ/).

Some African speakers of English, moreover, merge the vowels of DRESS and FACE, using a single [ɛ]-type vowel for both *red* and *raid*, *get* and *gate*, *pepper* and *paper*. This is reported in Nigeria for speakers whose first language is Efik, Nupe, Tiv, or Igbo; it is also frequently the case in East Africa and Southern Africa. In some areas, in addition, GOAT tends not to be distinguished from LOT–THOUGHT – NORTH – FORCE, so that *coat* may be homophonous with *court* (and *caught* and *cot*). Other, less usual, mergers include DRESS with TRAP (Fula) and KIT with NURSE (Efik) (Dunstan 1969: 69, 45).

In South Africa (according to the account in Lanham 1967b) the mergers are slightly different from those found further north, in that STRUT and START–BATH–PALM are merged as [a], and TRAP, DRESS, NURSE and SQUARE as [ɛ]. As elsewhere, [ɔ] covers LOT and THOUGHT –NORTH–FORCE, [i] FLEECE and KIT (meaning that South African *sister* [sista] sounds very different from the whites' [sɪstə ~ səstə]), and [u] FOOT and GOOSE. Although both Zulu and Xhosa have five-vowel systems, they include allophonic [e] and [o], used in English for FACE and GOAT respectively. The diphthongs PRICE, MOUTH, and CHOICE are equated with the Bantu sequences /a.ji, a.wu, o.ji/: hence *five* tends to be pronounced disyllabically, [fa.jiv]. (The usual way of saying 'it's ten past five' in Zulu, according to Rycroft & Ngcobo (1979: 117), is *nguthen'phas'-fayiv'*.)

9.2.4 Consonants

African languages tend to have relatively large consonant systems; but the consonants tend to be subject to severe phonotactic constraints. Hence in African English syllable-final consonants and consonant clusters suffer more first-language interference than do initial and intervocalic consonants.

Some West Africans (e.g. Efiks) tend to use a double-articulated labial-velar [k͡p] for English /p/ in initial position. Others (e.g. some Hausa speakers) use [f], thereby confusing /p/ and /f/.

Very much more widespread is difficulty with the dental fricatives, /θ/ and /ð/. It is very common for alveolar plosives to be used, thus [tik] *thick* (= *tick*), [dɛa] *their* (= *dare*). Less frequently, alveolar fricatives may be used, thus [sik] *thick* (= *sick*), [briz] *breathe* (= *breeze*). However, the dental fricatives constitute such a well-known problem in English pronunciation that most speakers with a reasonable command of English have acquired the ability to pronounce [θ] and [ð], at least in careful speech.

Other fricatives, too, may be subject to interference. The palato-alveolars, /ʃ/ and /ʒ/, constitute a difficulty for some, and may be confused with /s/ and /z/, or with /tʃ/ and /dʒ/; so that *ship* tends to be pronounced like *sip* or *chip*. The difference between /v/ and /b/ is a problem for speakers of Fula and Hausa, which makes them tend to pronounce *van* as [ban], identically with *ban*, or *vote* identically with *boat*. Distinctions of voicing in fricatives lead many speakers of Bantu and other languages to tend to confuse /f/ and /v/, /s/ and /z/, /ʃ/ and /ʒ/.

For some Africans – particularly speakers of certain Bantu languages in East and Southern Africa – the distinction between /l/ and /r/ constitutes a well-known difficulty. This may lead *light* to be pronounced identically with *right* or *belly* with *berry*. But the mere fact that it is well-known as a problem – just as with the dental fricatives – means that those with a good command of English are likely to have been drilled into overcoming it. (The realization of /r/ in African English may be either [ɹ] or [ɾ], generally depending upon what is found in the first language.)

Generally, though, it is not the articulation of particular consonants in themselves which suffers severe first-language interference in African English phonetics, but their combination in clusters and unfamiliar syllabic positions.

Most African languages admit only a small range of consonants in word-final position. Hence African English often exhibits neutralization of oppositions and reduction of clusters in this environment. Speakers of Yoruba, for example, do not always distinguish between voiced and voiceless final consonants, so that pairs súch as *leaf* and *leave*, *bus* and *buzz*, *leak* and *league* are pronounced identically. (In WAP the word for 'big, large' is /bik/; 'charge' is /tʃas/; and 'nose' is /nos/.) Some Africans pronounce *which* identically with *wish*, *reap* with *reef*, and *off* not only with *of* but also with *up*; thus exhibiting neutralization of other oppositions in this environment. Final consonants are also very commonly subject to regressive assimilation of voicing (which obviously involves neutralization of the voicing opposition) as in the examples [meg ðɛm] *make them*, [laif kol] *live coal*, [sev dɛpɔzit] *safe deposit*, [dʒas siŋga] *jazz singer*.

Difficult final clusters may be avoided either by reduction (deletion) or else by epenthesis. Examples of the first include [nos] *notes*, [spos] *sports*, [bus] *books*, [rũːz] *rooms*, ['perẽz] *parents* (all taken from the survey of the speech of first-year Nigerian undergraduates carried out by Tiffen (1974)). They all exemplify the tendency to delete earlier rather than later consonants in final clusters, something virtually unknown among speakers of English as a first language: thus the final /kst/ cluster of *next*, for example, is readily reduced to /ks/ in first-language English (in appropriate phonetic environments), but becomes /st/, losing /k/, only in African English.

Some Africans tend to pronounce [Ṽ] for final or preconsonantal /V/ plus nasal, thus [sĩ] *seen*, [dã] *done*, [mɔdã] *modern*, [fãi] *fine*, [ẽ] *aim*. This may of course lead to the loss of opposition between final nasals (*rum* = *run* = *rung*); but outright deletion of nasals, without compensatory nasalization of the vowel, seems not to occur.

Epenthesis of consonant clusters involves breaking them up by inserting vowels; this is commoner with initial clusters than with final, thus the much-quoted Hausa speakers' [sukuru direba] *screw driver*. The commonest use of inserted vowels to facilitate the pronunciation of final consonants is their addition at the ends of words, as [b(u)redi] *bread*. An extreme example (quoted by Farsi (1965)) is [ai kati maiselfu endi ai wozi bulidiŋgi] *I cut myself and I was bleeding*. Examples of cluster-internal epenthesis include [silik] *silk*, [bɛlɛt] *belt*. Once again, though, these are the sort of beginners' errors which are more or less successfully tackled in the classroom, so that educated adults succeed in avoiding them. Among Nigerian undergraduates, Tiffen concludes, '/θ/ and syllabic /l/ are the only two consonants that present serious problems from the point of view of intelligibility in connected speech' (1974: 265). (The mention of syllabic /l/ is somewhat surprising in this connexion: the Nigerians whose speech he was describing tended to pronounce it [ũ], thus ['litũ] *little*, ['sjuti'bũ] *suitable*, which differs from the common English vocalized syllabic /l/ only in its nasality.)

We have already mentioned the possibility of voicing assimilation. Several other types of assimilation of a kind not encountered, or rarely encountered, in first-language English are to be observed in African English. One often found in Nigeria is the place assimilation of final sibilants to a following dental, thus [tʃuð ði] *choose the*, [əproð ði] *approach the*.

One further, and very important, consideration affecting consonants is that of syllable structure. Most African languages have a strong preference for syllables of the structure /C₀V/ (zero or more consonants plus a vowel, with no final consonant). Thus the name *Zimbabwe* is locally syllabicated as /zi.mba.bwe/, and consists of free syllables (though speakers of English as a first language syllabicate it /zɪm.bɑːb.weɪ/). Similarly, many Africans tend to syllabicate *window* as *wi$ndow* [wi.ndo] rather than as *win$dow*, a tendency which may be reinforced by the syllable-by-syllable methods of teaching reading which many African pupils are exposed to. Hence *dark red* may be syllabicated [da.krɛd], *success* as [sɔ.ksɛs]. For those Africans whose first language is syllable-timed (as many are), the resultant pronunciation of a word such as *society* [sɔ.sai.jɛ.ti] is very different from what is heard in England or America; even a word such as *mother*, syllabicated /CV.CV/, sounds rather different from the usual /CVC.V/ type (African [ma.ða] etc., RP [mʌð.ə]).

There are also certain characteristically African spelling pronunciations. They include *comb* and *climb* with final /mb/ (in spite of what was said above about the avoidance of syllable-final clusters), thus [komb], [klaimb] (compare RP [kəʊm], [klaɪm]). Others are [listɛn] *listen* (RP [lɪsn̩]), [half] *half* (RP [hɑːf]). In the case of [kiŋg] *king* (RP [kɪŋ]), the result agrees with some first-language accents of English.

9.2.5 Prosodic characteristics

Many African languages are tone languages, using contrasts of pitch to make lexical or grammatical distinctions. There may be just a contrast between high tone and low tone, or a more complicated system involving high, mid, and low, or rising and falling tones, or the use of contrastive tonal downstep. English is not a tone language, and these distinctions are obviously not applicable in English; but some tone-language habits do tend to be carried over into English.

It is generally true to say that high tone is perceived by speakers of non-tonal stress languages (such as English) as stress, and that English stress is equated by speakers of tonal African languages with high tone. In each case the syllable in question is rendered more prominent auditorily. Thus English loan-words in Yoruba have high tone on the syllable which is stressed in English. But the difference between typical African and typical native-English patterns is greatest in unstressed syllables: a native-English intonation group tends to have a preponderance of level sequences of syllables, or of gentle downward or upward curves, the pattern being spread over both stressed and unstressed syllables, whereas the common African pattern is a succession of jumps from high to low and back to (not quite so) high and then to low again, as 'stressed' and 'unstressed' syllables alternate.

Most African languages have nothing corresponding to the 'sentence-stress' of English, i.e. the contrastive location of the intonation nucleus (vol. 1, 1.3.9). And the principles whereby some words in English running speech are accented but others not are far from self-evident to those whose first language makes no such distinctions. So African English is usually characterized by an intonation system lacking contrastive tonicity (nucleus location).

There may be other special factors. In Yoruba, for example, the relative *tí* is high-toned; this tends to mean that in Yoruba English all *wh*-words, the translation equivalents of *tí*, are also given a high tone (equivalent to being stressed). But in a phrase such as *the man who was talking* speakers of English as a first language would not normally stress *who*. In fact in African English as a whole it is very common for pronouns, auxiliary verbs, prepositions and so on to be stressed in running speech; and a further consequence of this is that no weak forms are used. Compare the sentence *She's a rascal, you know* in its West African syllable-timed form ['ʃi ze 'raskal 'ju no] ((['] = high tone, unmarked = low tone) and its English-English stress-timed form [ʃɪzə 'rɑːskļ jʊ nəʊ]. The use of tone rather than stress, and of syllable-timing rather than stress-timing, combine to make some African English strikingly different from other varieties in pitch and rhythm.

9.2.6 Interference and intelligibility

In a study of the speech of twenty-four first-year university students of Hausa or Yoruba mother tongue, Tiffen (1974) found, not surprisingly, that British listeners understood RP speakers very much better than they did the African speakers. In a test where an RP speaker was 99.4 per cent intelligible, the mean intelligibility of the Nigerians ranged from 92.7 down to only 29.9 per cent, with a mean of 64.4. Examples of misunderstandings include *secondary school* [sɛ'kɔndrɪ 'skuː] heard as *country school*, *come and queue up* ['kʌm 'ɛnd kju 'ʌp] heard as *come in the ???*, *work* ['wɔk] taken as *walk*, and *recent* ['rizənt] taken as *reasons*.

Studying intelligibility in the other direction, with African listeners, Brown (1968) found that Twi listeners correctly understood 83 per cent of an English text read aloud by other Twi speakers, but only 72 per cent when the readers were speakers of Ewe or RP; Ewe listeners scored 78 per cent with the Ewe readers, 73 per cent with Twi readers, and 70 per cent with RP readers. These figures seem to show that Africans do not understand other Africans speaking English with anything like the reliability that holds between those whose first language is English; and that Africans tend to be much less intelligible to English people (as represented by RP speakers) than English people are to Africans.

Tiffen (1974: 224) was led to conclude that the causes of intelligibility failure in connected speech (African speakers, British listeners) were, in order of importance, as follows:
(i) mispronunciation of vowels; (ii) incorrect rhythm; (iii) incorrect word stress; (iv) incorrect elision (for example, *supervision* ['spaviʃn], *books* [bus]); (v) mispronunciation of consonants; (vi) mispronunciation of consonant clusters; (plus various other less

important causes). 'All the rhythmic/stress failures . . . were usually accompanied, to a greater or lesser extent, by wrong intonation groupings and patterns. However, it was not possible to state categorically that these intelligibility failures were solely or mainly attributable to incorrect intonation, rhythmic and accentual deviations being prime' (Tiffen 1974: 238). It seems likely that generally similar results would be found in Eastern and Southern Africa.

It is as yet an unresolved issue whether black Africa should formally abandon a British (or for that matter American) pronunciation model in favour of a local standard. While there are obvious political, social, and practical arguments in favour of a local standard, it does unfortunately seem to entail both internal and external intelligibility problems.

9.3 The Far East

In this section we consider briefly three Far Eastern territories in which English is particularly well established as a second language: Singapore, the Philippines, and Hawaii. The first was colonized by the British, the others by the Americans; the first two have since become independent, while Hawaii has become part of the United States.

9.3.1 Singapore

Of the $2\frac{1}{4}$ million inhabitants of Singapore, three-quarters are ethnically Chinese, the remainder mostly Malay or Indian. English is one of four official languages, the others being Malay, Chinese (Mandarin), and Tamil. In 1975, some 70 per cent of schoolchildren were attending English-medium schools, even though many were more fluent in Chinese than in English. It was estimated in the same year that seven Singaporean teenagers out of eight could understand English.

Although the Singaporean Chinese share the single common Chinese literary tradition, they speak several mutually incomprehensible varieties of Chinese. Most of the phonetic characteristics of Singaporean English are obviously to be attributed to interference from the Chinese phonological common core (involving, for instance, limitations on the range of possible syllable-final consonants).

One of the most prominent features of Singaporean English is the use of syllable-timed rhythm, as against the stress-timed rhythm of other accents. This is something that applies throughout all that is said. There are also occasional unusual placements of word stress: *ad'vantageous, cha'racter, col'league, e'conomic, fa'culty*; the end-stressing of compound nouns (ˌ*door-'key*) also diverges from usage elsewhere.

The vowel system is clearly of the British type, being isomorphic with that of RP except for the absence of an opposition between LOT (RP /ɒ/) and THOUGHT (RP /ɔː/). Realizationally, though, there are several differences. In particular, the vowels of FACE and GOAT are monophthongal, [eː] and [oː] (= RP [eɪ, əʊ]), as are those of SQUARE ([ɛː], RP [ɛə]) and FORCE ([ɔː], some British [ɔə]).

In phonotactics, Singaporean English shows a marked tendency to avoid [ə], preferring strong vowels in many unstressed syllables, particularly those which are pretonic: [a]*vailable*, c[ɔ]*nclusion*, ʃ[æ]*miliar*, [o]*fficial*, [ʌ]*pon*.

Among the consonants, the non-release of word-final plosives is particularly noticeable: thus *li*[pˀ], *re*[dˀ], *tal*[kˀ]. The voicing distinction is often neutralized in this word-final position, all obstruents being made voiceless, so that *believe* and *belief* become homophones in [-f], *ones* = *once* [wʌns]. Medially, there is no neutralization, though there are reportedly some oddities of lexical incidence, e.g. *De*[z]*ember*.

All the foregoing relates to the English of those educated Singaporeans whose speech shows relatively little interference from the first language. Those with more limited education or of lower social status, showing somewhat greater interference, may lack /θ/ and /ð/, using /t/ and /d/ in their place; they tend to reduce the clusters /nt, nd, ld, sk, sθ/ by the loss of the second consonant (not only finally, but also for example in *hundred*); final plosives tend to be glottalled or entirely lost (so that *rip* = *rib* = *writ* = *rid* = *rick* = *rig* = *rich* = *ridge*, [ɹɪʔ ~ ɹɪ]). Those whose English is even more subject to first-language interference may further sometimes interchange [s] and [ʃ], or indeed not distinguish /r/ from /l/ (Chinese), /f/ from /p/ (Malay), or /v/ from /w/ (Indian).

9.3.2 The Philippines

Language has been a contentious issue in the Philippines. As a 'language of wider communication' Spanish, inherited from the Spanish colonial period, has now been more or less thoroughly displaced by English, introduced during the American period (1898–1935). Meanwhile, efforts to make the Tagalog-based Pilipino the national language of the entire archipelago have met with mixed success. Rather over half the population speak Tagalog; the remainder speak a variety of languages, including Bisayan (Cebuano, Hiligaynon, Waray), Ilokano, Bikolano, Panganisan, and Kapampangan, as well as the Spanish-based creoles Zamboangeño and Caviteño.

The Filipino is, in reality, multilingual, using a vernacular in his intimate familial interaction; a lingua franca (a regional vernacular and increasingly Tagalog-based Pilipino akin to the language of the Greater Manila area) in his urban communities and in his transactions with other ethnic groups; English in business, industry, academia, for negotiations in international circles and as a language of wider communication. (Gonzalez 1980: 149)

Llamzon (1969) has furnished an outline description of 'Standard Filipino English'. This is 'the type of English which educated Filipinos speak, and which is acceptable in educated Filipino circles'; it is to be distinguished from creolized or erroneous forms of English ('bamboo English') and from a type of speech which mixes Tagalog and English ('*halo-halo*', i.e. 'mix-mix'). This standard local version of English is found 'largely in urban areas and among the educated elites of Philippine society' (Gonzalez 1980: 150); on the whole it is a second language rather than a native one, although for many speakers it might be described as 'near-native' (Llamzon 1969: 4).

Rhythmically, Standard Filipino English is syllable-timed rather than stress-timed. It is spoken with 'a delivery which gives the impression of a clipped or staccato rhythm, rather than legato' (Llamzon 1969: 46). Word stress sometimes differs from that in other standard accents, tending to all on the penultimate in words of three or more syllables, thus *labora'tory, nece'ssary, to esti'mate* (all stressed on the first syllable in GenAm and RP).

The vowels of stressed syllables are like those of GenAm, comprising the ten monophthongs /i, ɪ, e, æ, a, ə, u, ʊ, o, ɔ/ and five diphthongs. Following Llamzon's description (1969: 35–7), we can divide them into part-systems as follows, depending on their distribution: (i) in stressed syllables only: /æ/ TRAP, /ɔ/ THOUGHT; (ii) in stressed syllables, and in unstressed syllables in formal style, but not in conversational: /ə/ STRUT; (iii) in stressed syllables, and in unstressed syllables in conversational style, but not in formal: /i/ FLEECE, /e/ DRESS, /a/ LOT, /o/ (in stressed syllables only as part of a diphthong), /u/ GOOSE; (iv) in stressed syllables, and in unstressed syllables in all styles: /ɪ/ KIT, /ʊ/ FOOT; (v) diphthongs: /ej/ FACE, /aj/ PRICE, /oj/ CHOICE, /aw/ MOUTH, /ow/ GOAT. Llamzon does not make explicit how NURSE words are pronounced; presumably they have /ər/. Nor does he give any examples involving NEAR, SQUARE, or FORCE words.

The vowels /i/ and /u/ have neither the length nor the diphthongal quality ([ɪi, ʊu]) found in most British and American accents.

As mentioned, the vowels in unstressed syllables vary considerably according to style. In formal and semi-formal style, [ə] is frequent: *sugar* ['ʃʊgər], *nation* ['nejʃən], *mother* ['məðər], *alcohol* ['alkəhəl]. But in conversational style [ə] is avoided in favour of peripheral vowels, in a pattern which evidently originated in spelling pronunciation, the same words being pronounced ['ʃʊgar], ['nejʃon], ['məðer], ['alkohol]. Thus the Filipinos, unlike the Americans and the British, appear to have more vowel weakening in formal style than in casual.

The consonants, too, exhibit a certain stylistic variability. Initial /p, t, k/ are aspirated in formal style, but not in conversational; final plosives, both voiceless and voiced, are released in formal style but not in conversational. Thus *cap* and *tick* are [kʰæp], [tʰɪk] in formal style, [k⁼æpˀ], [t⁼ɪkˀ] in conversational. In *dot* the only stylistic difference is with the final segment: formal [dat], conversational [datˀ]. Llamzon describes /t, d, n, l/ as dental, and states moreover that /l/ and the nasals /m, n, ŋ/ are 'unreleased' when in final position (in all styles). I have not had an opportunity to check what exactly this means: possibly a kind of (post)glottalization, thus *sing* [sɪŋʔ], *bill* [bɪlʔ], etc.

Filipino English, with its American parentage, is rhotic. The consonant /r/ is realized as a retroflex approximant in formal style, but as a rather unAmerican tap, [ɾ], in conversational style. Thus *rice* and *bar* are formally [ɹajs], [baɹ], conversationally [rajs], [baɾ]. For a Filipino to say as *a matter of* [p]*act*, under the influence of the local languages (which have no [f]), is to incur the charge, in Llamzon's view (1969: 14), of having committed an 'unacceptable lapse'.

9.3.3 Hawaii

The Hawaiian Islands have had a somewhat complicated demographic and linguistic history over the past two hundred years. Although they are now politically part of the United States and settling ever more firmly into the 'GenAm' accent mould, considerable traces of their pidgin and creole history remain in contemporary Hawaiian English.

The native Hawaiians found by Cook in 1778 spoke a Polynesian language. Its phonemic system is remarkably small: there are only eight consonants, which phonotactically neither enter into clusters nor occur word-finally (thus the names *Ho.no.lu.lu*, *Ka.ne.o.he* etc.; the names *Bruce* and *Frank* were Hawaiianized as *Pu.lu.ke* and *Pa.la.ni* respectively). In spite of severe decline, 'the Hawaiian tongue is far from extinct' (Reinecke 1969: 141). From the 1820s on, missionaries from New England taught English in the islands, and in 1840–50 there was a great craze for learning English. Hawaiians who had been taken on as seamen in the China trade also introduced vocabulary items, if nothing more, from Chinese Pidgin English, e.g. *kaukau* 'food' (Hawaiianized from *chow-chow*). By the end of the nineteenth century English had become the language of education and officialdom.

Meanwhile, there had occurred a massive immigration of speakers of languages other than Hawaiian and English. During the last quarter of the nineteenth century 46,000 Chinese, 17,500 Portuguese, and 61,000 Japanese settled in the Islands. They were followed in the first third of the twentieth century by smaller numbers of Puerto Ricans, Koreans, and Spanish, and by 120,000 Filipinos. The descendants of these 'sugar immigrants' now form over half the population of the state. The makeshift English of these new arrivals constituted a new pidgin; in the course of time it became creolized, and what is popularly known as 'pidgin' today in Hawaii is properly termed Hawaiian Creole English. Contemporary

English in the Islands exhibits a continuum of varieties extending from standard English, with a pronunciation locatable within the spectrum of GenAm, to Hawaiian Creole English, which has a restricted phonemic inventory, a smaller range of phonotactic possibilities, and its own rhythmic and intonational characteristics. Many speakers have active control over a range of varieties, and readily switch between a formal standard and an informal creole.

The accent of the standard end of the Hawaiian continuum, then, is a form of GenAm, similar to that spoken in the mid west and far west of the United States. It is rhotic, has unrounded [ɑ] in LOT, a well-established LOT–THOUGHT opposition (/ɑ/ vs. /ɔ/), and Yod Dropping in words such as *opportunity* /-tu-/, *during* /'dʊrɪŋ/, and *new* /nu/. Some speakers, at least, use /hw/ in *when, whine*, etc.

The principal phonetic characteristics in respect of which Hawaiian Creole differs from GenAm can be listed as follows. Among the vowels, the oppositions /i/ vs. /ɪ/ (FLEECE vs. KIT), /eɪ/ vs. /ɛ/ (FACE vs. DRESS), /æ/ vs. /ɛ/ (TRAP vs. DRESS), /u/ vs. /ʊ/ (GOOSE vs. FOOT), and /ɑ/ vs. /ʌ/ (LOT vs. STRUT) may be missing; in each pair it is the second which offers the 'difficulty', thus tending to be avoided in favour of the first. Among the consonants, similar considerations apply to the oppositions /t/ vs. /θ/, /d/ vs. /ð/, and /dʒ/ vs. /ʒ/. Furthermore, obstruents tend to be always voiceless in word-final position, thus [wəs] *was*, [θɪŋs] *things*, [reɪst] *raised* (= *raced*), [lɛk] *leg*. Consonant clusters tend to be simplified in accordance with principles similar to those operating in West Indian English (7.1.4 above, Cluster Reduction) and Black English (6.6.2 above), thus [læs] *last*, [ɛn] *end*. A drastic treatment of final consonants is reported by Glissmeyer (1973: 197), who mentions 'back clipping' (i.e. deletion) of final consonants in words such as *that, float, dog, animal*; she also mentions the possibility of variable Glottalling for the final consonants in *float, salt, drink, cloud, five, rain, fall* and other words (which is particularly interesting in view of the existence of a phoneme /ʔ/ in Hawaiian). Rhoticity is variable, the creole end of the continuum being non-rhotic; thus ['sɛntɑ] *center*, [kɛə] *care*, ['pɑːtɪ] *party*. The initial clusters in *train, drain*, and *strain* tend to be [tʃɹ, dʒɹ, ʃtʃɹ] respectively. Intersonorant /t/, as in *butter, mountain, kitten*, tends to be voiceless (as usually in British English but not in American). The use of peripheral vowels in what in standard accents are unstressed syllables means that *kitten* is phonetically ['kʰɪtʰɛn].

In the kind of speech which lies between the extremes of creole and standard, it is common for the phonemic oppositions mentioned to exist, but for certain 'relic' lexical items to retain the creole-type pronunciation: thus [bout] *both*, [da] *the*, [liv] *live* (= *leave*), for speakers who otherwise have perfectly viable /θ/, /ð/, and /ɪ/.

Rhythm varies from the stress-timing usual in English to the syllable-timing characteristic of much Hawaiian Creole (deriving from the stress-timed rhythm brought with them by Japanese and Filipino immigrants). It is often criticized by local teachers of English as 'choppy' or 'staccato', and involves not only timing but also stress. Carr (1972: 71) gives the example of the sentence *to see if I could get into lawschool*, with a standard pattern stressing only /si/, /gɛt/ and /lɔ/ (with a secondary stress on /skul/), but a creole syllable-timed rhythm involving stress on every word, and hesitation between *law* and *school* as the place of the intonation nucleus.

A special intonation usage characteristic of Hawaiian English (avoided, though, in formal standard speech) is a high fall on yes–no questions. Carr (1972: 51) exemplifies this with the question *Wanna go show to`night?* (high-level even-stressed staccato prenuclear pattern, high fall nucleus), as against the standard American pattern *Do you 'want to 'go to the 'show tonight?*

We may finally note that the name of the state is locally pronounced [hɑ'waiʔi], [hɑ'vaiʔi], or [hɑ'wai].

Sources and further reading

Other works which attempt a similar geographical coverage to the three volumes of *Accents of English* include Bähr 1974; Blunt 1967; Wächtler 1977; Wise 1957. The only one of these on which I have drawn is Bähr, and that very sparingly.

6   Useful surveys include McDavid 1958; Reed 1967; Shuy 1967; Thomas 1958: chs 21–2. Theoretically outmoded but still valuable: Hockett 1958: ch. 40; Trager & Smith 1951. Two excellent collections of readings: Allen & Underwood 1971; Williamson & Burke 1971. Sixty articles by the most eminent contemporary American dialectologist are collected in McDavid 1979; Davis 1972 is a festschrift compiled in McDavid's honour. Linguistic Atlas findings for the eastern US: *PEAS* (Kurath & McDavid 1961); for Minn., Ia., Neb. and the Dakotas, *LAUM* (Allen 1976). See also Kurath 1972. Accent, dialect, nomenclature: Berger 1968; McDavid 1967b, McMillan 1977.

6.1   BATH Raising: Bailey 1973: 56–70; Ferguson 1975; Labov 1966: 51 and passim, 1972c: 134–64. FORCE and NORTH: Kurath 1940. *Greasy*: Atwood 1950; Hempl 1896. Particular regions: Carmony 1970; DeCamp 1958–9; Foster & Hoffman 1966; Labov 1981; Labov *et al.* 1980; Labov, Yaeger & Steiner 1972; Pederson 1972; Reed 1961; Udell 1966.

6.2   Avis 1965, 1972; Chambers 1975; Léon & Martin 1979. McDavid 1954; Orkin 1971. Vowels: Gregg 1957a,b; Lehn 1959. PRICE, MOUTH Raising: Chambers 1973; Gregg 1973; Joos 1942. US–Canada differences: Allen 1959; Avis 1956; Hamilton 1958; Scargill 1955. Survey of Canadian English: Scargill & Warkentyne 1972; Warkentyne 1971. Lunenburg, NS: Emeneau 1935; Wilson 1959. Newfoundland: Drysdale 1959; Paddock 1966; Seary *et al.* 1968; Story 1957a,b.

6.3   Hubbell 1950a; Labov 1966. Also Bronstein 1962; Frank 1948; Labov 1972a; Labov *et al.* 1968; Lass 1976; *PEAS*; Sprague de Camp 1943, 1952; Thomas 1932, 1958: 219–22.

6.4   *PEAS*; Thomas 1961. Boston: Laferriere 1977; Parslow 1967. Martha's Vineyard: Labov 1963, 1972b. Short *o*: Avis 1961.

6.5   I have drawn particularly on Bailey 1969b; Jaffe 1973; McDavid 1955; Norman 1956; O'Cain 1972; Sledd 1955, 1966, 1958, 1965; also *PEAS*.

6.6 De Stefano 1973; Fasold & Wolfram 1973; Labov 1969a,b; Labov *et al.* 1968; Luelsdorff 1975; Williamson 1968; Wolfram 1969; Wolfram & Clarke 1971. Readable introductions: Burling 1973; Labov 1973. Gullah: Turner 1945, 1949.

7.1 History: Le Page 1957–8; Le Page & DeCamp 1960; Taylor 1977. Creole continuum: Bickerton 1975; DeCamp 1971; Stewart 1962. Pidgins and creoles: Alleyne 1980; Hall 1966; Hymes 1971; Reinecke 1975; Todd 1974.

7.2 Jamaica: Cassidy 1961; Cassidy & Le Page 1980; DeCamp 1969; Wells 1973. Trinidad: Warner 1967; Winford 1978. Guyana: Bickerton 1973; Allsopp 1958 (both mainly syntax). Barbados: Haynes 1973. Leewards: Cooper 1979; Farquhar 1974; Wells 1980. Bahamas: Holm 1979; Shilling 1975. Various: Le Page 1972.

8.1 Cochrane 1959; Delbridge 1970; Mitchell & Delbridge 1965; Turner 1966. Also: Adams 1969; Baker 1947; Mitchell 1946; Pilch 1971. Origins of Australian pronunciation: Bernard 1969; Blair 1975; Collins 1975; Turner 1960. Bibliography (by Blair): Ramson 1970. 'Strine': Lauder 1965, 1966, 1968, 1969.

8.2 Hawkins, 1973a,b, 1976, n.d.; Turner 1966, 1970. Also Bauer 1980; Bennett 1943; Kelly 1966.

8.3 Lanham 1967a, 1970, 1978b; Lanham & Macdonald 1979; Lanham & Traill 1962. Also Breckwoldt 1961; Hopwood 1928/1970. Demography and history of English in SA: Lanham 1978a; Watts 1976.

9.1 Bansal 1969; Nihalani *et al.* 1979. Also Masica & Dave 1972; Limaye 1965; Sethi 1980; Vermeer 1969. Sri Lanka: Fernando 1977. Anglo-Indians: Spencer 1966.

9.2 Dunstan 1969; Ladefoged *et al.* 1972; Spencer 1971; Tiffen 1974. Also Farsi 1965; Lanham 1967b; McGregor 1971; Perren 1956; Schachter 1962; Sey 1973. Liberia: Hancock 1971a, 1974. WAP: Mafeni 1965, 1971; Dwyer 1966; Schneider 1966.

9.3 Singapore: Tay 1979; also Platt 1977. Philippines: Llamzon 1969; also Gonzalez 1980; Sibayan 1977. Hawaii: Carr 1972; Glissmeyer 1973; Reinecke 1969; also Vanderslice & Pierson 1967. This sub-chapter is the only one in the book to be based wholly on secondary sources. (As this book was in proof I learnt of the publication of: Platt, J. & Weber, H. 1980. *English in Singapore and Malaysia.* Kuala Lumpur: Oxford University Press.)

References

Adams, C. M. 1969. A survey of Australian English intonation. *Phonetica* 20.81–130

Afolayan, A. 1968. The linguistic problems of Yoruba learners and users of English. PhD thesis, University of London

Allen, H. B. 1959. Canadian–American speech differences along the middle border. *Journal of the Canadian Linguistic Association* 5.1.17–24

Allen, H. B. 1976. *The linguistic atlas of the Upper Midwest. (LAUM)* Volume 3. Minneapolis: University of Minnesota Press

Allen, H. B. & Underwood, G. N. 1971. *Readings in American dialectology.* New York: Appleton-Century-Crofts

Alleyne, M. C. 1980. *Comparative Afro-American.* Ann Arbor, Mich.: Karoma

Allsopp, R. 1958. The English language in British Guiana. *English Language Teaching* 12.2.59–66

Allsopp, R. 1962. Expression of state and action in the dialect of English used in the Georgetown area of British Guiana. PhD thesis, University of London

Allsopp, R. 1972. Some suprasegmentals of Caribbean English. Paper presented to UWI/UNESCO Conference on Creole Languages and Educational Development, Trinidad

Amis, K. 1968. *I want it now.* London: Cape

Anshen, F. 1970. A sociolinguistic analysis of a sound change. *Language Sciences* 9.20–21

Atwood, E. B. 1950. *Grease* and *greasy*: a study of geographical variation. *Studies in English* (University of Texas) 29.249–60. Reprinted in Allen & Underwood 1971: 160–8

Atwood, E. B. 1951. Some Eastern Virginia pronunciation features. *University of Virginia Studies* 4.111–24. Reprinted in Williamson & Burke 1971: 255–67

Avis, W. S. 1956. Speech differences along the Ontario–US border, III. *Journal of the Canadian Linguistic Association* 2.2.41–59

Avis, W. S. 1961. The 'New England short *o*': a recessive phoneme. *Language* 37.544–58. Reprinted in Allen & Underwood 1971: 200–15; and in Williamson & Burke 1971: 389–405

Avis, W. S. 1965. *A bibliography of writings on Canadian English (1957–1965).* Toronto: Gage

Avis, W. 1972. The phonemic segments of an Edmonton idiolect. In Davis 1972: 239–50

Babbitt, E. H. 1896. The English of the lower classes in New York City and vicinity. *Dialect Notes* 1.457–64

Bähr, D. 1974. *Standard English und seine geographischen Varianten.* Munich: Wilhelm Fink

Bailey, B.L. 1966. *Jamaican Creole syntax.* Cambridge University Press

Bailey, C.-J. N. 1968a. Is there a 'Midland' dialect of American English? Washington: Center for Applied Linguistics, ERIC doc. ED 021 240

Bailey, C.-J. N. 1968b. Dialectal differences in the syllabication of non-nasal sonorants in American English. *General Linguistics* 8.79–91

Bailey, C.-J. N. 1969a. An exploratory investigation of variation in the accepted outputs of underlying short vowels in a dialect of Southern States English. *University of Hawaii Working Papers in Linguistics* 1.57–63

Bailey, C.-J. N. 1969b. Introduction to Southern States phonetics. *University of Hawaii Working Papers in Linguistics* 4.81–144; 5.107–89; 6.105–203; 7.75–95; 8.139–79; 9.61–147; 11.143–76

Bailey, C.-J. N. 1973. *Variation and linguistic theory.* Arlington, Va.: Center for Applied Linguistics

Bailey, R. W. & Robinson, J. L. 1973. *Varieties of present-day English.* New York: Macmillan

Baker, S. J. 1947. *Australian pronunciation: a guide to good speech.* Sydney: Angus & Robertson

Bamgboṣe, A. 1969. Yoruba. In Dunstan 1969

Bamgboṣe, A. 1971. The English language in Nigeria. In Spencer 1971: 35–48

Bansal, R. K. 1969. *The intelligibility of Indian English.* Hyderabad: Central Institute of English

Bauer, L. 1980. The second Great Vowel Shift? *Journal of the International Phonetic Association* 9.2

Bennett, J. A. W. 1943. English as it is spoken in New Zealand. *American Speech* 18.2.8.95. Reprinted in Ramson 1970: 69–83

Berger, M. D. 1968. Accent, pattern, and dialect in North American English. *Word* 24.55–61

Bernard, J. R. L-B. 1969. On the uniformity of spoken Australian English. *Orbis* 18.1.62–73

Berry, J. 1961. English loanwords and adaptations in Sierra Leone Krio. In Le Page 1961

Berry, J. 1976. Tone and intonation in Guyanese English. In Juilland 1976: 263–70.

Bickerton, D. 1973. The nature of a creole continuum. *Language* 49: 640–69

Bickerton, D. 1975. *Dynamics of a creole system.* Cambridge University Press

Blair, D. 1975. On the origins of Australian pronunciation. *Working*

Papers of the Speech and Language Research Centre, Macquarie University, July 1975

Bloch, B. 1939. Postvocalic *r* in New England speech, a study in American dialect geography. *Actes du quartième Congrès Internationale de linguistes*, 195–9. Copenhagen: Munksgaard. Reprinted in Allen & Underwood 1971: 196–9

Blunt, J. 1967. *Stage dialects*. San Francisco: Chandler Pub. Co.

Breckwoldt, G. H. 1961. Some aspects of the phonetics of vowels in South African English. *Maître Phonétique* 115.5–12

Bright, J. A. & McGregor, G. P. 1970. *Teaching English as a second language*. London: Longman

Bronstein, A. J. 1960. *The pronunciation of American English*. Englewood Cliffs, NJ: Prentice-Hall

Bronstein, A. J. 1962. Let's take another look at New York City speech. *American Speech* 37.13–26

Bronstein, A. J. *et al.* (eds) 1970. *Essays in honor of C.M. Wise*. Hannibal, Missouri: Standard, for the Speech Association of America

Brown, K. 1968. Intelligibility. In Davies 1968: 180–91

Bruce, L. 1975. *The essential Lenny Bruce*. Edited by J. Cohen. St Albans: Panther

Bruck, A., Fox, R. A., & LaGaly, M. W. (eds) 1974. *Papers from the parasession on natural phonology*. Chicago, Ill.: Chicago Linguistic Society

Burling, R. 1973. *English in black and white*. New York: Holt, Rinehart and Winston

Caffee, N. M. 1940. Southern 'L' plus a consonant. *American Speech* 15.259–61

Caffee, N. & Kirby, T. A. (eds) 1940. *Studies for William A. Read*. University, La: Louisiana State University Press

Carmony, M. 1970. Some phonological rules of an Indiana dialect. In Griffith & Miner 1970

Carr, E. B. 1972. *Da kine talk. From Pidgin to Standard English in Hawaii*. Honolulu: University Press of Hawaii

Carter, H. & Kahari, G. P. 1979. *Kuverenga ChiShóna*. London: School of Oriental and African Studies

Cassidy, F. G. 1961. *Jamaica talk: three hundred years of the English language in Jamaica*. London: Macmillan

Cassidy, F. G. & Le Page, R. B. 1980. *Dictionary of Jamaican English*. Second edn. Cambridge University Press.

Cearley, A. 1974. The only phonological rule ordering principle. In Bruck *et al.* 1974: 30–41

Chambers, J. K. 1973. Canadian raising. *Canadian Journal of Linguistics* 18.2.113–35

Chambers, J. K. 1975. *Canadian English*. Agincourt, Ont.: Methuen

Chomsky, N. 1964. *Current issues in linguistics*. The Hague: Mouton

Chomsky, N. & Halle, M. 1968. *The sound pattern of English. (SPE)* New York: Harper & Row

Cochrane, G. R. 1959. The Australian English vowels as a diasystem. *Word* 15.1.69–88

Collins, H. E. 1975. The sources of Australian pronunciation. *Working Papers* of the Speech and Language Research Centre, Macquarie University, January 1975

Collymore, F. A. 1970. *Notes for a glossary of words and phrases of Barbadian dialect.* Bridgetown, Barbados: Advocate Co/Barbados National Trust (Cover title is just *Barbadian Dialect*)

Cook, S. 1969. Language change and the emergence of an urban dialect in Utah. PhD diss., University of Utah

Cooper, V. O'M. 1979. Basilectal creole, decreolization, and autonomous language change in St Kitts-Nevis. PhD diss., Princeton University

Crewe, W. J. (ed.) 1977. *The English Language in Singapore.* Singapore: Eastern Universities Press

Dalby, D. 1972. The African element in Black American English. In Kochman 1972

Davies, A. (ed.) 1968. *Language testing symposium.* London: Oxford University Press

Davis, L. M. 1970. Some social aspects of the speech of central Kentucky. *Orbis* 19.2.337–41. Reprinted in Williamson & Burke 1971: 335–40

Davis, L. M. (ed.) 1972. *Studies in linguistics in honor of Raven I. McDavid, Jr.* University, Alabama: University of Alabama Press

DeCamp, D. 1958–9. The pronunciation of English in San Francisco. *Orbis* 7.372–91, 8.54–77. Parts III and IV reprinted in Williamson & Burke 1971: 549–69

DeCamp, D. 1961. Social and geographical factors in Jamaican dialects. In Le Page 1961: 61–84

DeCamp, D. 1969. Diasystem vs. overall pattern: the Jamaican syllabic nuclei. In *Studies in language, literature and culture of the middle ages and later* (ed. Atwood, E. B. & Hill, A. A.), Austin: University of Texas

DeCamp, D. 1971. Towards a generative analysis of a post-creole continuum. In Hymes 1971: 349–70

Delbridge, A. 1970. The recent study of spoken Australian English. In Ramson 1970

DeStefano, J. D. (ed.) 1973. *Language, society, and education: a profile of Black English.* Worthington, Ohio: Charles A. Jones

De Villiers, A. (ed.) 1976. *English-speaking South Africa today.* Cape Town: Oxford University Press

Dillard, J. L. 1972. *Black English: its history and usage in the United States.* New York: Random House

Dillard, J. (ed.) 1975. *Perspectives on Black English.* The Hague: Mouton

Dingwall, W. O. (ed.) 1971. *A survey of linguistic science.* College Park,

Md.: University of Maryland

Drysdale, P. D. 1959. A first approach to Newfoundland phonemics. *Journal of the Canadian Linguistic Association* 5.1.25–34

Dunstan, E. (ed.) 1969. *Twelve Nigerian Languages.* London: Longman

Dwyer, D. [1966]. *An introduction to West African Pidgin English.* Supervised by D. Smith. [East Lansing:] African Studies Center, Michigan State University, for the US Peace Corps

Emeneau, M. B. 1935. The dialect of Lunenburg, Nova Scotia. *Language* 11.12.140–7

Evertts, E. L. (ed.) 1967. *Dimensions of dialect.* Champaign, Illinois: National Council of Teachers of English

Farquhar, B. B. 1974. A grammar of Antiguan Creole. PhD diss., Cornell University

Farsi, A. A. 1965. Some pronunciation problems of Swahili-speaking students. *English Language Teaching* 20.2.136–40

Fasold, R. W. & Shuy, R. W. (eds) 1970. *Teaching Standard English in the inner city.* Washington: Center for Applied Linguistics

Fasold, R. W. & Shuy, R. W. (eds) 1977. *Studies in language variation: semantics, syntax, phonology, pragmatics, social situations, ethnographic approaches.* Washington, DC: Georgetown University Press

Fasold, R. W. & Wolfram, W. 1973. Some linguistic features of Negro dialect. In Fasold & Shuy 1970. Reprinted in DeStefano 1973

Feagin, C. 1979. *Variation and change in Alabama English.* A sociolinguistic study of the white community. Washington, DC: Georgetown University Press

Fergus, H. A. 1975. *History of Alliouagana. A short history of Montserrat.* Plymouth, Montserrat: the author

Ferguson, C. 1975. 'Short *a*' in Philadelphia English. In *Studies in linguistics in honor of George L. Trager* (ed. Smith, M. E.). The Hague: Mouton

Fernando, C. 1977. English in Ceylon: a case study of a bilingual community. *Language in Society* 6.3.341–60

Foster, D. W. & Hoffman, R. J. 1966. Some observations on the vowels of Pacific North West English (Seattle area). *American Speech* 41.119–22

Francis, W. N. 1958. *The structure of American English.* New York: Ronald Press

Frank, Y. H. 1948. The speech of New York City. Diss., University of Michigan

Glissmeyer, G. 1973. Some characteristics of English in Hawaii. In Bailey & Robinson 1973: 190–225

Gonzalez, A. B. 1980. *Language and nationalism. The Philippine experience thus far.* Quezon City: Ateneo de Manila University Press

Gregg, R. J. 1957a. Notes on the pronunciation of Canadian English as spoken in Vancouver, BC. *Journal of the Canadian Linguistic Association* 3.1.20–6

Gregg, R. J. 1957b. Neutralization and fusion of vocalic phonemes in Canadian English as spoken in the Vancouver area. *Journal of the Canadian Linguistic Association* 3.2.78–83

Gregg, R. J. 1973. The diphthongs əi and aɪ in Scottish, Scotch-Irish and Canadian English. *Canadian Journal of Linguistics* 18.2.136–45

Griffith, J. & Miner L. E. 1970. *The First Lincolnland Conference on Dialectology*. University, Alabama: University of Alabama Press

Hall, R. A., Jr 1966. *Pidgin and creole languages*. Ithaca, NY: Cornell University Press

Hamilton, D. E. 1958. Notes on Montreal English. *Journal of the Canadian Linguistic Association* 4.2.70–9

Hancock, I. F. 1971a. Some aspects of Liberian English. *Liberian Studies Journal* 3.2. Reprinted in Dillard 1975: 248–71, with an appendix on the Liberian English of Cape Palmas

Hancock, I. 1971b. A survey of the pidgins and creoles of the world. In Hymes 1971

Hancock, I. F. 1974. English in Liberia. *American Speech* 49.3–4.224–9

Hankey, C. T. 1972. Notes on West Penn-Ohio phonology. In Davis 1972: 49–79

Hanks, P. (ed.) 1979. *Collins dictionary of the English language*. London & Glasgow: Collins

Hawkins, P. 1973a. The sound patterns of NZ English. *Proceedings of the 15th AULLA Congress*, Sydney, 13.1–8

Hawkins, P. 1973b. A phonemic transcription for NZ English. *Te Reo* 16

Hawkins, P. 1976. The role of NZ English in a binary feature analysis of English short vowels. *Journal of the International Phonetic Association* 6.2.50–66

Hawkins, P. n.d. The New Zealand accent and its role in the analysis of some phonological problems of English. Mimeo

Haynes, L. 1973. Language in Barbados and Guyana. Attitudes, behaviours, and comparisons. PhD diss., Stanford University

Hempl, G. 1896. *Grease* and *greasy*. *Dialect Notes* 1.438–44. Reprinted in Allen & Underwood 1971: 154–9

Hockett, C. F. 1958. *A course in modern linguistics*. New York: Macmillan

Holder, M. 1972. Word accentual patterns in Guyanese English (GE) compared with British English (RP norm). *Proceedings of the 7th International Congress of Phonetic Sciences, Montreal, 1971*: 897–9. The Hague: Mouton

Holm, J. 1979. African features in white Bahamian English. Mimeo

Hooper, A. G. 1945. A preliminary report of an investigation of spoken English in South Africa. *South African Journal of Science* 41.476–84

Hopwood, D. 1928. South African English pronunciation. Reprinted 1970, College Park, Md: McGrath Pub. Co.

Howren, R. R. 1958. The speech of Louisville, Kentucky. PhD diss.,

Indiana University

Howren, R. R. 1962. The speech of Ocracoke, North Carolina. *American Speech* 37.161–75. Reprinted in Williamson & Burke 1971: 280–93; and in Shores & Hines 1977: 61–72

Hubbell, A. F. 1950a. *The pronunciation of English in New York City: consonants and vowels.* New York: Octagon Books

Hubbell, A. F. 1950b. The phonemic analysis of unstressed vowels. *American Speech* 25.105–11

Hymes, D. (ed.) 1966. *Language in culture and society.* New York: Harper and Row

Hymes, D. (ed.) 1971. *Pidginization and creolization of languages.* Cambridge University Press

Jaffe, H. 1973. The speech of the central coast of North Carolina: the Carteret county version of the Banks 'Brogue'. *Publications of the American Dialect Society* 60

Jones, E. 1971. Krio: an English-based language of Sierra Leone. In Spencer 1971

Joos, M. 1942. A phonological dilemma in Canadian English. *Language* 18.141–4

Juilland, A. (ed) 1976. *Linguistic studies offered to Joseph Greenberg, II: Phonology.* Saratoga, Ca: Anma Libri

Kelly, L. G. 1966. The phonemes of New Zealand English. *Canadian Journal of Linguistics* 2.2.79–52

Kenyon, J. S. 1958. *American pronunciation.* Tenth edn. Ann Arbor, Mich.: George Wahr (First edn 1924)

Kenyon, J. S. & Knott, T. A. 1953. *A pronouncing dictionary of American English.* Springfield, Mass.: Merriam

Kochman, T. (ed.) 1972. *Rappin' and stylin' out: communication in urban black America.* Urbana: University of Illinois Press

Kurath, H. 1940. *Mourning* and *morning.* In Caffee & Kirby 1940: 166–73. Reprinted in Williamson & Burke 1971: 417–23

Kurath, H. 1949. *A word geography of the eastern United States.* Ann Arbor: University of Michigan Press

Kurath, H. 1972. *Studies in area linguistics.* Bloomington: Indiana University Press

Kurath, H. & McDavid, R. I., Jr 1961. *The pronunciation of English in the Atlantic states (PEAS).* Ann Arbor: University of Michigan Press

Labov, W. 1963. The social motivation of a sound change. *Word* 19.273–309. Reprinted as ch. 1 of Labov 1972a

Labov, W. 1966. *The social stratification of English in New York City.* Washington, DC: Center for Applied Linguistics

Labov, W. 1969a. Contraction, deletion, and inherent variability of the English copula. *Language* 45.4.715.62. Reprinted with modifications in Labov 1972d

Labov, W. 1969b. The logic of nonstandard English. *Georgetown*

Monographs in Languages and Linguistics no. 22. Reprinted in
Labov 1972d, and in Bailey & Robinson 1973: 319–54
Labov, W. 1971. Methodology. In Dingwall 1971: 412–97
Labov, W. 1972a. *Sociolinguistic patterns*. Philadelphia: University of
Pennsylvania Press (British edn 1978, Oxford: Blackwell)
Labov, W. 1972b. The recent history of some dialect markers on the
island of Martha's Vineyard, Mass. In Davis 1972: 81–121
Labov, W. 1972c. The internal evolution of linguistic rules. In Stock-
well & Macaulay 1972
Labov, W. 1972d. *Language in the inner city. Studies in the Black English
Vernacular*. Philadelphia: University of Pennsylvania Press (British
edn 1977, Oxford: Blackwell)
Labov, W. 1973. Some features of the English of black Americans. In
Bailey & Robinson 1973: 236–55
Labov, W. (ed.) 1981. *Locating language in time and space*. New York
and London: Academic Press
Labov, W. *et al.* 1980. Social determinants of sound change. (Final
report on NSF SOC-75-00245.) Philadelphia: US Regional Survey
Labov, W., Cohen, P., Robins, C., & Lewis, J. 1968. *A study of the
nonstandard English of Negro and Puerto Rican speakers in New York
City*. Vol. I, *Phonological and grammatical analysis*. Vol. II, *The use
of language in the speech community*. Final Report, Cooperative
Research Project No. 3288. Washington, DC: Office of Education
Labov, W., Yaeger, M. & Steiner, R. 1972. A quantitative study of
sound change in progress. Philadelphia: US Regional Survey
Ladefoged, P., Glick, R., & Criper, C. 1972. *Language in Uganda*.
London: Oxford University Press
Laferriere, M. 1977. Boston short *a*: social variation as historical residue.
In Fasold & Shuy 1977: 100–7
Lanham, L. W. 1967a. *The pronunciation of South African English*. Cape
Town: Balkema
Lanham, L. W. 1967b. *Teaching English in Bantu primary schools. Final
report on research in Johannesburg schools*. Johannesburg: The
English Academy of South Africa
Lanham, L. W. 1970. South African English as an index of social his-
tory. *English Studies in Africa* 13.1.251–64
Lanham, L. W. 1978a. An outline history of the languages of southern
Africa. In Lanham & Prinsloo 1978
Lanham, L. W. 1978b. South African English. In Lanham & Prinsloo
1978
Lanham, L. W. & Macdonald, C. A. 1979. *The standard in South
African English and its social history*. Heidelberg: Julius Gross
Lanham, L. W. & Prinsloo, K. P. (eds) 1978. *Language and communi-
cation studies in South Africa. Current issues and directions in research
and enquiry*. Cape Town: Oxford University Press
Lanham, L. W. & Traill, A. 1962. South African English pronunciation.

References

English Studies in Africa 5.2.171–208

Lass, R. 1976. *English phonology and phonological theory.* Cambridge University Press

'Lauder, Afferbeck' 1965. *Let stalk Strine.* Sydney: Ure Smith; London: Wolfe

'Lauder, Afferbeck' 1966. *Nose tone unturned.* Sydney and London: Ure Smith

'Lauder, Afferbeck' 1968. *Fraffly well spoken.* Sydney: Ure Smith; London: Wolfe

'Lauder, Afferbeck' 1969. *Fraffly suite.* Sydney: Ure Smith; London: Wolfe

LAUM = Allen 1976

Lehn, W. 1959. Vowel contrasts in a Saskatchewan English dialect. *Journal of the Canadian Linguistic Association* 5.2.90–8

Léon, P. R. & Martin, P. J. (eds) 1979. *Toronto English. Studies in phonetics to honour C. D. Rouillard.* Ottawa: Didier

Le Page, R. B. 1957–8. General outlines of Creole English dialects in the British Caribbean. *Orbis* 6.2.373–91, 7.1.54–64

Le Page, R. B. (ed.) 1961. *Proceedings of the Conference on Creole Language Studies.* Creole Language Studies II. London: Macmillan

Le Page, R. B. 1972. *Sample West Indian texts.* Mimeo. York: Dept. of Language, University of York

Le Page, R. B. & DeCamp, D. 1960. *Jamaican Creole.* London: Macmillan

Levine, L. & Crockett, H. J. 1966. Speech variation in a Piedmont community: postvocalic r. *Sociological Inquiry* 36.204–26. Reprinted in Lieberson 1966: 91–109; and in Williamson & Burke 1971: 437–60

Lieberson, S. (ed.) 1966. Explorations in sociolinguistics. Publication 44, *International Journal of Applied Linguistics*

Limaye, M. R. 1965. 'H' for a Marathi speaker of English. (The problem of aspiration). *English Language Teaching* 20.1.72–5

Llamzon, T. A. 1969. *Standard Filipino English.* Manila: Ateneo University Press

Luelsdorff, P. 1975. *A segmental phonology of Black English.* The Hague: Mouton

McDavid, R. I., Jr 1948. Postvocalic -r in South Carolina: a social analysis. *American Speech* 23.194–203. Reprinted with revisions by the author in Hymes 1966; and in McDavid 1979: 136–42

McDavid, R. I., Jr 1954. Linguistic geography in Canada: an introduction, *Journal of the Canadian Linguistic Association* 1.1.3–8

McDavid, R. I., Jr 1955. The position of the Charleston dialect. *Publications of the American Dialect Society* 23.35–49. Reprinted in McDavid 1979: 272–81

McDavid, R. I., Jr 1958. American English dialects. In Francis 1958

McDavid, R. I., Jr 1965. American social dialects. *College English* 26.254–60. Reprinted in McDavid 1979: 126–30

McDavid, R. I., Jr 1966. Review of Thomas 1958 & Bronstein 1960. *Language* 42.149–55. Reprinted in McDavid 1979: 381–4

McDavid, R. I., Jr 1967a. Needed research in Southern dialects. In Thompson 1967: 113–24. Reprinted in McDavid 1979: 288–94

McDavid, R. I., Jr 1967b. A checklist of significant features for discriminating social dialects. In Evertts 1967: 7–10. Reprinted in Allen & Underwood 1971: 468–72

McDavid, R. I., Jr 1970. Changing patterns of Southern dialects. In Bronstein 1970: 206–28. Reprinted with updating in McDavid 1979: 295–308

McDavid, R. I., Jr 1979. *Dialects in culture: essays in general dialectology.* Edited by W. A. Kretzschmar, Jr. University, Alabama: University of Alabama Press

McDavid, R. I., Jr & McDavid, V. G. 1951. The relationship of the speech of American Negroes to the speech of whites. *American Speech* 26.3–17. Reprinted with addendum in Wolfram & Clarke 1971; and in McDavid 1979: 43–51

McGregor, G. P. 1971. *English in Africa.* London: Heinemann

Mackiewicz-Krassowska, H. 1976. Nasality in Australian English. *Working Papers* of the Speech and Language Research Centre, Macquarie University, January 1976

McMillan, J. B. 1939. Vowel nasality as a sandhi-form of the morphemes -nt and -ing in Southern American. *American Speech* 14.120–3. Reprinted in Williamson & Burke 1971: 489–95

McMillan, J. B. 1946. Phonology of the Standard English of East Central Alabama. PhD diss., University of Chicago

McMillan, J. B. 1977. The naming of American dialects. In Shores & Hines 1977

Mafeni, B. O. W. 1965. Some aspects of the phonetics and phonology of Nigerian Pidgin. MLitt thesis, University of Edinburgh

Mafeni, B. 1971. Nigerian Pidgin. In Spencer 1971: 95–112

Masica, C. & Dave, P. B. 1972. *The sound system of Indian English.* Hyderabad: Central Institute of English

Mencken, H. L. 1963. *The American language.* Fourth edition, with two supplements, abridged and annotated by R. I. McDavid, Jr. New York: Alfred A. Knopf

Miller, V. R. 1953. Present-day use of the broad A in eastern Massachusetts. *Speech Monographs* 20.4.235–46

Mitchell, A. G. 1946 (revised edn 1965). *The pronunciation of English in Australia.* Sydney: Angus & Robertson

Mitchell, A. G. & Delbridge, A. 1965. *The speech of Australian adolescents. A survey.* Sydney: Angus & Robertson

Morgan, L. C. 1969. North Carolina accents. *Southern Speech Journal* 34.223–9. Reprinted with additional material in Williamson & Burke 1971: 268–78

Nihalani, P., Tongue, R. K., & Hosali, P. 1979. *Indian and British*

English. A handbook of usage and pronunciation. Delhi: Oxford
University Press (India)
Norman, A. M. Z. 1956. A southeast Texas dialect study. *Orbis* 5.61–79.
Reprinted with corrections in Allen & Underwood 1971: 135–51
O'Cain, R. K. 1972. A social dialect survey of Charleston, South
Carolina. Diss., University of Chicago
Orkin, M. M. 1971. *Speaking Canadian English*. London: Routledge
& Kegan Paul
Pace, G. B. 1960. Linguistic geography and names ending in ⟨i⟩.
American Speech 35.175–87. Reprinted in Allen & Underwood 1971
Paddock, H. J. 1966. A dialect survey of Carbonear, Newfoundland. MA
thesis, Memorial University of Newfoundland
Parslow, R. L. 1967. The pronunciation of English in Boston, Mass.:
vowels and consonants. PhD diss., University of Michigan. One
chapter reprinted in Williamson & Burke 1971
Pascasio, E. M. (ed.) 1977. *The Filipino bilingual. Studies on Philippino
bilingualism and bilingual education*. Quezon City: Ateneo de Manila
University Press
PEAS = Kurath & McDavid 1961
Pederson, L. A. 1965. The pronunciation of English in metropolitan
Chicago. *Publications of the American Dialect Society* 44. Reprinted
in Williamson & Burke 1971: 528–48
Pederson, L. 1972. Black speech, white speech, and the Al Smith syn-
drome. In Davis 1972: 123–34
Perren, G. E. 1956. Some problems of oral English in East Africa.
English Language Teaching 11.1.3–10
Pilch, H. 1971. Some phonemic peculiarities of Australian English. In
Form and Substance (ed. Hammerich, L., Jakobson, R., &
Zwirner, E.), Copenhagen, 269–76
Platt, J. T. 1977. The subvarieties of Singapore English: their sociolectal
and functional status. In Crewe 1977: 83–95
Ramson, W. S. (ed.) 1970. *English transported. Essays on Australasian
English*. Canberra: Australian National University Press
Reed, C. E. 1961. The pronunciation of English in the Pacific
Northwest. *Language* 37.559–64. Reprinted in Allen & Underwood
1971: 115–21; and in Williamson & Burke 1971: 379–86
Reed, C. E. 1967. *Dialects of American English*. Cleveland, Ohio: World
Pub. Co. Second printing, 1973: University of Massachusetts Press
Reed, C. E. & Reed, D. W. 1972. Problems of English speech mixture in
California and Nevada. In Davis 1972: 135–43
Reinecke, J. E. 1969. *Language and dialect in Hawaii*. Honolulu:
University of Hawaii Press
Reinecke, J. E. 1975. *A bibliography of pidgin and creole languages*.
Honolulu: University Press of Hawaii
Richards, J. C. (ed.) 1979. *New varieties of English: issues and approaches*.
Singapore: Seameo Regional Language Centre

Rycroft, D. K. 1980. Tone and depression in Nguni. *Occasional Papers* 8, Department of African Languages, Rhodes University, Grahamstown

Rycroft, D. K. & Ngcobo, A. B. 1979. *Say it in Zulu*. London: School of Oriental and African Studies

Scargill, M. H. 1955. Canadian English and Canadian culture in Alberta. *Journal of the Canadian Linguistic Association* 1.1. (reg.). 26–9

Scargill, M. H. 1974. *Modern Canadian English usage*. Toronto: McClelland & Stewart

Scargill, M. H. & Warkentyne, H. J. 1972. The survey of Canadian English: a report. *English Quarterly* 5.3.47–104

Schachter, P. 1962. *Teaching English pronunciation to the Twi-speaking student*. Legon: Ghana University Press

Schneider, G. D. 1966. *West African Pidgin English*. Athens, Ohio: the author

Scott, N. C. 1939. Canadian *caught* and *cot*. *Maître Phonétique* 66.22

Seary, E. R., Story, G. M. & Kirwin, W. J. 1968. The Avalon peninsula of Newfoundland: an ethnolinguistic study. Ottawa: National Museum of Canada, Bulletin no. 219

Sethi, J. 1980. The vowel system in educated Punjabi-speakers' English. *Journal of the International Phonetic Association*. 10.64–73

Sey, K. A. 1973. *Ghanaian English*. London: Macmillan

Shafer, M. 1970. A phonological study of some aspects of the English pronunciation of a group of Yoruba primary school children. MPhil. thesis, University of London

Shilling, A. 1975. Bahamian English – a non-continuum? Paper contributed to the 1975 International Conference on Pidgins and Creoles, Hawaii

Shores, D. L. & Hines, C. P. 1977. *Papers in language variation*. SAMLA-ADS Collection. University, Alabama: University of Alabama Press

Shuy, R. W. 1967. *Discovering American dialects*. Champaign, Ill.: National Council of Teachers of English

Sibayan, B. P. 1977. A tentative typology of Philippine bilingualism. In Pascasio 1977: 27–33

Sledd, J. H. 1955. Review of Trager & Smith 1951. *Language* 31.312–45

Sledd, J. H. 1958. Some questions of English phonology. *Language* 34.252–60

Sledd, J. H. 1965. Review of Kurath 1964. *American Speech* 40.3.201–22

Sledd, J. H. 1966. Breaking, umlaut, and the southern drawl. *Language* 42.18–41. Reprinted in Williamson & Burke 1971: 461–88

Sledd, J. H. 1973. Review of DeStefano 1973. *American Speech* 48.3–4. 258–69

SPE = Chomsky & Halle 1968

Spencer, J. 1966. The Anglo-Indians and their speech. *Lingua* 16.57–70

Spencer, J. (ed.), 1971. *The English language in West Africa*. London: Longman

Spencer, J. 1979. English in Africa. In Hanks 1979: xxviii-xxix

Sprague de Camp, L. 1943, 1952. [Specimens,] New York City dialect. *Maître Phonétique* 79.11–12; 98.34–5

Stewart, W. A. 1962. Creole languages in the Caribbean. In Rice, F.L.A. (ed.), *Study of the role of second languages in Asia, Africa and Latin America*. Washington, DC: Center for Applied Linguistics

Stewart, W. A. 1967. Sociolinguistic factors in the history of American Negro dialects. *The Florida FL Reporter* 5.2.1–7. Reprinted in Allen & Underwood 1971: 444–53

Stewart, W. A. 1968. Continuity and change in American Negro dialects. *The Florida FL Reporter* 6.1.3–4, 14–16, 18. Reprinted in Allen & Underwood 1971: 454–67

Stockwell, R. P. & Macaulay, R. K. S. (eds) 1972. *Linguistic change and generative theory*. Essays from the UCLA Conference on Historical Linguistics in the Perspective of Transformational Theory, February 1969. Bloomington, Ind.: Indiana University Press

Stolz, W. & Bills, G. 1968. An investigation of the standard–nonstandard dimension of Central Texan English. Part of the Final Report, Office of Economic Opportunity, contract OEO-4115

Story, G. M. 1957a. Research in the language and place names of Newfoundland. *Journal of the Canadian Language Association* 3.1.47–55

Story, G. M. 1957b. Newfoundland English usage. *Encyclopaedia Canadiana* 7.321–2. Ottawa

Tay, M. W. J. 1979. The uses, users, and features of English in Singapore. In Richards 1979: 91–111

Taylor, D. 1977. *Languages of the West Indies*. Baltimore, Md: The Johns Hopkins University Press

Thomas, C. K. 1932. Jewish dialect and New York dialect. *American Speech* 7.321–6

Thomas, C. K. 1958. *Phonetics of American English*. New York: Ronald

Thomas, C. K. 1961. The phonology of New England English. *Speech monographs* 28.223–32. Reprinted in Allen & Underwood 1971: 57–66

Thompson, E. T. (ed.) 1967. *Perspectives on the South*. Durham, NC: Duke University Press

Tiffen, B. W. 1974. The intelligibility of Nigerian English. PhD thesis, University of London

Todd, L. 1974. *Pidgins and creoles*. London: Routledge & Kegan Paul

Trager, G. L. 1930. The pronunciation of 'short *a*' in American Standard English. *American Speech* 5.396–400

Trager, G. L. 1934. What conditions limit variants of a phoneme? *American Speech* 9.313–15

Trager, G. L. 1940. One phonemic entity becomes two: the case of 'short *a*'. *American Speech* 15.255–8

Trager, G. L. 1941. ə 'nəwt on æ ənd æˑˑ in ə'merikən 'iŋgliʃ. *Maître Phonétique* 17–19

Trager, G. L. & Smith, H. L., Jr 1951. *An outline of English structure.* Third edn 1957. Washington, DC: American Council of Learned Societies

Tsuzaki, S. M. & Reinecke, J. E. 1966. *English in Hawaii: an annotated bibliography.* Honolulu: Pacific and Asian Languages Institute

Tucker, G. R. & Lambert, W. E. 1969. White and Negro listeners' reactions to various American English dialects. *Social Forces* 47.463–8. Reprinted in Dillard 1975: 369–77

Turner, G. W. 1960. On the origin of Australian vowel sounds. *AUMLA* 13.33–45

Turner, G. W. 1966. *The English language in Australia and New Zealand.* London: Longman

Turner, G. W. 1970. New Zealand English today. In Ramson 1970

Turner, L. D. 1945. Notes on the sounds and vocabulary of Gullah. *Publications of the American Dialect Society* 3.13–28. Reprinted in Williamson & Burke 1971: 121–35

Turner, L. D. 1949. *Africanisms in the Gullah dialect.* Chicago: University of Chicago Press

Udell, G. R. 1966. The speech of Akron, Ohio: a study in urbanization. PhD diss., University of Chicago

Uldall, E. 1958. American 'molar' *r* and 'flapped' *t*. *Revista do Laboratório de Fonética Experimental da Faculdada de Letras da Universidade de Coimbra* 4.3–6

Vanderslice, R. & Pierson, L. S. 1967. Prosodic features of Hawaiian English. *Quarterly Journal of Speech* 53.156–65

Vermeer, H. J. 1969. *Das Indo-Englische. Situation und linguistische Bedeutung (mit Bibliographie).* Heidelberg: Julius Groos

Viereck, W. 1975. *Regionale und soziale Erscheinungsformen des britischen und amerikanischen Englisch.* Tübingen: Max Niemeyer

Wächtler, K. 1977. *Geographie und Stratifikation der englischen Sprache.* Düsseldorf: Bagel, and Munich: Francke

Warkentyne, H. J. 1971. Contemporary Canadian English. *American Speech* 46.193–9

Warner, M. P. 1967. Language in Trinidad, with special reference to English. MPhil thesis, University of York

Watts, H. L. 1976. A social and demographic portrait of English-speaking white South Africans. In De Villiers 1976

Wells, J. C. 1973. *Jamaican pronunciation in London.* Oxford: Blackwell

Wells, J. C. 1980. The brogue that isn't. *Journal of the International Phonetic Association* 10.74–9

Wetmore, T. H. 1959. The low-central and low-back vowels in the English of the eastern United States. *Publications of the American Dialect Society* 32. Introduction and ch. 9, 'Western Pennsylvania', reprinted in Williamson & Burke 1971

References

White, E. 1980. *States of desire*. London: André Deutsch
Williamson, J. V. 1968. A phonological and morphological study of the speech of the Negro of Memphis, Tennessee. *Publications of the American Dialect Society* 50
Williamson, J. V. 1970. Selected features of speech: Black and White. *Journal of the Canadian Linguistic Association* 13.4.420–3.
Reprinted in Williamson & Burke 1971: 496–507
Williamson, J. V. & Burke, V. M. 1971. *A various language: perspectives on American dialects*. New York: Holt, Rinehart and Winston
Wilson, H. R. 1959. The dialect of Lunenburg County, Nova Scotia: a study of the English of the county, with reference to its sources, preservation of relics and vestiges of bilingualism. PhD diss., University of Michigan
Winford, D. 1978. Phonological hypercorrection in the process of decreolization – the case of Trinidadian English. *Journal of Linguistics* 14.129–375
Wolfram, W. A. 1969. *A sociolinguistic description of Detroit Negro speech*. Washington, DC: Center for Applied Linguistics
Wolfram, W. A. & Clarke, N. 1971. *Black-white speech relationships*. Arlington, Va: Center for Applied Linguistics
Wood, G. R. 1972. *Vocabulary change: a study of variation in regional words in eight of the Southern states*. Carbondale, Ill.: Southern Illinois University Press

Index

669

CPSIA information can be obtained at www.ICGtesting.com
Printed in the USA
LVOW08s0057231215

467416LV00001B/91/P